WHITE MAN'S COUNTRY

WHITE MAN'S COUNTRY

LORD DELAMERE AND
THE MAKING OF KENYA

BY
ELSPETH HUXLEY

VOLUME TWO
1914-1931

CHATTO AND WINDUS
LONDON

PUBLISHED BY
Chatto and Windus Ltd
40 WILLIAM IV STREET
LONDON WC2

*

Clarke, Irwin & Co Ltd
TORONTO

First published 1935
New Edition 1953
Reprinted 1956
Reprinted with a new preface 1968
First issued in this paperback edition 1980

© Elspeth Huxley 1935

All rights reserved. No part of this publication may be reproduced, stored in a retrieval system, or transmitted in any form, or by any means, electronic, mechanical, photocopying, recording or otherwise, without the prior permission of Chatto & Windus Ltd.

ISBN 0 7011 0834 7

PRINTED AND BOUND IN GREAT BRITAIN BY
REDWOOD BURN LIMITED
TROWBRIDGE AND ESHER

CONTENTS

Volume II

CHAPTER		PAGE
XIV	The Campaign	3
XV	War-Time in the Protectorate	26
XVI	Protectorate into Colony	50
XVII	Reconstruction	82
XVIII	The Indian Question	110
XIX	Deputation to Downing Street	140
XX	Spotlight on Kenya	167
XXI	Tanganyika Interlude	187
XXII	The Federation Issue	213
XXIII	The Sunbeam Period	235
XXIV	Locusts bring Trouble	255
XXV	In Defence of Settlement	275
XXVI	World Depression	303
	Appendix. Chronology of Secretaries of State and Governors, 1895-1931	325
	Index	327

MAPS

1. East Africa Campaign, 1914-1917   13
2. Kenya Colony, 1933   50
3. East Africa in 1926   198

VOLUME II

For in truth the problems of East Africa are the problems of the world.   WINSTON CHURCHILL.

CHAPTER XIV

THE CAMPAIGN
1914–1917

I

ON the outbreak of war the white population converged on Nairobi. The capital was humming with unfounded rumours. No one knew, even, whether there was going to be a war in East Africa at all. Many people thought that both sides would abstain from staging a display of the legalised slaughter of whites by whites for the edification of an overwhelming black population, and even more that they would avoid training natives to shoot Europeans. It was hoped at first that Britain and Germany would agree to fight it out in Europe. Some such arrangement might, in fact, have been made, had not the bombardment of Dar-es-Salaam by two British cruisers, the *Astraea* and the *Pegasus*, on August 8th forced the issue. This was the first hostile act of the campaign.

One battalion of the King's African Rifles in Nairobi was the Protectorate's sole military force. There was no organised reserve or defence force. And the Uganda railway ran within fifty miles of the unguarded Anglo-German border. The line was alarmingly vulnerable. By destroying a few bridges the Germans could cut the highlands off completely from the sea.

On August 4th a volunteer enlistment office was opened in Nairobi House. The first wave of excitement washed hundreds of settlers through its doors. Some had paused only to seize a rifle and pocketful of ammunition and to saddle up a mule before riding in to the capital. Many of the Uasin Gishu settlers arrived in a body. The news reached them in the midst of an agricultural meeting at Eldoret. They leapt on to their waiting mules, rode through part of the night to the nearest station at Londiani, boarded a train and arrived some thirty-six hours later—hungry, unshaved, without clothes or money, but full of ardour. Some of them were Boers who had fought against the British fourteen years before. The Uasin Gishu contingent formed themselves into a regiment of their own, the Plateau South Africans.

No one knew what was going to happen. There was no organisation ready, no unit to join. A few settlers raised commandos of their own, as some of them had done before in South Africa. Others took the first ship home to join in England.

In a few days an astonishing variety of miniature regiments had sprung to life — Bowker's Horse, Arnoldi's Scouts, Ross's Scouts, Wessell's Scouts and others. All these were finally merged into the East African Mounted Rifles.

The volunteers brought their own rifles, ranging from huge double-barrelled elephant guns to light carbines. Some were provided with ammunition, some were not. Uniform varied according to each man's taste. His hat might be a khaki helmet, a battered felt with an ostrich feather tucked into one side, or even a cloth cap. His shirt was generally a sort of tunic with huge pockets, and sleeves chopped off at the elbow. He might wear shorts, breeches or slacks; gaiters, puttees or even tennis shoes. A bright handkerchief was often knotted round his neck, a bush-knife stuck into his belt. His mount was often a mule and generally a vicious, obstinate and uncontrolled one at that. He was hung about with home-made bandoliers, water-bottles, tins and anything that occurred to him as potentially useful. Of discipline there was none.

In a few days Nairobi was crowded with these peculiar free-lance troopers, waiting for news and instructions.

What was happening on the border? everyone asked. There was as yet no Intelligence service. The Chief Secretary issued instructions to district Commissioners to send out scouts near Vanga, Moshi and Taveta. These were the danger spots, for there was a strong German post at Moshi and regular troops just over the border.

On August 5th martial law was declared. The Indians on the railway remained out on strike against poll-tax. Regular trains were suspended. A small K.A.R. patrol left on the afternoon of the 5th by special train for Voi. The sale of ammunition was stopped. The price of petrol went up to 4s. a gallon. German nationals were arrested and placed under guard. Eight hundred Somalis met in the tin village near Muthaiga and marched down to Nairobi House in a body to offer their services to the Government. They were organised into a troop of mounted scouts under Delamere's brother-in-law, Mr. Berkeley Cole.

News from Europe began to trickle in. The Belgians had repulsed the Germans at Liège; the Royal Naval Reserve had been called out; the Germans had invaded France.

The Governor dashed off to Mombasa, protected day and night by a Town Guard hastily organised by Nairobi business men. A mysterious tug was seen outside the harbour flying no flag. The *Koenigsberg* was on the way to bombard Mombasa; the Germans were advancing on Voi; Nairobi was in danger; enemy aeroplanes had been seen flying at night over the capital.

The Dar-es-Salaam wireless station had been destroyed; the town had been evacuated; the British had sunk a survey ship in the mouth of the harbour; they had captured the *Tabora*; the *Koenigsberg* had escaped; the Germans were advancing from Moshi. No one knew what to believe, or what was happening. Rumours fattened on uncertainty.

2

The Anglo-German border ran through a waste of bush; there were no British government stations between Taveta and the Mara river. Troops could break through anywhere. The Masai alone knew the country. Their loyalty and co-operation as scouts was vital.

Delamere at once decided that he could help most effectively by organising the *moran* into scouting parties to patrol the border. On August 5th he telegraphed from Elmenteita to the chief staff officer of the volunteers:

May I act under your orders as Intelligence along German Masai border. Can talk Masai and know the people really well. Can guarantee complete control. Can find own outfit, transport and Masai, but Masai only engaged for work within Protectorate except for voluntary service.

Headquarters wired back:

Your offer gratefully accepted. O.C. Troops has been informed.

An Intelligence department was being hastily organised in Nairobi. Its nucleus was the Game department which already had a staff of native spies (one of whom was normally attached to each safari to see that the game laws were not infringed) and a corps of informers to detect ivory poaching. Captain R. B. Woosnam, the chief game ranger, was placed in charge and Delamere was appointed O.C. Intelligence on the Masai border. His instructions read as follows:

Get into communication with Van de Weyer as soon as possible at his store on the Narosera river. He will have some carrier pigeons and will tell you what he has arranged and how they are to be used. When sending a message by pigeon send a duplicate also by runner or motor cycle. If runners have to be used tell them to come in to the game office (elephant skull outside the door).

Judd and Postma and Hitching will come down later to work in conjunction with you and under your orders. They will come via Van de Weyer's store to Lady G. Mackenzie's camp at Sonzo near Natron. If you can get the country between Natron and Laitokitok under observation so much the better; it is at present being looked after by Magadi. Judd and Postma know this country and I think would be able to establish an observation post there.

As soon as you get going down there we should like some news sent back even if only negative to say all quiet. Try and send some Dorobo across the border to find out if there is any concentration of German troops taking place. When doing so try and get them to distinguish between black and white troops and whether mounted or on foot and if they have artillery or maxims.

The country between the Amala River (*Engabei* of the Masai) and the lake will be worked by Cotter and Fey, also under your orders if necessary.

Woodhouse with twelve mounted Somalis is at Taveta working between Lake Jipi and Kitirus. Seth-Smith is working between Lake Jipi and Shimoui on the coast.

There is a Govt. *boma* on the Amala river with R. W. Hemsted, D.C. in charge of the Masai reserve, and he knows the whole country well. Another Govt. *boma* is on the Ngari Narok in charge of Talbot-Smith, and E. D. Browne is A.D.C. Ngong and knows the country very well.

R. B. WOOSNAM,
Intelligence Officer

Delamere disappeared into the border country on a mule with a few faithful Masai, some blankets, cooking pots and saddle-bags of flour, sugar, chocolate and tea, to take over the job of organising patrols and scouts along 200 miles of unguarded frontier. "They were the hardest six months' work of my life," he afterwards wrote.

3

At the outbreak of war the number of able-bodied white men of military age was approximately the same in German and in British East Africa—a little over 3500. The Germans had a larger force under arms. But while the British were sure of quick reinforcements—the first detachments from India could arrive within a few weeks—the Germans were cut off from any help. British command of the sea isolated the tiny white force in German East Africa from reservoirs of man-power in the Fatherland. Their one chance was to strike before British reinforcements could reach Mombasa. They took the offensive; and East Africa was the only part of the British Empire to be invaded by the enemy.

On August 24th a German patrol, armed with dynamite and bombs, got through to the Uganda railway. They had, however, rashly used British maps in planning their attack. The maps were inaccurate and the party struck the railway at the wrong spot, miles from the bridge they had intended to destroy. They had counted on replenishing their water supplies at the river. They were found by a British patrol staggering, half dead from thirst, towards Voi, and were brought in triumph to Nairobi—the first captives.

In the capital the East African Mounted Rifles were undergoing training before being moved down to guard the border. The difficulty was that the officers knew no more about training and drill than the men. A camp was formed on the racecourse; but most of the troopers lived either in one of the hotels, in the recently opened country club, with Nairobi friends or even at Government House.

"Where are Troopers Ridley and Thompson?" enquired the second-in-command who was inspecting the camp one evening, observing that two of the sentries were missing. "Oh, they're dining at Government House," the sergeant replied, "but H.E.'s promised to send them home early in his car."

The E.A.M.R. were divided into six squadrons, with a machine-gun and a signalling section. The most aristocratic squadron was known as "Monica's Own" after the Governor's youngest daughter. The commander was an ex-Lancer, and he insisted on arming his squadron with lances. These were hastily made in the railway workshops out of bamboo shafts. They were adorned with red and white pennons which fluttered gaily in the breeze when the squadron turned out on parade, but which were very disconcerting to the mules. The lances only saw service once and that was at Nairobi House. A lawyer who occupied an office there tried to get in after hours. The guard, acting under instructions to allow no civilian entry at night, poked a lance into his well-covered stomach and forced him to retreat.

This queerly assorted regiment embraced men of every type and nationality. There were elephant poachers, prospectors, store-keepers, transport riders, white hunters and plain settlers; there were Australians, Americans, Boers, Swedes, Italians, Swiss and even a Turk, until someone discovered that the Empire was at war with Turkey, and he was hastily interned. There was no uniform and no proper equipment. There was an acute shortage of ammunition. When the regiment left for the front each man had only a hundred rounds and there was nothing in reserve. There was, however, an artillery section possessing a few antiquated guns drawn by Ford cars, including a couple of Hotchkiss guns from Uganda. These had not seen service since the Uganda war of 1891, and even then they had been used more for display than for violence.

Nairobi was still believed to be in danger, principally from aircraft. For some reason the enemy was credited with a large air force. (There was, in fact, one aeroplane in German territory at the outbreak of war; it had been brought over for an exhibition at Dar-es-Salaam but crashed on its first flight.) This and other even more imaginary machines were seen, repeatedly and unmistakably, flying towards Nairobi, always at night and carrying a bright light.

The climax came when an order from headquarters was issued in the middle of the night instructing a patrol to proceed with all speed to Kijabe, about forty miles away, where an aeroplane had been seen by a staff officer. The patrol galloped to the spot as fast as the troopers could urge their reluctant mules; but there was no aeroplane. The planet Venus, exceptionally bright at that time of the year, was, however, observed to be rising just above the hills in the direction from which the aeroplane had been seen approaching.

The aeroplane scare persisted for some weeks. A recruit who was placed under arrest for firing off his rifle in the night replied to the charge: "Sir, I fired at the person who was flying at me in his aeroplane". A rhyme on the subject was soon invented:

> I thought I saw an aeroplane
> Upon the Athi plain:
> I looked again and saw it was
> A Kavirondo crane.

4

The first real fight took place on September 4th. The Germans had occupied a post at Taveta abandoned by the British as untenable on the outbreak of war. From there a small force advanced through waterless thorn scrub on Tsavo on the Uganda railway. It was intercepted and harried by a Nubian mounted company of the K.A.R. and forced to retreat.

After this the E.A.M.R. were moved to the front (they had received less than a month's training at Nairobi) to patrol the border and prevent other German parties from breaking through. Before they left a full-dress parade was held, and the Governor and Commander-in-Chief inspected the regiment. It was hard to know whether he or his troops excelled in unconventionality of military dress. The Governor took the salute in a Norfolk shooting jacket, a pair of cycling breeches and a white helmet. The parade passed off fairly smoothly until three cheers for the Governor was raised when most of the mules endeavoured to bolt, shedding pots and tins, water-bottles and loose cartridges and occasionally their riders as they went.

The squadrons derailed at Kajiado and marched towards the border, sending scouting parties through the thick bush into German territory. No transport had been organised; the men had no food, and lived entirely off game which they shot and then stewed in such tins and pots as the older hands had brought. At one time the whole regiment was forced to subsist on one meal a day consisting solely of soup made from dried kongoni meat.

The E.A.M.R.'s first engagement with the enemy, curiously enough, was a naval one. The Germans tried to break through to the railway at the other end of the border, near Kisumu on the lake, where practically no defensive line had been organised. A detachment marched into British territory but was intercepted by a company of K.A.R. at Kisii and beaten off on September 12th. A squadron (Bowker's Horse) of the E.A.M.R. was rushed back from Kajiado and railed to Kisumu, where the men embarked on a lake steamer, the s.s. *Winifred*. They were to be taken to a landing place south of Kisumu called Karungu Bay, in British territory, and to march from there to Kisii to reinforce the K.A.R.

But they found Karungu in German hands and were greeted with machine-gun fire. They retaliated with the *Winifred's* Hotchkiss but were driven off by the more powerfully armed German gunboat *Mwanza*. The next morning they returned with an escort, the British gunboat *Kavirondo*, and found that the Germans had evacuated Karungu by night. The E.A.M.R. considered that their first victory had been won.

The war became more serious after that. The E.A.M.R. were strung out along the border in thick rhino and lion-infested bush, so thick that at any moment patrols might stumble into an enemy ambush or the camp might be rushed by a raiding party. The sentries could not see more than a few yards through the scrub. Lions prowled round the camp all night and the sentries dared not fire for fear of giving away their position; the Germans, for all they knew, might be scouting a hundred yards away. All they could do to discourage the lions was to throw stones at them. Rhinos frequently charged from a few yards away, stampeding all the mules and sometimes knocking over troopers. There was no camp equipment, and hyenas were known to slink up to a man sleeping (as they all did) in the open, and seize the mule saddle doing duty as a pillow from under his head. Nerves became jumpy and on edge, until the sharp bark of an invisible zebra sounded to strained ears like the hoarse command of a German askari, and a stampeding mule was magnified into a charging rhino.

Scouting was done mainly at night, by moonlight, and the risk of losing the way in the waterless bush and dying of thirst by agonising degrees was never far away. There were no medical arrangements, no dressing station or field hospital, no stretcher-bearers to get the wounded in from some disastrous ambush twenty miles away in the bush. And wounds festered as fast as dead flesh mortified in that hot, low-lying country. Malaria was rampant and blackwater, almost always fatal, was common.

The volunteers had joined up full of enthusiasm. They were going to march down to German East and conquer it for the Empire. They would occupy Tabora—the chief German post, on the Central railway from Dar-es-Salaam to Lake Tanganyika—in a few weeks. The E.A.M.R. had a bellicose song which they used to bawl to the tune of "Marching Through Georgia":

> Hurray! Hurray! We're off to G.E.A.
> Hurray! Hurray! The squareheads we will slay.
> And so we sing this happy song
> Upon this happy day—
> As we go marching to Tabora.

Now it appeared that the programme was to be quite different. They began to learn the reality of war in Africa:

that it was fought not against Germans but against a more intangible and destructive enemy—against the germs of malaria and blackwater and dysentery and tsetse fly, reinforced by floods and savage sun; against the hopelessness of organising transport; against thirst and hunger, sickness, gangrene and exhaustion.

5

In September the first Indian troops arrived and Indian generals took over the high command. Punjabis and Kapurthalas joined the E.A.M.R. on the border. The Germans were strongly entrenched on a hill called Longido, covered with thick bush and forest. It was decided to dislodge the enemy and then to attack Taveta, the key to the border. Two columns were to advance on Longido from each side and a mounted column (Bowker's Horse) to cut off retreat from behind.

The plan miscarried. The attacking British columns were driven off the mountain and Bowker's Horse, misled by Masai guides, were raked from above with machine-gun fire and retired with serious losses. The attack was a failure, the first British reverse in the campaign.

This was on November 2nd. Two days later the fiasco at Tanga occurred. Two British warships carrying reinforcements from Bombay anchored opposite the German port intending to land troops and occupy the town. They gave notice of their intent so as to allow the Germans to evacuate. The next day some of the troops landed a little way along the beach and bathed, but no attempt was made to capture Tanga. On the following day the troops (the Loyal North Lancs, the 101st Grenadiers and the Kashmir Rifles) were disembarked and advanced on the town through thick bush.

The Germans, by that time, had had two clear days in which to fortify themselves. They had not neglected to do so. The British were received with heavy well-placed fire. As they tore their way through the dense thorny bush they tripped over cleverly concealed cords stretched over the ground. Some of these were attached to flags which, jerked into the air, gave the defenders an accurate range; others tipped over native bee-hives hidden in trees and released a stream of angry bees which attacked the British troops with a terrible ferocity. It was the bees, more than the machine-gun fire, which turned the advance. The troops withdrew at dusk after struggling for two and a half hours in the bush. They re-embarked, leaving behind heavy casualties, hundreds

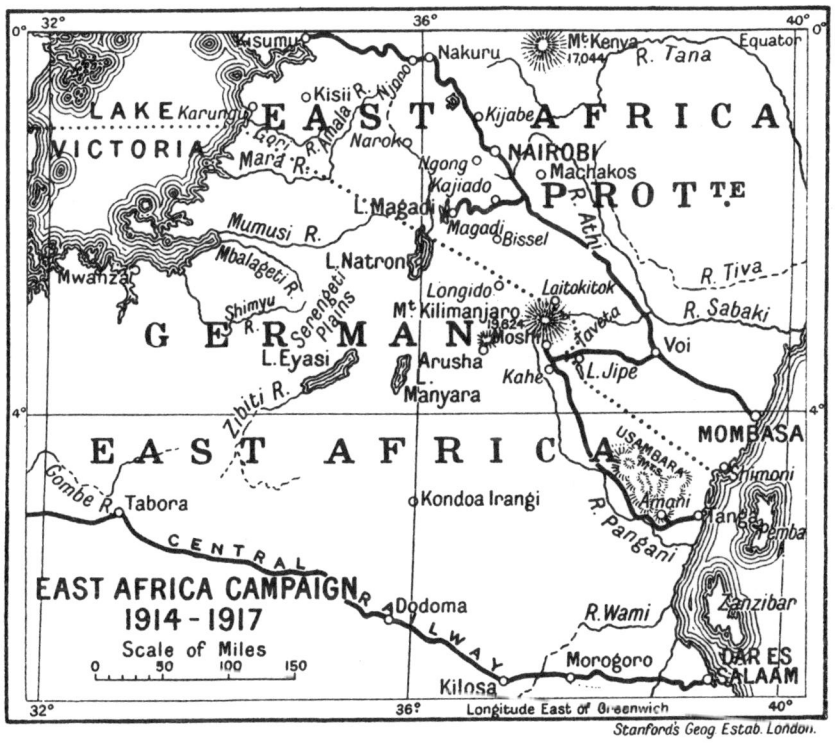

of rifles and sixteen machine-guns; and the warships sailed away.

Tanga was not captured until July 7th, 1916, when General Smuts advanced upon it with immense transport difficulties and at a heavy cost in casualties, sickness and expenditure. He had to fight his way through the Usambara mountains from Taveta to reach the port.

When the Indian troops arrived the *raison d'être* of the E.A.M.R. largely vanished. They had held the border at a critical time when there was no one else, save one battalion of K.A.R., to do it. Now that progress seemed to have halted, and unlimited Indian soldiers were everywhere, they began to get anxious about their farms.

They had left, most of them, at a moment's notice. They had had no chance to return even for a day to put their affairs in order. No arrangements had been made even for paying wages in their absence. Some of them had left wives in charge. Many had felt nervous about leaving their womenfolk unguarded, fearing that natives might seize the chance to raid the farms, carry off stock and perhaps threaten the safety of isolated women. It was an ideal opportunity for natives suffering from grievances to pay off old scores. But their fears had been groundless. In spite of this sudden exodus of the majority of the able-bodied males in settled areas, the preoccupation of the officials and the complete defencelessness of the farms, no European estates were raided, no women harmed and no native outbreaks occurred. This spoke well for the relations existing between settler and native.

In many cases, where no womenfolk or assistants had been left in charge, native headmen simply carried on as best they could. If no wages were forthcoming at the end of the month the natives were for the most part content to wait until their master returned, as they never doubted he would. Nor did they doubt that whatever was owing to them would be paid.

In some other parts of Africa native outbreaks did in fact occur. In January 1915 a native Baptist clergyman headed a serious rising in Nyasaland and European farms between Blantyre and Zomba were attacked. Three Scotsmen were murdered and their women and children carried off by the rebels. Other bands of natives attacked stores and mission-stations, and women and children were brought into laagers. The whole country was on the brink of revolt. The movement avowedly aimed at driving the Europeans out of the Shiré highlands. Eventually the leader was shot and order restored.

Early in 1915 the campaign entered a watching and waiting phase in the bush. Many of the E.A.M.R. men were granted "indefinite leave" and went back to their farms to try to straighten things out. The rest remained for eight months at Bissel on the border, camped in the bush and sending out continual patrols.

The E.A.M.R. had a special value, out of proportion to their numbers, to the military. The Indian troops were at first as lost as a Polar bear in the Sahara. They spoke no native language—a serious matter when so much depended on native guides. They were strangers to African thorn bush, they lost their way, they knew nothing of the technique of dealing with lions and kindred beasts. The E.A.M.R. troopers knew the country, the natives, the language, the conditions.

The E.A.M.R. men were in great demand among other units. Many were taken to organise scouting sections, for Captain F. O'B. Wilson's scouts had won a particularly high reputation for efficiency and courage. Gradually the regiment shrank as it was drafted away in twos and threes. A large number of its members became staff officers. One squadron (Arnoldi's Scouts) became the nucleus of the East African Transport Corps.

In 1916, when Smuts took over and the offensive passed to the British, the remnants of the E.A.M.R. helped to drive the enemy out of the Usambara mountains, to advance along the Tanga railway and to strike down to the Central railway. Many of the troopers were killed on active service. Others died from malaria, which riddled the troops as they advanced steadily into more and more unhealthy country, their resistance weakened by lack of supplies (at one time even the game gave out and roast rats were the only food) and by long marches in the deadly sun.

By the end of 1916 the E.A.M.R. had dwindled to a major, a sergeant and two troopers. It was never disbanded. It simply faded away. It left no records; it appeared in no army lists. The only relic that remains is a list of names carved on the cavalry war memorial in Hyde Park among the Lancers and Hussars, an august company to which the regiment's humble mules gave it entry.[1]

---

[1] For this fact and for other information about the E.A.M.R. the author is indebted to M. G. Granville Squiers' account of the regiment's adventures published in *East Africa* in 1927 under the title "The Army that Found Itself".

6

Delamere remained in the Masai reserve until January 1915. His bases were a scattered chain of traders' stores along the border. Masai scouts came to these huts in the bush to report, and Delamere forwarded the information by runner or carrier pigeon to Nairobi.

The pigeons had been a trader's idea, evolved before the war to save time in ordering supplies from Nairobi. Now they became of great value. But they were troubled by hawks. If the pigeons encountered a hawk near home they would turn and fly back for their lives, sometimes darting into their wooden towers so close to their pursuer that the hawk would crash against the wall unable to check its flight. One day two pigeons returned completely plucked, as bare as roast chickens, from the hawks' attacks. They recovered, and grew another set of feathers. But in the end all the pigeons were killed on active service and communications had to be established by heliograph stations.

Delamere's job was to keep Intelligence headquarters informed as to the movement of enemy troops. He had some narrow escapes, for the Germans were playing the same game, and sometimes scouting parties took each other unawares in the bush. One of his men, Postma, was captured and effected an escape. He was surprised with two unarmed Dorobo natives by an enemy patrol and taken to the German camp. He was marched for several days into enemy country, handcuffed and guarded. One evening, in camp, he asked his guard to get him a cup. The man walked off, Postma seized a gun leaning against the side of a hut and fired it from his hip. The askaris, who had stacked their rifles, took cover and one of Postma's Dorobo cut through his handcuffs with an axe. He escaped, and the Dorobo guided him back to the British side of the border.

Shortly afterwards the same man had a less successful adventure. It was reported to Delamere by another of his scouts as follows:

26th November 1914
MORGAN'S CAMP

I very much regret having to report that Postma got badly mauled by a lioness to-day. He was riding back to camp, and was about half-way between Smith's and Morgan's camp when he suddenly came on to five lionesses. The horse shied badly and Postma got off, and one lioness that had cubs came for him and got him down, biting him badly in one thigh and clawing him on the other thigh. The lioness was dragging him along when he managed to kill her with his revolver. He was alone as he was riding on ahead of his boys, but he managed to get to his pony and made Morgan's camp. I have dressed the wounds and intend taking him to Nairobi *via* Lumbwa.

It was a hard life of continual movement and no rest. The strain proved too much for Delamere's strength. He had returned from a visit to England, undertaken solely on account of his health, less than three months before war was declared. He had been told to nurse his strength; but for six months he spent twelve hours a day or more in the saddle, often sleeping out at night in the dew, unable to light a fire for fear of giving away his position to the enemy, and dining off maize meal and chocolate. He contracted malaria and lived largely on quinine.

The climax came when he strained his heart running up a hill in the heat of the day to reach an observation post. He had a collapse, malaria gained control, and symptoms of dysentery appeared. He made his way back to Nairobi in an ox-cart and took a train for Elmenteita. He arrived at Soysambu half dead from a strained heart and malaria.

His manager insisted on wiring for a doctor—a famous character in Nairobi, the possessor of an Irish brogue, a brusque and somewhat ghoulish surgical manner, and a weakness for blood-letting. He prescribed a drastic arsenical injection which was given in the old way. Alternate doses of the drug and distilled water were pumped into a vein in the patient's arm. The manager stood on a rickety chair pouring the mixture from a cup into Delamere's arm, while the doctor ejaculated at intervals "Don't let in a drop of air, or ye'll kill the man!" until full two quarts had found its way into the patient's blood-stream.

VOL. II

It was a long time before Delamere recovered from the severe strain on his heart. He was moved down to the Scott Sanatorium, outside Nairobi, where he spent several months in bed.

He became involved, even from his bed, in a semi-political crisis. There were difficulties over recruitment of volunteers. The Government had given the impression that it did not need the settlers' help as soldiers in the prosecution of the war. It also refused to allow all but a very few of its officials to join. Volunteers fell off, and the military authorities accused both the Government and the civil population of failing to "do their bit". There was dissatisfaction all round, and no organisation.

Early in 1915 an appeal for 500 more volunteers was issued by the G.O.C. The terms of service were limited to two months training and two months' active service. The Governor refused to allow officials to go. "I cannot", he wrote, "sanction any such wider scale of recruitment of government servants as would seriously impair the efficiency of administrative machinery, neither do I see my way to suggest to the Imperial Government that the interests of the Protectorate should be set aside even temporarily in furtherance of the contemplated scheme of military operations."

This decision was unfavourably commented on by the unofficial population, who felt that the obligation to help win the war rested just as much on officials as on themselves. The Government refused even to close down the Survey department, although its principal object was the delineation of farms for new settlers of whom there were, naturally, none. The settlers felt that they were not wanted, and so the appeal for 500 more men was not met with the readiness anticipated by the military.

Delamere was asked to throw his influence on the side of the military. He wrote to the *East African Standard* and took other steps to persuade such settlers as were left to join.

A certain number responded; but the Government intervened. It pointed out that 500 men could not be spared if the business of the country was to be carried on. A further depletion of man-power could only result in the closing down of farms and businesses, and this at a time when increased home production was urgently required to feed the ever-expanding army, and when the shipping shortage was making it increasingly hard to secure supplies from overseas. As a result of government pressure the appeal for 500 infantrymen was abandoned by the military.

7

By the spring of 1915 Nairobi had become full of Indian generals and troops. The coast was blockaded by British warships and the Germans were cut off from supplies of ammunition as well as from reinforcements. Two ships, however, managed to run the blockade and landed ammunition, leather, rubber and spirits at Tanga.

These were the last supplies received by the Germans in the war. After February 1915 they had to live on the country. They were cut off from anything they did not themselves produce—from oil, tea, quinine, medicines, cotton goods, blankets, spirits and the thousand other things to which the British troops had access. They could get no ammunition, no more rifles, no big guns, no motor transport. They were fighting against hopeless odds, but they called on all their ingenuity to stave off surrender.

They produced their own gunpowder and manufactured home-made cartridges. They had established, as long ago as 1902, an exceptionally fine research station behind Tanga, in the Usambara mountains, whose object was to introduce plants of economic value and to study agricultural problems puzzling their settlers. This station, Amani, was turned with remarkable versatility into a scientific factory for producing an astonishing range of products and substitutes. During the first eighteen months of the war Amani prepared from its own resources sixteen varieties of medicine, five varieties of rubber products and many miscellaneous objects such as boots, tooth-powder, 10,000 pieces of soap, 15,000 bottles of whisky and other spirits, candles, and earthenware vessels.[1] When General Smuts drove the Germans out of the Usambara mountains Amani had to be abandoned, and that was perhaps one of the most deadly blows of the campaign.

[1] From the report of the East Africa commission, 1924, Cmd. 2387 of 1925.

During the summer of 1915 German troops continued to raid into British territory. South African and Rhodesian battalions were brought up to help. In July the Navy at last destroyed the *Koenigsberg*. The *Chatham* held her bottled up in a creek at the mouth of the Rufiji river until two monitors specially sent for from England arrived and, with the help of two aeroplanes and after an attack lasting for several days, succeeded in setting fire to the cruiser. The crew escaped with nearly all the guns and joined Von Lettow Vorbeck, the German commander. But the great advance into German East which everyone had anticipated so eagerly remained as far off as ever.

Towards the end of 1915 Delamere left for England. His heart was worse. He was practically unable to walk. He had strained a valve in his heart—it was the beginning of the trouble which caused his death sixteen years later—and was told by doctors in England that he must not, in future, live in East Africa for more than three months at a stretch on account of the altitude.

While he was in a nursing home in London he was obliged to refuse an invitation to join the staff of Sir H. Smith-Dorrien, who was sent out to take charge of the East African campaign. Smith-Dorrien fell sick at the Cape, and General Smuts took his place.

It was six months before Delamere could walk. As soon as he was strong enough, in the middle of 1916, he returned to East Africa to take over the management of his farms, and so release his manager for active service. To relations who protested that his way of life would fatally affect his heart he replied: "I shall be all right—I can't afford to die yet".

Njoro had been practically closed down. No more wheat was grown after 1914. Plant-breeding experiments were abandoned when the scientist in charge, Mr. Evans, enlisted. The hybrid wheat varieties became scattered and their identity lost. Delamere himself was fully occupied at Soysambu, where he looked after the cattle and sheep single-handed until Mr. E. C. Long returned after the war from active service in France.

8

During Delamere's absence the internal situation had changed. At first, relations between military, Government and settlers had become more strained. There was no machinery of co-operation between the civil and military authorities. Generals complained that the Government seemed to have washed its hands of the war, and that the Protectorate's population was not supplying enough volunteers. The settlers were equally dissatisfied with the Government's apparent lack of policy. The situation came to a head on September 7th, 1915. A mass meeting of settlers and commercial men from all districts—the largest ever held in the Protectorate—assembled in Nairobi to urge the Government to adopt some definite line of action in regard to the war.

They considered that the civil side of the campaign was very incompetently run. The Government, they said, had not proved equal to the emergency. If they wanted more help, then the settlers must have some say in the running of the country. On the one hand, the military were accusing the settlers of hanging back from their duty; on the other, the Government were telling them to stay on their farms. If they were expected to enlist in greater numbers, they said, some organisation must be formed to enable them to leave their properties in the knowledge that everything would not be looted by natives or irreparably damaged in other ways in their absence.

A rousing recruiting speech by Captain E. S. Grogan swung the meeting. He told his audience, in plain terms, that they were rabbits. In an hour the packed hall was hot with cheering and a resolution had been passed unanimously, with immense enthusiasm, placing the whole European population and the resources of the country unreservedly at the Governor's disposal for military service, and calling upon the Government to make immediate preparations for conscription.

The Government thereupon agreed to cut the knot of friction between administration, military and unofficial population by forming a War Council, on which all would be represented, to reorganise the country on a war basis. It was to be a sort of war cabinet.

On the day following the mass meeting the Governor appointed the War Council. Its chairman was the Chief Secretary. Its other members were two officials, a representative of the military, and three settlers.

The settlers asked if they might elect their representatives. The Governor consented. "I regard it as of the utmost importance", he said, "that the country should recognise the constitution of the War Council as really representative." The Council passed a resolution at its first meeting recommending that its membership should be increased by three elected members.

The right of the unofficial community to electoral representation was, therefore, officially recognised in 1915. The Governor had no alternative but to agree. Matters had reached a stage when the country could not be organised for war without the full co-operation of the unofficials, settlers and traders alike. But such co-operation could only be secured if the unofficials were given some say in the policy of the country and in its execution.

9

The issue was an important one because it exposed the basic weakness of Crown colony government. This form of government rests ultimately upon moral authority. There are only two ways of imposing authority: by force—the dictatorship method; or with the mandate of the majority—the democratic method. In a colony with rigidly limited resources force is impracticable because it is too expensive; and under the British system it is theoretically repugnant. At the same time ballot-box democracy, with a huge uneducated and uninformed population, is impossible. The government, therefore, must secure the backing of the majority of the people they are ruling by goodwill and mutual agreement. If they fail in this they must either capitulate or resort to force of arms.

In a Crown colony the government is engaged in carrying out a policy laid down not by the people of the country but by someone else—the Colonial Office, and ultimately the British Parliament. The method of government is, in fact, a dictatorship without the power behind all such movements, a militant party of supporters pledged to the dictator's cause. Sooner or later there comes a time when the government's policy—or lack of one—becomes repugnant to the people under the government's rule. The government must then either modify that policy, giving the people to whom it is to be applied a chance of suggesting their own improvements, or they must be prepared to enforce their will by military strength.

In the first real emergency the country had had to face since it was settled, the system of government broke down, as it always will when the emergency is of vital importance to the population and when government and people do not see eye to eye. (This was the first time: it broke down again before two subsequent emergencies, one economic and the other political.) The Governor saw that he could not impose a drastic measure such, for example, as conscription, unless he had the settlers on his side. "No taxation without representation" is a powerful, if hackneyed, cry. The issue was a bigger one than taxation; it was a question not of paying duties but of offering lives; and so the demand for representation had even more force.

The Governor realised, also, that by giving the settlers some voice in matters which, after all, touched their whole lives and futures he would replace grudging acquiescence—perhaps open non-co-operation—by enthusiastic initiative. The settlers, given responsibility, would go much further than the Government would have dared to go.

So electoral privileges were granted. The country was divided into three areas, and a representative from each area was elected by the settlers to the War Council. This body then had a clear unofficial majority.

The Council was only advisory but on no important issue did the Governor ignore its advice. Its objects were to devise machinery for applying a registration ordinance to the country, to consider how conscription might be introduced, and generally to organise the community on a war footing. In a month it had galvanised the Protectorate into activity and changed the whole attitude of the Europeans towards the Government and the local campaign.

The registration ordinance was introduced into the Legislative Council in September 1915. A network of district committees was set up. The district Commissioner was the *ex-officio* chairman of each committee and the rest of the members were elected by the settlers. Each committee compiled a register of every European in the district and made recommendations to the War Council as to who could be spared for military service and who was indispensable. Certificates were issued to those in the indispensable class, and everyone else was required to enlist. The committee also catalogued the country's resources by taking inventories of cattle, buildings and crops.

In the first month of the War Council's existence it released a considerable number of men, both settlers and officials, for service. It closed down the Game department. Every day for two months the Council met and passed resolutions at the rate of over one a day. Almost all of these were put into effect by the Government. Conscription was passed into law in March 1916. East Africa was the first country in the Empire to legalise conscription.

10

The military situation, too, had changed by the time that Delamere returned to East Africa.

General Smuts arrived at the beginning of 1916 and took over the supreme command, with General Van Deventer to assist. Within a fortnight he had surveyed the position and planned an offensive. He had, under his command, two battalions of K.A.R., the 2nd Rhodesian Rifles, the E.A.M.R. and the East African Pioneers, the South African Field Artillery and the 2nd South African Infantry. There were also Indian troops, mountain batteries, an armoured-car battery, howitzers, signallers and a field ambulance.

The offensive started from Longido. In March 1916 Smuts captured the German base at Taveta. Then Moshi fell. Next, he marched down the Pangani river to Tanga, clearing as he went the Tanga-to-Taveta railway.

Throughout a season of abnormal rains he pushed the Germans steadily southwards towards the Central railway. Von Lettow Vorbeck retreated to Kondoa Irangi, 140 miles south of Moshi. Van Deventer followed and captured Kondoa Irangi after marching for sixteen days in succession in heavy rain without provisions. It was impossible to keep in touch with the transport, which had to hack its painful way through walls of bush, leaving a pitiful trail of dead and dying oxen stricken with tsetse-fly infection.

From Kondoa Irangi Van Deventer pushed southwards again, making for Dodoma on the Central railway. Von Lettow retreated, crossed the railway and disappeared to the south. Van Deventer entered Dodoma in July.

General Smuts, meanwhile, had cleared the Usambara mountains south of the Pangani river. This evil country was almost uninhabited. It was clothed in dense bush, fever-ridden, so thick with tsetse that the flies bit the hands and feet of the men all day as they rode and no animal lived longer than a fortnight. "The very air seemed to throb with fever," wrote a historian of the campaign, "and men withered away like parched flowers."

The Belgians, in the meantime, had occupied Mwanza and so gained control of Lake Victoria. A Belgian column marched down to Lake Tanganyika and occupied Ujiji. Tabora, the seat of government, was threatened from east and west and its connection with the coast cut off by Van Deventer at Dodoma. And, from the south, General Northey was steadily advancing from Nyasaland, clearing the enemy out of the southern highlands, whose capital, Iringa, he occupied in August.

Columns were hemming in the Germans from all sides. Von Lettow, reduced to less than 2000 white troops and about 14,000 blacks, was playing a desperate running game. He dodged about the bush with the mobility of a leopard, dragging his *Koenigsberg* guns after him and checking the inevitable advance first in one direction and then in another, having insects as allies to inflict casualties on a scale that he could never hope to approach.

CHAPTER XV

WAR-TIME IN THE PROTECTORATE
1917–1919

I

EAST AFRICAN producers, unlike farmers in almost every other combatant country, had little opportunity of making money out of the war. Prices were tantalising but the market out of reach. In the shipping crisis so remote a corner of the world as East Africa was of very minor importance. Coffee, flax, sisal, wool and other locally unconsumable products accumulated in the country and could not be exported.

When world shipping difficulties became acute committees were set up in different parts of the Empire to allocate essential exports to the limited hold space available. East Africa's ration of shipping accommodation was settled by a committee in Cape Town composed of representatives of the shipping companies and of the Union Government. It was only natural that East Africa's allocation should be exceedingly low.

The local Government appealed to the Imperial Controller of Shipping for a larger allowance. In 1917 the Controller decided that shipments from the Protectorate should be confined to maize, ground-nuts, copra, hides and wattle-bark. The War Council pointed out that none of these products, with the exception of hides, were available for export, and asked whether the space could not be used for industries "essential to the Protectorate's life and development, such as coffee, sisal and flax".

As a result of these representations the Protectorate was allocated 500 tons in each steamer loading for the United Kingdom—they were few and far between—and the War Council was allowed to fix the nature of the goods to be exported. Some of the accumulated coffee was sent off, but shortly afterwards the space allowance was docked to 100 tons in each ship. The Protectorate was thus virtually cut off from its market.

The worst blow fell on March 1st, 1917, when coffee was listed as a prohibited import into the United Kingdom. Thousands of tons were lying economically frozen in inadequate stores. The planters, unable to sell their crops, were unable also to find the money to harvest the next one and to maintain their plantations. Their situation became so bad that the Government was forced to advance them money out of a special loan on the security of their unsaleable crops.

The difficulty over imports was equally acute. Implements of all sorts were unobtainable. No British firm could export a plough or a tractor without permission from the director of Munitions and, owing to the relative insignificance of East Africa, this was refused. Farmers were desperately handicapped by being unable to renew their equipment. There were no spare parts for tractors or engines, no ploughs, no more machinery for preparing flax, sisal or coffee.

Economically, therefore, East Africa lost ground during the war, whereas older countries were able, in the immediate and narrow sense, to profit by it. Their wool and wheat, fibres and vegetable oils, tea and sugar fetched immense prices, and the farmers who remained on their land were able to take full advantage of wartime prosperity.

2

Delamere suffered with the rest of the East African farmers from the economic stagnation of the war. He was unable, for example, to ship his wool to England.

From the summer of 1916 until the end of the war he remained at Soysambu, producing meat for the troops and trying to prevent his sheep from dying of heartwater. The shortage of meat was such that he had, to his great regret, to slaughter the game hitherto preserved on the farm. During a single fortnight he sent the carcases of 1200 Thomson's gazelle to Nairobi.

As a result of the meat shortage Soysambu became so seriously understocked that in 1917 he made an effort to buy more cattle. But they were almost unobtainable. He sent Somalis with boxes of silver rupees to the north to buy Boran cows. They met with little success. Next he bought 1300 head from a Greek at Mwanza—captured enemy cattle—but before he could take delivery they were commandeered by the military.

During the whole of 1917 and 1918 Delamere ran Soysambu entirely single-handed with his Masai herds. (After the war, when it was making money and expanding, eight Europeans were employed on the estate.) There were about 23,000 sheep on the place in 1916, and 1600 cattle. All these sheep had to be dosed, marked, drafted, shorn and so on; Delamere counted the sheep himself every week during 1918. Standing in the blazing sun and watching an endless stream of white, woolly backs filing through a pen all day was tiring work and a strain on the eyes, and Delamere suffered from severe headaches as a result.

There were other worries. It was exceedingly difficult to import pure-bred bulls needed for the continual grading-up of stock. In 1917 Delamere did at last manage, after many disappointments, to procure six fine Shorthorns. Their fate was described by a neighbour:

July 29, 1917

I told you, I think, what difficulty there always is in getting bulls. The last effort was the most disastrous yet. Delamere got six bulls from Australia, and we had arranged that I should take over three of them on arrival. After much trouble and expense they were safely landed about a month ago. Bearing in mind what happened to the last lot of six which I landed, all of which died within a year of their arrival, we thought we would send those to the government laboratory near Nairobi to be inoculated with various diseases. We were told that there was not much risk, but we might perhaps lose one out of the lot.

They have however killed the whole six and this within a month of their arrival, so that's settled that lot pretty effectively. They cost us about £70 each landed. I don't so much mind the actual loss in money, but what I do mind is being left without any bulls. That is where the real loss lies.

This same neighbour, who knew Delamere well, wrote the following vivid sketch of his character:

May 13, 1917

I expect Delamere will come over to-day. He often comes over here nowadays. He's bored over there, I think. He is a very interesting man to talk to when he's by himself, full of original ideas. Sometimes I think he's the most brilliantly clever person I know. Marvellously quick to understand things, but he shuts his mind to all the things except those which actually have to do with the material side of life with the utmost determination, and although, as I say, he's so interesting to talk to, this discounting of all things except those material leaves a sort of gap, a something rather hollow in his company.

He's the sort of person you would hesitate to express a thought to that seemed perhaps a little far fetched, not that he wouldn't understand it, he would, no one better; but he would dismiss it probably with ridicule. His perception, his keen wit and an amazing faculty he has for, so to speak, detaching himself and *never* giving himself away make him very strong in dealing with most people and all sorts of material things. You never really get to know him. I doubt if anybody ever has. He won't be known but he likes to know others. It's rather "take all and give nothing" with him. . . .

Delamere came over to get me to come and help him to class his rams out, and so I went over there and I've been doing this all day. This is the time of year the rams are mated with the ewes and different rams are put into different flocks. This mating of the right rams with the ewes is an important point as one has to avoid inbreeding. He has the most complicated system of ear-marking I ever saw. It looks grand on paper but there it ends. There are far too many different sorts of ear-marks. It leads to confusion. I like a much simpler system. Some of these rams of his have so many marks on their ears to denote age, family, etc. etc., that their ears look as if they'd been nibbled by rats. We did the best we could, but I don't think much of the result myself.

That's rather a dreary place over there. There's something about it that always depresses me and somehow there's a sort of bareness about Delamere's surroundings that I can't explain.

3

Stock diseases, always the farmers' worst enemy in Africa, seized the opportunity afforded them by the disorganisation brought about by the war. The veterinary staff, fighting a hopeless battle to keep army transport animals alive, had little time to spare for producers' troubles. Native stock was moved about to meet urgent military needs and there was no one to enforce the quarantine restrictions.

Disease spread into the settled areas. Pleuro-pneumonia was rampant in the north and in 1916 rinderpest, the dreaded cattle plague that had decimated Masai herds and the game when it first swept down from Aden in 1898, reappeared. Heartwater, a fatal disease carried by ticks, attacked the sheep at Soysambu for the first time on a serious scale in 1916. It killed off thousands of sheep. The only means of checking it was by dipping. This entailed capital expenditure for the building of dips. The sheep also suffered severely from threadworms, and in 1917 the lamb mortality was 25 per cent.

At about the same time a disease called streptotricosis appeared among the cattle and began to spread dangerously. In 1917 regular dipping of cattle was started to combat it.

Long has gone home to fight and I am alone here [Delamere wrote in October 1916]. I have nearly 9000 ewes just starting to lamb and my cows calve in September-October-November. And now the rinderpest. I have been seruming myself, but am now going in for the double inoculation. It has given a lot of work.

This double inoculation, a new method introduced into East Africa by the government laboratory during the war, proved, in the beginning, not a blessing but a disaster.

The agent which causes rinderpest is a virus, one of a group of minute specks of matter—perhaps the smallest units that can possess the force of life—which enter the blood stream of men and animals. When an animal becomes infected with the rinderpest virus its blood cells mobilise a defence force of antibodies to fight the invader. If these antibodies win the action, then the animal recovers.

In the rinderpest inoculation, serum from an animal which has conquered the disease is injected into a susceptible animal. This provides the animal it is desired to immunise with a ready-made supply of antibodies. At the same time virulent blood, full of rinderpest virus, from a sick beast is injected. A battle between virus and antibodies takes place:

the antibodies win: and the susceptible beast becomes immune.

When the double inoculation for rinderpest became general, towards the end of the war, it was noticed that outbreaks of redwater occurred wherever it was applied. Investigations were made. The virulent blood injected into the susceptible cattle was all taken from native beasts. Then it was realised that redwater was endemic and almost all native cattle had suffered from the disease in their youth. They still carried the parasite in their blood—harmless to them, but capable of passing on infection to a beast which had never contracted the disease.

This, then, was what the veterinary laboratory had been doing — spreading redwater throughout the high-grade herds of the Protectorate, sending out the infection with their rinderpest serum. As soon as the connection between redwater and the double inoculation was realised, the laboratory set to work to build up a herd of cattle free from redwater to provide a reservoir of rinderpest serum. But many cattle were lost before this scientific tragedy was discovered.

4

Early in 1917 Delamere was elected to the War Council. One of its first actions after he joined it was to meet a demand from the military authorities for another 300 men. This almost squeezed the country dry. The situation was not, as Delamere pointed out, comparable to that in European countries with a reserve of women and older men.

I know of no country where it has been thought wise policy to leave farms lying without occupants, especially at this time when the supply of foodstuffs and raw materials is one of the gravest problems. The burden and strain on the few people remaining is in some cases more than they can bear and carry on.

In a new country like this it is quite impossible, as in England or other old countries, for all the young men to go to the front on a clean cut for age, as there is no one to take their place. A farm cannot possibly be locked up and left behind like a house or an office without grave permanent detriment to the country as well as to the individual.

It must be bad policy to wreck a producing country, except as a last resort perhaps, for the sake of the very small number of men that would be made available by such action.

In spite of these very serious difficulties, production somehow carried on. The Protectorate's war record was, considering the circumstances, a remarkable one. On the outbreak of war the male population of fighting age, including Civil servants, missionaries and aliens, numbered 2321. Of these 1987—over 85 per cent—joined up for military service.

Delamere was anxious that the War Council should become an instrument for planning for the future as well as for organising the present. The country that was most prepared for peace and its readjustments, he pointed out, would be the first to take advantage of post-war conditions. He outlined his ideas on the action which the Government ought to take in a long letter to the War Council written in October 1917.

"This country can, like all new countries of this sort," he said, "produce grain and meat at a much less expenditure of European man-power than most, and our wisest course would appear to be to plank on production." The first step, he continued, was to equip the Protectorate to supply, to a greater extent, its own local market. This would not only reduce expenditure on imports but it would also help, in a small way, to save valuable shipping space, and it would free for Britain—where the food shortage was at its worst—foodstuffs which would otherwise have to be bought from India, Australia or elsewhere.

Rice at the coast and wheat up-country were the two crops which, Delamere urged, the Government should most encourage. He believed that European growers should be forced by government decree to plant a certain percentage of their cultivated land with these cereals. "It has been found necessary in England to give arbitrary powers to local committees to bring about the growing of produce," he said. "I am sure the same thing has got to be done here." The Government, he suggested, should take over the running of the flour mills, fix a minimum price for wheat and restrict imports as the local supply met the demand.

Immediate action was taken on Delamere's suggestions with regard to wheat. One of the results, through no fault of the Government, was to send his flour mill, Unga Ltd., practically into bankruptcy.

In 1917 large quantities of wheat had to be imported at an exceedingly high cost. The local price was so inflated that there was a danger of an insufficient amount being held back for seed, and regulations under martial law were issued to govern the disposal of the 1917 crop. The Government also guaranteed to take over all locally grown wheat at a fixed price of 20 rupees a bag for three years from January 1st, 1919. During these three years wheat was to be imported only under licence. Unga Ltd. agreed to buy the entire crop at the price fixed by the Government.

A greatly increased acreage was planted, but the widespread drought of 1918 seriously reduced the crop. Imports of wheat, as a result, were not restricted. Indian wheat poured into the country and undersold the local product, but Unga Ltd. was still bound by its agreement to buy the East African crop at a fixed figure very much higher than the market price. It honoured its promise, but was almost ruined as a result.

5

Much of Delamere's time during 1917 was spent in touring the country with the Economic commission appointed by Sir Henry Belfield in March 1917. Its members included two officials, the Treasurer and the Commissioner of Customs; three settlers, of whom Delamere was one; and three commercial men. Its object was to take stock of all the Protectorate's resources and to suggest an economic policy for post-war reconstruction.

Evidence was collected from every district and from all classes of producer, trader and official. The result was a summary of fifteen years of development. The report showed that the total trade of the Protectorate had risen in value during this short period from nil to £7,800,000.

The rapidity of this expansion, the commission considered, was due to the policy of European settlement.

The function of Europeans in middle Africa [it suggested] is to act as a yeast leavening the inert dough of Africa's indigenous peoples. Where one white immigrant into Canada represents merely one additional participant in Canada's development, one white immigrant into East Africa may galvanise a thousand economically speaking "dead" Africans into active participation in imperial trade.

The report showed up the weak point in East African finances throughout their history—the high ratio of government expenditure to exports. East Africa's prosperity depended wholly on exports. Its internal trade was relatively insignificant. Yet in 1917 the Government's expenditure was only slightly less than the total value of all exports. Revenue was exceeded and a deficit was beginning to pile up.

Many recommendations were made. One was the establishment of a board of economic development composed of officials and unofficials which would suggest methods of opening up the country by means of such schemes as irrigation, boring for water in the Northern Frontier deserts, and finding a market for native cattle. Another suggestion was the setting up of a bank with government aid and control to finance big enterprises such as the development of fisheries and industrial alcohol.

Much could be done, the report said, to increase prosperity in the coastal belt. Once, under the Arabs, it was one of the richest strips of Africa, probably of the world. Vasco da Gama recorded that at Mombasa he had been given "fowls, sheep, sugar canes, citrons, lemons and large sweet oranges, the best that had ever been seen", and also "cakes of rice, butter and honey and plenty of fruit". At Malindi he had enjoyed a luxurious feast of "cauldrons of boiled rice, very fat sheep roasted whole and boiled, and much good butter, and then cakes of wheat and rice-flour, and many fowls boiled and roast stuffed with rice inside; also much vegetables and figs, coconuts and sugar canes". Now, under the British, the coast had languished until it produced little beyond copra—and the coconut beetle was rapidly destroying the remaining plantations—some mangrove bark and poles and a little grain for home consumption. The British had abolished slavery and so ruined the once wealthy Arab planters; no constructive steps had been taken to build a new policy of production on a less repugnant foundation.

The reform of the fiscal system was one of the report's main recommendations. The Protectorate was bound by the Brussels Convention to limit its import duties to a maximum of 10 per cent. One of the most valuable sources of revenue in any new country was therefore dammed, and money had to be raised as best it might be in other ways, such as a tax on exports. The abrogation of the Convention was strongly urged and numerous specific plans for expansion were outlined.

6

Delamere took an active part in framing this report. It filled much of his time and cost him a threshing machine. When the commission reached, on its list of witnesses, an association of wheat-growers on the Uasin Gishu plateau, Delamere protested that he could not spare the time to go all the way to Eldoret. A deputation of wheat-growers was therefore asked to come to Nairobi. The farmers, busy on their land, refused to do so. After an acrimonious exchange of telegrams they were subpoenaed and travelled morosely to Nairobi. Delamere, sympathising with their point of view, presented them with his threshing machine to put them in a better humour.

The Economic commission was a part of the Protectorate's preparations for peace. Another advisory body appointed by Sir Henry Belfield at about the same time was also instructed to draw up plans for reorganisation after the war. This was a committee which sat during 1917 to consider the best method of introducing a system of electoral representation for Europeans.

After the principle had been conceded over the War Council the grant of this privilege, once hostilities were over, became inevitable. The Imperial Government's promise, given by Mr. Bonar Law, was actually announced by Sir Henry Belfield in October 1916. "It is impossible for me to over-estimate the personal satisfaction with which I have received that announcement", he said. "It is no longer necessary for me to disguise the fact that to the best of my ability I have supported the request of the community through its succeeding stages."

The committee divided the country into ten electoral areas, each of which was entitled to return one member to the Legislative Council. There were also to be two Indian nominated members.

This scheme was discussed at intervals in 1917 and 1918 and criticised by a section of the settlers on the grounds that it did not go far enough. Certain "left-wing" extremists cried loudly for the moon in the shape of an unofficial majority on the Council. Delamere defended the committee's scheme in a speech delivered in 1918 which showed the relative moderation of his view:

> I cannot agree that it would be wise at present to put more responsibility on a community engaged in laying the foundations of agricultural and commercial prosperity. I believe it will be difficult enough at present to find people with leisure to carry out properly their duties as legislators; the duties of administration and an executive can best be carried out for the time by the Crown.
>
> I agree that minority advisory councils are never really satisfactory, but I think it is the best the country can do at present with regard to the main legislature, and in the meanwhile the widest possible measure of self-government should be given to all local and municipal bodies. The really important thing to my mind is that the Colonial Office should avoid interference in the local affairs of this Protectorate. I simply use the word interference because at the moment I can find no other; the word is not used in an offensive sense.
>
> Certain matters such as agriculture and education should be treated by the Colonial Office as transferred subjects and should be left entirely to the local legislature. On all other subjects the Secretary of State should rule that only matters of extreme importance affecting class legislation, native policy and finance should be referred to him.
>
> The Imperial Parliament through the Secretary of State should of course have the last word, but surely it can be laid down that except where members of Parliament raise questions, no effort will be made by the Colonial Office to interfere in matters of local concern, except where they affect other classes of the population, and finance. It is impossible for people living thousands of miles away, however capable they may be, really to keep in touch with the requirements of the country.

7

During 1917 the campaign in German East Africa achieved its object. The enemy were dislodged from their last bases and driven out of their colony.

It had been an arduous and expensive task. Smuts and Van Deventer drove the Germans steadily south. Smuts occupied Morogoro, the administrative capital, in August 1916. Then Portuguese troops, under British command, crossed the Rovuma, marched up the coast and occupied Dar-es-Salaam without resistance in September. The South African troops, or what was left of them after fever and dysentery had done their work, were sent home and replaced by native troops from Nigeria and the Gold Coast.

A final advance from north, east and west was launched on New Year's day 1917. The Germans, always just ahead somewhere in the bush, slipped away to the south through the encircling forces and crossed the Rufiji river. Then the rains set in, unduly early, and transport became impossible. The last seventy miles of Allied communications ran through black cotton soil which degenerated into a vast swamp.

The spring of 1917 was one of the wettest ever known. Bridges were carried away, fever raged, food was short, everybody was perpetually soaked and intermittently ill; but still the advance went on. General Smuts left to attend the Imperial Conference. The campaign deteriorated into an attempt to round up three little slippery German columns, without transport and apparently almost without food or ammunition, amounting in all to about 1000 Europeans and 7000 natives. It was like chasing three active tadpoles in a muddy pond. One of these columns wriggled away to the north, marched through hundreds of miles of territory conquered and held by the Allies, appeared near Kondoa Irangi, repulsed a Belgian attack near Mwanza, passed north of Moshi—almost on the British border—and finally surrendered to the Cape Corps in the Usambara mountains. There were fourteen Europeans and 150 askaris, and they had marched over 2000 miles through wild and cruel bush, from Nyasaland to the British East African border, between February and October.

Von Lettow retreated steadily towards the Portuguese border, fighting as he went, often incurring heavy losses. In October the last battle of the campaign was fought. It lasted four days. The British attacked Von Lettow's position and were eventually forced to withdraw after sustaining 2700 casualties out of the 4000 infantry engaged. The advance was held up for nearly a month.

In November half Von Lettow's forces surrendered. But the German commander himself escaped across the Rovuma into Portuguese territory with the remnants of his army, 300 Europeans and 1200 natives. A few days later the third German column under Tafel, 92 Europeans and 1100 natives, surrendered on the Rovuma.

There were now no enemy forces left in German East Africa. The territory was declared an Allied Protectorate in December 1917. A civil administration was established.

Von Lettow held out to the last. At the end of 1917 he captured a Portuguese post held by 700 men with his tiny, battered, almost exhausted force. He re-equipped with machine-guns, British rifles and ammunition, clothing and the first canned food his men had tasted for a year or more. Then he entered Nyasaland, recrossed the Rovuma, marched up nearly to Tabora, turned south again, invaded Northern Rhodesia—still pursued by British troops—and attacked Fife on November 1st, 1918.

On November 13th he prepared to attack another British post. His men fired into a factory at Chambesi and exchanged shots with British askaris. Later in the morning the news of the Armistice came through. Von Lettow was told. He agreed to march to Abercorn to surrender. It took him ten days to collect his scattered forces and on November 25th he surrendered formally with 30 officers, 125 white troopers, 1165 askaris and a mob of porters and hangers-on. He and his officers were permitted to retain their arms as a tribute to the courage and endurance which his Allied opponents had come to regard with astonishment and respect.

8

Before the war ended a further incident occurred in British East Africa in which Delamere took a leading part. It concerned the recruitment of natives for active service.

As the British forces pursued the enemy south into tsetse-fly infested bush, transport with oxen became more and more impossible. The army fell back on native porters and the administration were asked to supply the men.

For some time this was done without compulsion through the co-operation of the chiefs. Thousands of natives were recruited. It was estimated that in the course of the war 200,000 Africans served in the Carrier Corps—not, of course, at one time—and that about 46,000 of them died.

At first no attempt was made to call up any of the Masai who, almost alone among the major tribes of the Protectorate, had hitherto taken little active part in the war. Some Masai—particularly members of one section, the Loita—had done useful scouting work on the border, but they had supplied no recruits for the Carrier Corps and no askaris for the K.A.R. Other tribes of the same way of living, such as the Nandi, had responded willingly and made excellent soldiers. The Masai, who always boasted of their courage and military prowess, had simply boycotted the war so far as active service was concerned. They did not want to leave their own country and they objected strongly to military discipline, feeling it to be beneath their dignity. The behaviour of the Masai, the Government felt, was unfair to the other tribes who were sending their young men in thousands into the field.

Delamere was quick to come to the defence of his beloved Masai. It was true that they had shown no desire to join in the fighting; but their part, he suggested, was the equally vital one of supplying food to the troops. Their record in this respect, considering their well-known reluctance to part with stock, was good. Over 20,000 sheep had been commandeered from Masai flocks during the first eighteen months of the war. At the end of 1915 it was decided to purchase stock from the Masai and over 40,000 animals were obtained, without difficulty and for a poor price, in four months. Several officials who knew the Masai supported Delamere's contention that the tribe had not shirked its part in the campaign. "If the Masai have proved a failure in the war so far as man-power is concerned," said an official report on the reserve, "it must be remembered to their great and everlasting credit that they have largely furnished a most important munition of war in the form of beef and mutton. Not only the troops but also the public have drawn their supplies of fresh meat mainly from the Masai."

The Government made various tentative attempts to enlist *moran*, but the K.A.R. were not at first anxious to have them. A Masai company had been raised in 1902, but it had not proved a success and had been disbanded five years later. In 1916 a K.A.R. officer had attempted to secure some recruits without success. The K.A.R. did not press for the enlistment of Masai and administrative officers therefore took no active steps to persuade the *moran* to join.

9

In 1918 the question was raised again. Conscription had by this time been applied among the natives. The Government decided that an exception could no longer be made in favour of the Masai. A scheme for the compulsory recruitment of 300 *moran* was drawn up by the K.A.R. The young men, once obtained, were to be taken to a peninsula jutting out into Lake Victoria, near Bukoba, and a double company of regular troops was to be posted behind them to prevent them from deserting during training.

The officer-in-charge of the reserve, Mr. R. W. Hemsted, objected strongly to this scheme. He knew that it would arouse intense resentment among the Masai. No tribe was more easily offended, and the posting of troops to prevent desertion would have touched their pride on the raw and destroyed all hope of their co-operation. He believed that the 300 *moran* could be recruited voluntarily by his administrative officers. He drew up a scheme for enlisting the young men and concentrating them at Ngong for their training.

Before it could be put into force he went on leave and an officer with no previous experience of the tribe and no knowledge of the language took his place. This was unfortunate, for the Masai will as a rule only co-operate with men whom they know and trust, and are apt to read into some often innocent phrase or action a discourteous or arbitrary meaning.

The Government then decided to adopt the K.A.R.'s compulsory scheme. An officer was sent to the reserve with instructions to obtain the *moran*.

The administration knew nothing of the Government's plans until the K.A.R. officer arrived at Narok one Sunday morning and asked: "Where are my men?" The new officer-in-charge of the reserve, Mr. R. Weeks, was somewhat nonplussed. He wired to the acting Governor, Mr. (now Sir) Charles Bowring, asking that a conference might be held between the Government, the military and the administrative officers before the K.A.R. scheme was put into force. This request was refused. Mr. Weeks had no alternative but to carry out his orders.

Narok was in the centre of the country occupied by the Purko clan, the most independent and powerful of all the sections—and the one, moreover, that had been moved by the Government from Laikipia. The *moran* paid no attention to Mr. Weeks' orders and refused to come in. The elders professed themselves unable to influence the young men.

This amounted to deliberate defiance of the Government. To withdraw the demand for 300 men at this stage would have meant capitulation to the Purko *moran* and a collapse of government prestige. It was decided that the Government's authority must be upheld. At the end of August a company of the K.A.R., with two machine-guns, marched to Narok.

The *moran* retired into the forest near Melelo and refused to emerge even for a discussion. They had no intention of obeying the Government, they said; they had dismissed their elders and were going to live in the forest. They would rather die than join the K.A.R.

The next step was to find the ringleaders responsible for this defiance; but there were no *moran* to be seen. They were all hidden in the forest—acting on the principle so aptly expressed in one of their own riddles: "What is it that escapes the veld fire? The bare ground where no grass grows." The situation seemed to have reached stalemate.

A few days later news was received that a party of the rebellious *moran* were sleeping in some huts near a place called Ol-Alunga, a few miles from the K.A.R. camp. It was decided to arrest them. The huts were surrounded by the military on the night of September 9th and at dawn the officer-in-charge of the reserve and his assistant, Mr. Welby, entered the little village. It was deserted save for a few women and some cattle.

Then a disaster occurred. The askaris outside opened fire, without orders. Nearly 300 rounds were fired into the village and the administrative officers inside narrowly escaped being killed. The company commander took cover behind an ant-hill and blew frantically on his whistle. Before the askaris could be stopped they had killed two women and ten cattle and wounded two more women, an old man and a friendly *moran*.

10

As soon as Delamere heard of this he wired a protest in the following terms to the commandant of the K.A.R.:

Hope you will protest against needless use of K.A.R. to conscript people by force who would be useless when got. No precedent forcible conscription in face of opinion of whole people.

Left matter after Government moved in the hope that a collision might be avoided by Masai climbing down, but now position clearly indicates that they will not be conscripted although they wish to avoid hostilities. Cannot believe wanton attack on whole people to get useless conscripts justified. Suggest their part of doing their bit should be supplying cattle as before.

He followed this up with a telegram to the Chief Secretary which read:

Consider conscription of Purko *moran* bad policy except with their consent, and should have supposed that they were useless to military. Understand Masai say that they do not want to fight and will not be conscripted.

Situation now means that Government have to either order attack or hope for collision to simplify position, or withdraw. Consider strong Government should withdraw troops to border for fear of collision, and then appoint military civil board with some knowledge of people to go into question with the heads of the *moran*. Very willing serve if any use.

The Chief Secretary accepted Delamere's offer and summoned him to Nairobi for discussion. As a result he was asked to undertake negotiations with the Masai on behalf of the Government and was given a *carte blanche* to find a way out without further bloodshed. Orders were issued to delay further action until he arrived.

The Government were by now thoroughly alarmed. At any moment a general revolt of all sections of the Masai might, they feared, take place. They hoped that Delamere, who spoke the language fluently and who had the confidence of the tribe, might succeed in calming them down.

He left for Narok on September 15th, 1918. Three days before, an event had occurred which made his task seem almost hopeless. A large force of Purko *moran*, infuriated by the slaughter of the old women in the deserted village at Ol-Alunga, rushed the K.A.R. camp at dawn and stormed it with spears. They were beaten off by rifle and machine-gun fire and retired, leaving behind fourteen dead and carrying away many wounded.

The *moran* did not go back to the forest. Instead, they dispersed and roamed the country in armed, infuriated bands. Within the next few days over fifty stores in the Narok and Mara districts were pillaged and burned and several of the unarmed Indian owners murdered. (The damage was estimated later by a commission at £24,000.) The telegraph line from Narok to Elmenteita was cut. All Somali traders and their sheep were ordered out of the reserve. Settlers along the boundary applied to the police for protection, and their Kikuyu labourers started to desert in fright.

A system of mounted patrols was improvised. Several stores belonging to Europeans in the reserve were attacked and burnt. The *moran* population was quivering with resentment and on the verge of revolt. Every Purko *moran* was on the war-path with his spear greased and ready.

A single provocative action might have plunged the reserve, from Kajiado to the Mara, into rebellion.

The position was therefore critical when Delamere started from Elmenteita to Narok. It was also dangerous. Delamere was well known, at least by sight and name, to most of the *moran*; but the Masai are subject to fits of excitement almost amounting to hysteria, and there was more than a chance that in their present frame of mind they would attack a solitary white man on sight.

Delamere selected some of his most trusted herds from Soysambu to act as an escort and to conduct negotiations. He depended most on one called Mesobero, the head shepherd, renowned for his bravery in dealing with lions and devoted to his employer. Delamere went off on a pony with no other protection save half a dozen of his Masai, one Kavirondo and a revolver in his holster.

11

He started in the dark, at about three in the morning of September 15th. At dawn he was accosted by a roving band of *moran* who sprang out of the bush on to the path, spears uplifted, and ordered him to halt. It was an anxious moment. Mesobero and the other herds explained that they had come to make peace and the *moran* lowered their spears. One of the leaders urged the warriors to attack, waving his spear as he harangued them. Delamere spoke to him in Masai. The *moran* recognised him and quieted down.

A long discussion followed. The warriors explained their grievances. They had not, they said, intended to attack the K.A.R. camp until the shooting of the old women drove them into a frenzy and they attempted to retaliate according to the custom of the tribe—blood must be avenged by blood. Now some *moran* had been killed as well, and they would resist the Government to the last.

The sun came up and the discussion continued well into the morning. In the midst of it Mesobero suddenly appeared to throw a fit. His normal dignified calm gave way to a spasm of uncontrolled frenzy. He had just heard that his brother had been one of the fourteen *moran* killed by machine-gun fire during the attack on the K.A.R. camp. It was a bad omen for Delamere's chances of obtaining a settlement—his chief negotiator frenzied and then sullen with grief and anger at the death of his brother at the Government's hands.

Narok was safely reached late that night. Delamere found the occupants in a state of nerves, expecting to be attacked at any moment. The K.A.R. officer was anxious to go out and inflict a lesson on the *moran*. Delamere agreed with the administrative officers that this would only provoke the Masai into general revolt.

Most of the *moran* had left the Narok district, he discovered, and gone to the Mara, further west. He followed them there and established contact with scattered bands. His position made it possible for him to do this where a government officer would have failed. The Masai refused to meet any of the officers in charge of them; but they knew that he was not a government man, that he was their friend and that he had nearly always taken their side against the Government and sometimes got their grievances straightened out. Mesobero's loyalty was greater than his resentment. He did invaluable work in pacifying the young men.

Delamere succeeded in getting into touch with Legalishu, the head of the senior age-group of the Purko Masai and, therefore, one of the principal leaders. After a meeting on September 24th Delamere reported:

I have met a good many *moran* and they are in a nervous, excited state but I hope things will improve.

Legalishu himself is anxious that the *moran* should come into line but is very upset about the accident—the shooting of women and cattle.

He says he made blood-brotherhood with the Government years ago, and that meant that you and he were of one blood and would not spill each other's, but that this accident has upset that. I do not myself believe that any actual collision would have occurred unless the men who had lost mothers and cattle had not led the *moran* in, although surrounding villages is naturally always liable to lead to a collision. Orders having originally been given to get the *moran*, and they having refused, there seems to be no blame attaching to anyone here, but the matter has I think been rushed.

Ten days after his arrival Delamere was able to send a fairly encouraging report to Nairobi. He had succeeded in getting delegates from two of the age-groups—*sirits*—into which Masai warriors are divided to come into his camp for a conference. They repeated that they had not intended to fight until the women were shot and they lost control, and that they desired to remain on friendly terms with the Government as before.

Since coming here [he wrote] and going into everything, I see that the only way to do the Masai a good turn themselves (apart altogether from the desirability of adding to the numbers of the K.A.R.) is to make every effort to get them to agree voluntarily (more or less) to going out as soldiers. It makes the whole thing easier if they go with the consent, and under the control, of the *sirits* [age-groups].

I told the representatives of the two *sirits* that our people were in the middle of the greatest war we had ever known and were inclined to look on those who did not actively help as almost enemies, and that Government had said three things: (1) that they must produce men for soldiers; (2) that they must pay for the damage done to shops, etc.; (3) that Government was considering what should be done to the *moran* for having disobeyed orders.

I said I was sure that Government would enforce the first two, but that I hoped that prompt acceptance of these and the explanation of the causes of the trouble *might* induce Government to forego the third as they were still considering it. . . . I advised them to make up their own minds that they would voluntarily give the men, and to influence the other delegates accordingly.

Some days later *moran* of all the different age-groups assembled, by now in a quieter frame of mind, on the Mara river. A long meeting followed. Agreement was reached. Delamere returned to Narok and telegraphed a brief report to the Secretariat:

Representative meeting of Purko *moran* held at Mara agreed to find men for K.A.R. . . . I came to Narok to ask Mr. Welby to come out and satisfy himself that it is genuine. They wish to select the men themselves and replace rejects. . . .
Strongly urge all past matters wiped out. Surrender of men agreed unconditionally, but *moran* ask that the men going into the K.A.R.

should not have cattle commandeered for military during period of service because they are unable to look after them while away. I think that if this is answered in the affirmative it will ease matters, and hope you will agree to this.

12

A further report was sent in after Delamere returned to his farm. He gave his version of the causes of the trouble in the following words:

I firmly believe that the *moran* had no intention of actually fighting. They knew quite well the power of rifles, the Kassaroni [an age-group] for instance having lost a lot of men only a year or two ago in German East Africa.

Then the accident happened at the village. That upset the relations and friends of the women who were killed, and they attacked in desperation (as they say) knowing that they had no chance. They have realised now that the shooting of the women was a pure accident.

I am sure that no question of fighting was ever settled among them, although it is likely that the catching of *moran* would have led to fighting in individual cases. If it had been settled in advance the *sirits* from Subugo, Loita and Siana would have been fully represented and everyone in the country would have known where the *moran* had sent to get medicine for fighting.

I can find no evidence at all of this.

It is very unlucky:

(1) That Hemsted was away and Weeks new to the Masai.

(2) That the matter was rushed, instead of the *moran* being given time to talk matters over.

(3) That no official in the reserve knows the language of the people. All *shauris* are done through interpreters and hangers-on, and the *moran* and others bitterly complain that the truth frequently does not reach the *boma* undiluted. The headman at the village at Narok is a Damat, and the Purko believe that he and his people prejudice the Government against them.[1]

(4) That Government did not ask Hemsted to stop till his scheme was through, or wait till he came back from leave.

[1] The Masai are divided into thirteen tribal divisions or clans. Of these the Purko is the largest and most important. The Damat form a separate division, but they were defeated some years ago by the Purko and subsequently lived in the same part of the reserve more or less subject to their conquerors.

(5) That in addition to the disagreeable requests necessitated by the war the Masai should have been worried with questions of policy which might well have been left till after the war.

I am not saying anything against Mr. Weeks. I am sure he is a very capable officer, but he cannot know the people in the time.

As soon as Delamere's telegraphic report arrived, the acting Governor held a meeting with his senior officials and the suggested terms for a settlement of the case were approved and passed through Executive Council on the same day. It was decided to allow the age-groups to select the men themselves, as they had requested; to promise that cattle should not be commandeered from *moran* on active service; to impose a communal fine which would cover all damage done to property during the outbreak of looting and to exact blood-money for the murdered storekeepers; and to let the Masai off any punishment for attacking the K.A.R. in view of the provocation they had sustained.

The possibility of a widespread Masai rising was thus averted. Such a rebellion, coming at that stage of the war when most of the K.A.R. were hundreds of miles away in conquered territory, might well have been disastrous.

The last trick went to the Masai. Delamere went home, the K.A.R. retired, and the *moran* dispersed again. They did not attack any more stores; nor did they produce any soldiers. "The rank and file of the *moran*", says the official report of the incident, "continued a policy of passive resistance, avoiding all intercourse with government officers." Before the Government decided whether or not to take further action the Armistice was signed and the need for more recruits passed.

Later, the Masai worked off their feelings in several large-scale raids over the border into the ex-German colony. The K.A.R. were called on once more to pursue elusive and intractable *moran* over the Masai plains. This time a detachment of mounted infantry was sent to the reserve. It proved far more effective than the somewhat cumbrous infantry. The raiding was checked and the chief primarily responsible, Sendeyo, was evicted from the reserve and deported to Meru. A heavy fine was imposed and paid to make good part of the damage done when the stores were sacked by Purko *moran*.

There was comparative peace again, after that, until 1922, when an effort to modify the military organisation of the tribe and persuade the *moran* to marry and settle down in villages instead of roaming the country in bands, clad in warriors' pigtails and armed with spears (an effort which Sir Charles Eliot had prophesied would eventually have to be made if the Masai were to be kept under control) resulted in a further though less serious outbreak, and to its aftermath of a collective fine.

Two months after the K.A.R.'s abortive attempt to recruit Masai soldiers the war came to an end. By Article 119 of the Treaty of Versailles Germany renounced all her rights in her overseas possessions to the Allied and Associated Powers.

CHAPTER XVI

PROTECTORATE INTO COLONY
1919–1921

1

A NEW age, new hope, new faith, new blood—these were the promises of 1919. The waste of the war was ended; now for something useful—production, progress, expansion. More land under the plough, more coffee, more flax, more wheat, more stock—the world was crying out for these things, and paying well for them. This was the Empire's chance; East Africa would never look back.

Settlers hurried home from the conquered territory or, if they could somehow squeeze into a boat, from Europe, to find their farms in havoc. Ploughed land was covered with couch grass, once flourishing young coffee trees smothered in a jungle of weeds. The drooping yellow fruit of the sodom-apple stared like a fixed and baleful eye through the curtain of tangled creepers screening the once cultivated ground; innumerable burrs clung tenaciously to the passer-by as he trampled through the undergrowth that obliterated his flower-beds. Implements were rusted or stolen, trees cut down by native squatters, and even houses, sometimes, half-devoured by white ants.

Often it meant a new start. Years of hard work had been wiped out, money lost, by four years of absence. Their capital gone, settlers turned to the banks. The faces of the bank managers were shining with confidence. Overdrafts were settled with a wave of the hand. A mere 8 per cent was nothing. Expensive coffee and flax machinery reared itself on overdrafts; tractors ran on them, houses were built with them. In two or three years, when profits came in, they would vanish (the borrowers thought) like the scaffolding of a completed house.

PROTECTORATE INTO COLONY

The administration of the country needed a new start, too. It was in a bad way. Reconstruction from the foundations was essential. Everything was rickety. The railway had been hopelessly neglected; the permanent way was almost crumbling and hundreds of thousands were wanted to restore it. Bridges were verging on the unsafe; roads had been rubbed out by rain, dust and rocks; the one little pier at Kilindini was chronically congested; stores and sheds were inadequate and confusion reigned at the port. The Civil service was understaffed, underpaid and discontented. A deficit for three years running had exhausted the surplus balances and disorganised the budget; the campaign had cost the country at least a million pounds over and above what had been paid by the Imperial Government; expenditure had risen by about 60 per cent since 1913.

In 1918 there had been a drought and a severe famine. The Government had imported maize, but in spite of all it could do thousands of natives died from epidemics which followed on the heels of hunger. The labour supply was badly depleted and native production in the reserves at a standstill. There was a shortage of everything that was most needed—wagons, oxen, tents, lorries, implements, petrol. The country was, in short, in a state of confusion and disorganisation; its greatest need was for a decisive and energetic man who would put it right.

The Governorship had been vacant since Sir Henry Belfield's retirement in 1917. The choice of a good man was of the utmost importance. The settlers were afraid that the Colonial Office would take one of their standard colonial governors out of the stock-room, dust him, and ship him out with a kind word or two to do his best. This, they believed, would be fatal. Only a man with initiative and organising capacity could hope to clear up the muddle left by the war.

In 1918 the Convention of Associations cabled to the Colonial Office a request for the appointment of a military Governor. The Secretary of State for the Colonies, Mr. (afterwards Viscount) Long, agreed, and in June the appointment of Major-General Sir Edward Northey, who had won a high military reputation for his direction of the Nyasaland campaign, was announced.

2

The new Governor arrived in January 1919—a dapper, monocled and autocratic herald of the new era of prosperity whose triumphal procession through the fat years would (so everyone hoped) soon follow in his wake. He was greeted warmly by the settlers. The Convention of Associations gave for him the biggest dinner yet seen in Nairobi on the night following his arrival.

The difficulties facing Sir Edward Northey were immense. Perhaps even now their extent has not been realised. His achievement in reconstructing the country from top to bottom, pulling it together and placing it on a sound financial footing, all in less than four years, was a remarkable piece of administration.

The next few years were perhaps the most eventful and significant in the history of the Protectorate. In Sir Edward Northey's short régime seven major steps of lasting importance were taken.

A new Legislative Council was set up with elected members representing the settler and commercial communities. The ex-soldier settlement scheme was launched and, in spite of set-backs, acknowledged to be the most successful postwar settlement project in the Empire. The Protectorate graduated to Crown colony status in June 1920.

The railway was completely reorganised. Its finances were separated from those of the Protectorate, Uganda's well-justified grievances were removed and the railway system was placed on a business footing under the control of an inter-colonial council. The first big loan was raised and out of it a new railway built and harbour works begun. The Civil service was reorganised and the rates of pay raised so as to place them on equal terms with other colonial services. The budget was balanced and swollen expenditure drastically cut so as to bring the country's coat within the measure of its cloth.

New lines of policy, afterwards developed until they became the framework of the country's political structure, were enforced for the first time. Sir Edward Northey divided the country, for example, into settled and native areas, separating administration into two branches and placing resident magistrates in charge of settled areas and district Commissioners under a chief Native Commissioner in control of the reserves. (These arrangements had first been recommended by the Native Labour commission on which Delamere sat in 1912.)

The office of chief Native Commissioner was created and most of the reserves were demarcated. The principle, confirmed by successive Governors, was laid down that the Government expected every able-bodied young African to work—either in his own reserve, or for the Government or the settlers.

These steps paved the way for the beginnings of decentralisation: for the setting up of native councils with limited powers of taxation and self-government in Sir Robert Coryndon's time, and for the introduction of municipal and district councils in the settled areas in Sir Edward Grigg's. They laid the foundations of the "dual policy" afterwards defined and elaborated by both succeeding Governors.

Three shadows fell across the political life of the colony (as it had by then become) during this eventful period. One was the disastrous stabilisation of the exchange; another an acute labour shortage, the worst ever experienced; and the third was the Indian question. All three had a serious effect on the country's recovery from the paralysis of the war.

Sir Edward Northey came with a lump of sugar in his pocket to reward the colonists for their good behaviour in the war. This was the long-awaited grant of the franchise. A definite announcement was made in his opening address to the Legislative Council in February 1919.

A bill was introduced in 1919 providing for the election of members on the lines suggested by the committee appointed by Sir Henry Belfield two years before. Nairobi was given two representatives; eleven electoral areas were therefore established instead of ten. At the same time the Governor announced that two unofficial members would be placed on the Executive Council; and in April 1919 he appointed Delamere and Mr. T. A. Wood, one to represent the settlers and the other the commercial interests.

The first election was held in January 1920. The settlers

drew one conclusion: that another step on the road to self-government had been taken.

3

Early in 1919 the Government launched its second official attempt to fill up the empty spaces with settlers—potential taxpayers and producers of wealth.

A scheme for settling ex-soldiers on the land when hostilities were over had been put forward as long ago as 1915 by the War Council. The idea that lay behind it at the time was not so much patriotic or even economic as strategic.

It was generally thought, in the early days of the war, that the East African campaign would have a highly unsettling effect on the native population. The white man's prestige must, it was said, be severely shaken, and natives who had not only seen Europeans shoot each other on an impressive scale but had themselves done some of the shooting would return to their reserves with disturbing ideas about the vulnerability of white men, and even with an acquired taste for killing them. The only insurance for safety, it was felt, lay in doubling the white population and filling in as many as possible of the gaps.

The idea was put up to the Secretary of State. He did not squash it, although he made it quite clear that any idea of financial help from the Imperial Government must be ruled out. Sir Henry Belfield appointed a Land commission to draw up a provisional scheme. Delamere was a member.

The arguments in favour of a settlement project had strengthened by the time the commission began to sit. As insatiate armies sucked up civilian populations with ever increasing velocity, it became clear that hundreds of thousands of men would be stranded, after the war, jobless and restless, wondering how to settle down. If East Africa could provide for a few of them farms, a healthy life and a chance of making good, it would be doing a service to the Empire as well as to itself.

The Land commission reported in January 1919. It recommended that all the land that had already been surveyed for alienation should be thrown open for the scheme. Ex-soldiers were to be given land free of purchase price on a

999 years' lease for an annual rental of 10 cents of a rupee per acre.

Within two months of Sir Edward Northey's assumption of office a definite scheme had been drawn up. It differed from the original project mainly in that it required most of the ex-soldiers to buy their land on easy terms. It was felt that the Protectorate could not afford to give away its only real asset. Settlers were to be divided into two classes: those who were to be given free farms of up to 160 acres and those who were to purchase larger blocks. About 250 small and 800 larger farms were set aside. The allotment was to be made by ballot and selection boards were set up in London and in Nairobi to examine the records and approve the characters of all applicants. Only those approved as suitable settlers by these boards were allowed to take part in the draw.

Applications poured in to both boards. Over two thousand had reached Nairobi by the end of May and many applicants were turned down. The local draw took place in June in the Theatre Royal. The scene resembled a miniature Irish sweep. Two revolving drums were kept busy all day while the audience watched their future being gambled away on the dismantled stage. A name was drawn, then a number. The number showed the order in which the applicant could chose his farm from a descriptive list issued by the Government. In London, a similar draw took place at the Colonial Office a few weeks later.

The number drawn and the farm chosen, the intending settler had still to reach his land. London was crammed with irritated men from the Dominions trying to find berths in scarce and overcrowded ships. East Africans were making valiant attempts to reach their homes by way of the Cape. At last a ship was found. In November 1919 an army of some 1500 settlers and settlers' families left England in the *Garth Castle* on their new adventure.

The local Government made it clear from the outset that practically nothing was being given away. It arranged for a hostel containing fifty beds to be made available at Kabete, offered to sell new-comers tents at cost price and issued a return ticket to Mombasa for the price of a single. There was considerable local feeling that this was not enough.

The Government refused to waive customs duties on such of the new settlers' household goods as were dutiable, and it was felt that the prices of the farms, based as they were on Nairobi land agents' sanguine estimates of the market value, were too high.

There were other complaints. Some of the farms, located with difficulty, proved to be devoid of water; some, it was said, had even been marked out on the parched volcanic floor of Menengai crater and on the glaciers of Mount Kenya. But others were more promising; and gradually the wave of ex-soldiers which swept into Nairobi in four special boat trains in December rippled up-country in ox-wagons and mule-carts and second-hand motor cars and came to rest on the sheep plains of Nanyuki, the flax and coffee land of Kericho, the cattle country round Kiu and the maize areas of the Trans Nzoia. The Government's second settlement scheme had been carried through. Eight years later it was estimated that 75 per cent of the ex-soldiers had made good and were still settled on the land.[1]

The struggle to make good in the next few years was a severe one. Like others before them, in many lands, the settlers had to suffer the bitter shattering of one of the world's greatest and most persistent illusions—that farming is a simple, straightforward business, readily learnt. They bought their knowledge slowly and with many disappointments. Their inexperience was balanced by courage and enterprise; they had no government or other backing to support them. Nearly all the soldier-settlers were small farmers with very limited capital. They started dairying and pig production, grew maize and flax.

For some of them it was flax that proved their undoing.

---

[1] Out of 1031 farms allotted under the scheme, 770 were still in possession of the original owners in 1927. Another 225 had been transferred to other owners, and the balance had reverted to Government.

About 4,736,000 acres of land had been alienated before 1919; the ex-soldier settlement scheme added 2,880,000 acres more. The total of alienated land was then 12,212 square miles out of an area for the whole Protectorate of just under 240,000 square miles.

The native reserves were estimated to embrace 31,250 square miles. When the boundaries of the reserves were gazetted in 1925 another 11,000,000 acres, or over 17,000 square miles, were added, bringing the total area of the native reserves to 48,345 square miles.

In the summer of 1919 it was worth well over £300 a ton. In August 1920 a Miss Smith of Lumbwa obtained the record price of £590 a ton for flax and £340 for the tow. Young coffee trees were being rooted up to make room for flax. The acute shortage of fibre on the English market, due to the sudden drying up of supplies from Russia, seemed likely to continue and there was no apparent reason why prices should fall.

The British East Africa disabled officers' colony, a gallant attempt to found a co-operative farming community financed out of the pooled savings of their semi-crippled members, gambled everything on flax. They secured a block of 25,000 acres near Kericho, bought up some army tractors that had done duty in France, broke a large area of virgin land and put it down to flax.

Then came the sudden post-war slump. Flax fell to less than £100 a ton—well below the cost of production at the time—and the disabled officers' colony, broken now in fortune as well as in health, was ultimately dispersed. Later, their land was found to be excellent for tea and the company that bought it from them planned to establish there one of the biggest tea-gardens in the world. Had a lucky chance led the ex-soldiers to experiment with tea instead of with flax at the beginning, they might have been saved a second breaking on the wheel of world events far outside their control.

4

The influx of soldier-settlers, combined with the effects on the native population of war, famine and influenza, created a labour crisis for the second time in the country's history.

On this occasion there was a third complication. The Government—always by far the biggest employer—upset the labour market by a sudden demand for men to build the new Uasin Gishu railway. Thousands who would otherwise have sought work with private individuals were kept busy laying rails; and the Government found itself faced with the very problems which, at periodic intervals, so vexed the settlers.

The question was whether both Government and settlers

should let themselves be crippled and (in the case of the farmers) even ruined, or whether some pressure should be brought to bear on natives to stimulate them to work.

Three factors entered into the situation which had not been present at the time of the previous labour crisis of 1908. In the first place, the Government had a more direct responsibility towards the colonists than before. The ex-soldier settlement scheme was a Government one, the Government had invited the settlers to come, and there was a feeling that ex-service men, still heroes in 1920, deserved special consideration.

In the second place, the fear that demobilised askaris and carriers would return to their reserves in a restless and unsettled mood to stir up trouble was still present in everybody's minds. Safety could only be secured, people thought, by giving them jobs as soon as possible to keep them occupied. It would be courting disaster to let them stay idle in the reserves, out of touch with Europeans, drinking beer and thinking of the strange things they had seen south of the Pangani river.

The third factor was the economic state of the country. This had never yet been really strong; now it was almost desperate. The costs of government were twice as large as the total annual sum realised for exports. Economically the position was untenable. The administration was like a pyramid balanced on its apex. Unless production could be increased immediately and drastically the Protectorate would be bankrupt and the Imperial Government would have to be called to the rescue with a grant-in-aid.

The damage done by the war had to be repaired at once. It was no good saying "we will be patient and carry on as best we can for three or four years; by that time the young men may have tired of life in the reserves and be ready to find work". Budgets had got to be balanced at once, not three or four years hence; nor would the banks wait for their interest, the railway for its freight, the crops for their harvest.

The natives' interests, as much as those of the Europeans, were bound up in the country's economic revival. Missionaries, educationalists, officials and the Convention of Associations were continually urging the Government to spend more on native services—hospitals, education, agriculture and the rest.[1] Indeed, few people questioned that these services had been sadly neglected and that a progressive scheme of native betterment was overdue.

But, as a poet once remarked in picturing a Platonic heaven: "How shall we wind these wreaths of ours where there are neither heads nor flowers?" There must be money to pay for these desirable but expensive projects.

The native's principal contribution to the revenue, hut tax, was derived mainly from wages paid to him by settlers. His receipts from production in the reserves were still of secondary importance. Unless natives went out to work, therefore, money could not enter the reserves in any quantity and hut tax could not be collected. More money must be made to circulate before the Government could raise the larger revenue it so badly needed.

Above all, it was essential that exports should be immediately increased. This was a question of urgency. It was believed that the quickest results would be obtained by ensuring that the new settlers who were everywhere putting fresh land under cultivation should be able to obtain sufficient labour to carry out their programmes. The stimulation of production in the reserves was part of a long-range policy. It must certainly be applied, but it could not give noticeable results for several years. There was a groundwork of education to be laid before exports of saleable produce from the reserves could be expected materially to increase. On European farms, on the other hand, alleviation of the labour shortage would result in increased exports within a year.

[1] The Convention passed resolutions pressing for further medical facilities for natives at frequent intervals, mainly in the interests of the labour supply. For example, in January 1919 they agreed: "that it is essential that every facility for medical treatment and medicines be given to the native population in outlying districts, and that quarantine and other necessary accommodation be provided"; and again that "the proper care medically of natives in the reserves and on farms closely affects the diseases of syphilis and yaws which are appallingly prevalent; by the use of an effective drug these diseases can be combated and the country benefits". At the same meeting a resolution was passed: "that this Convention urges the Government to take immediate steps to further the industrial education of the native population".

5

These considerations lay behind the issue of the so-called "Ainsworth circular" which aroused an outburst of indignation in some quarters in England. The chief Native Commissioner, like Cranmer, lighted a candle which was to burn fiercely for many years. Even the dampers applied by several impartial commissions failed to extinguish it completely, and its flame still flickers in speeches and writings richer in eloquence than in accuracy.

It was ironical that this circular should have been signed by a man renowned, for twenty-five years, for his active interest in native welfare, a man who had incurred constant criticism and occasional abuse from the settlers on the grounds of being unduly "pro-native"—of persistently favouring the native's interests, that is, before those of any other class of the community. So unpopular had he become for the alleged one-sidedness of his attitude that the Convention of Associations had passed a resolution asking specifically for his removal.

The final responsibility for the circular belonged, of course, to the Governor. Mr. Ainsworth drafted the circular and Sir Edward Northey approved it with a few minor alterations.

Its object was to lay down a uniform labour policy for the whole country. Before it appeared, each district Commissioner acted as he thought best. This lack of consistency led inevitably to friction. The circular was meant to clear the matter up.

His Excellency trusts [the controversial passage stated] that those officers who are in charge of what are termed labour-supplying districts are doing what they can to induce an augmentation of the supply of labour for the various farms and plantations in the Protectorate; and he feels assured that all officers will agree with him that the larger and more continuous the flow of labour is from the reserves, the more satisfactory will be the relations as between the native peoples and the settlers and between the latter and the Government.

The necessity for an increased supply of labour cannot be brought too frequently before the various native authorities, nor can they be too often reminded that it is in their own interests to see that their young men become wage-earners and do not remain idle for the greater part of the year.

At the same time as the issue of this circular, government measures for the protection of labour were strengthened. An amendment to the Masters' and Servants' ordinance was passed providing for labour inspectors who would travel round continuously to farms seeing that good conditions were maintained. All natives going out to work were first to be certified as medically fit by government doctors. The main ordinance, passed in 1910, already laid down conditions of housing, rationing, provision of blankets and so on, and now these were to be properly enforced. A Resident Native ordinance was passed to regulate the growing custom by which natives voluntarily left their reserves with their wives and families, cattle, goats and all their possessions to settle as "squatters" on the uncultivated parts of European farms. In return for free land, grazing, water, firewood, medical attention and so on, the hut-holder contracted to work for half the year at the ordinary rate of pay for the European farmer on whose land he squatted.

One further government action was taken to ease the labour situation. This was the enforcement of the Native Registration ordinance passed in 1915. The measure laid down that every native who left his reserve and entered employment should carry with him a certificate of identification. The only way by which illiterate natives could be identified was by means of finger-prints, and these were recorded on his certificate.

6

In authorising the issue of the Ainsworth circular Sir Edward Northey was not making any new departure in policy. The Government was already fully committed, by repeated promises, to encourage natives to work. Sir Edward Northey's predecessor had pronounced in 1917:

> It cannot be too widely known that it is the declared policy of the Government to give the fullest encouragement to settlers and natives alike to arrange for the introduction and maintenance on farms of a

supply of labour sufficient to meet the varying requirements of different proprietors. If any impression exists that the legitimate requirements of the farmer are to be subordinated to the policy of confining the native to his reserve, I trust that these words will be sufficient to dispel that impression. . . .

I am prepared to state definitely that we desire to make of the native a useful citizen, and that we consider the best means of doing so is to induce him to work for a period of his life for the European.

Sir Edward Northey's policy was a continuation of that professed for many years by changing Governors and Secretaries of State. The only novelty lay in the fact that he proposed to put the accepted policy into practice. His own views, as summarised in his first speech to the Legislative Council, were no more strongly expressed than those of Sir Henry Belfield. "It is a duty", Northey remarked, "to encourage the energies of all communities to produce from these rich lands the raw products and foodstuffs that the Empire requires. . . . I believe that there is a great future for this country, but only if a steady flow of natives out of the reserves, working willingly for a good wage, well housed and fed, under European control and supervision, can be properly organised."

There are two points to consider [he wrote later in a circular defining his policy on labour]: firstly, that native labour is required for the proper development of the country; and secondly, that we must educate the native to come and work for his own sake, because nothing is worse for a young native than to remain idle in the reserve. . . .

In the old days the young man was constantly on the warpath and led a healthy life of outdoor exercise; nowadays, unless he works, he has no compensation for the loss of the raids and fights of those old days. For the good of the country and for his own welfare he must be brought out to work. . . .

Having got the native out to work we must see that he is properly looked after by initial medical examination and subsequent medical care, by proper feeding and housing and by provision of reasonable comfort when travelling by road or rail. There should be compensation in cases of accidents while employed, general conservation of health and prevention of employment of immature youths.

Neither the Governor nor the majority of his officials doubted that it was both mentally and physically good for the native to go out to work. Mentally, because the native could learn at first hand the elements of better farming—the advantages of ploughs, for example, the principles of stock breeding and the conception of manuring. Working for a European was, for an intelligent native, a practical education. Physically, because men from those tribes that lived on deficient, inadequate diets quickly grew fatter, stronger and healthier on the regular and sufficient supplies of food issued by their employer. Farmers who recruited labourers from one of the poorer and more remote reserves often visited by famines could see their gang of skinny weaklings filling out, putting on weight and losing the pinched look born of malnutrition, within the period of the contract.

Sir Edward Northey was not a little taken aback at the reception of the Ainsworth circular in England. The Aborigines Protection Society and the conference of Missionary Societies protested to the Secretary of State. The Archbishop of Canterbury launched a spirited attack on the circular in the House of Lords, referring darkly to "sjamboks and ropes". The circular was denounced as giving official sanction to "forced labour". The cry was taken up and an impression gained ground that the Protectorate Government was turning out forced labour under legal compulsion for the benefit of private individuals.

Opposition to the tone of the circular from within the Protectorate was naturally better informed. The Bishops of Mombasa and Uganda and Dr. Arthur, head of the Church of Scotland Mission, signed a joint memorandum to the Governor protesting against the excessive amount of power placed in the hands of the native chiefs and headmen, who were, in the words of the circular, to be "repeatedly reminded that it is part of their duty to advise and encourage all unemployed young men . . . to go out and work". The Bishops held that the reliance to be placed on chiefs and headmen would lead to abuses. The chiefs, anxious to gain government approval, would virtually force the young men to work against their will.

The Bishops' memorandum recommended a system of

carefully controlled and legalised compulsory labour instead of the use of administrative pressure, which they believed to be more open to abuse.

We recognise that much in this circular is good and indeed necessary [they wrote]. Compulsory labour is not in itself an evil and we would favour some form of compulsion, at any rate for work of national importance, provided that it was frankly recognised as compulsion and legalised as such, that it was confined to able-bodied men, that good conditions should be guaranteed by the Government and that the time of employment should be defined and limited.

Given these and other provision the Bishops announced themselves to—

favour compulsory labour, as long as it is clearly a necessity. . . . We believe that ideally all labour should be voluntary. We recognise that, at present, this is impossible, and that some form of pressure must be exerted if an adequate supply of labour for the development of the country is to be secured.

7

The heads of the Church thus objected to the circular on the ground that it did not go far enough—that it did not frankly institute compulsory labour—rather than on the ground that its premises were repugnant. They quarrelled with the Government over the method, not the principle. Their views were supported by other leading missionaries. Archdeacon Owen—head of the Church Missionary Society's station in north Kavirondo and a renowned champion of native rights—advocated forced labour in the following terms:

Supposing that the settlers and all the commercial men did not exist in Kenya Colony, the native could not get a market for his labour without going outside the colony; or in other words, he would be at a great disadvantage. All he would have then for sale would be the fruits of the land.

The Power which undertook the task of civilising the natives of Kenya would then have to do its utmost to make the native grow a sufficiency of such crops, for sale in Europe and elsewhere, as would enable the native to pay for the cost of civilising him. A railway would be required, roads would have to be made, and transport of crops arranged for. A much larger body of soldiery would be required in order to give that impression of might necessary to prevent outbreaks, which is produced to-day by commercial men and settlers.

It is doubtful whether the natives of Kenya could shoulder such costs. Therefore it follows that unless the civilising Power were prepared to spend money every year for which it would get no return, the progress of the natives towards civilisation would be very slow. . . .

Boiled down to a small compass it comes to this, that the native wants to pay for civilisation in his own way, and in the method most convenient to himself. When he has plenty of the fruits of the earth, he will offer them, but will offer little labour; when the fruits of the earth fail him, he will offer an excess of labour. And the colonist of this country, who be it remembered has made the labour market and made it possible for the native to have something to fall back on if harvests fail him, refuses to be made a convenience of in this way, and demands that there must be a stable supply of labour.

And he is quite right too. He has made the labour market, and he deserves consideration. He cannot carry on when left to the caprice of natives who do not understand the situation.

I would suggest that for a period of ten years compulsion be used to secure a continuous supply of native labour at a rate of remuneration fixed by the home authorities after full consideration of the facts, and with every possible safeguard that human ingenuity can suggest. But I should only suggest this if at the same time there be also initiated a really effective policy of development and civilisation in the reserves, on the lines which any government would have been forced to adopt had commerce and settlers never entered the country.[1]

In the discussion which raged in England over "forced labour" considerable confusion arose through failure to distinguish between compulsory labour for government purposes and compulsory labour for private employers.

Never, at any time, was any legal compulsion brought to bear on natives to work for European farmers. There was, however, a clause in the Native Authority ordinance of 1912 entitling the Government to call out young men for six days a quarter to perform labour on communal works which would benefit the whole tribe. This provision was inserted

[1] *The East African Standard*, September 1920.

to legalise the traditional and almost universal native custom by which chiefs could call upon their tribesmen to perform necessary communal tasks. When the Government assumed authority over the chiefs this custom had to be controlled and supervised. Such free labour was used for the building of bridges and roads and other essential works.

The same traditional obligations to provide free labour for the tribe existed in other East African territories and similar laws had been passed to control it. The Uganda law provided for the use of compulsory labour by the Government for a greater number of purposes and it allowed the men to be called out for thirty days a year, six days longer than was permitted in Kenya. In addition to this month of unpaid labour to which the Uganda native was liable, the Government of Uganda made considerable use of compulsory paid labour for public purposes. There was no provision allowing for this form of labour to be employed in Kenya at all.

Professor Buell, in his book *The Native Problem in Africa*, commented:

Before 1921 practically all the labour required for government purposes [in Uganda] was secured by a form of compulsion under a system of *kasanvu* labour. No serious effort to obtain voluntary labour was made; men were called out under the Native Authority ordinance under which they could be required to do work "of a public nature" for not more than sixty days in any year, unless employed for a period of three months in any other occupation.

It is estimated that twenty thousand men were annually obliged to submit to this obligation . . . at present [1927] but a small proportion of the unskilled labour employed by government departments is voluntary.

8

Early in 1920 the East Africa Protectorate decided to bring its legislation on this subject into line with that of Uganda. It was virtually compelled to take this step in order to recruit labour to build the new railways which were being planned. An amendment to the Native Authority ordinance, exactly modelled upon the law already in force in Uganda, was passed.

No one in England had paid any attention to the Uganda law. But as soon as it was imitated in Kenya an indignant outcry arose. There were questions in the House, letters to the press, sermons in the pulpits. The natives of Kenya were being ruthlessly exploited: "forced labour" and slavery were almost synonymous terms. Kenya became a sort of Bluebeard of the Empire, hiding the most horrible evils in its secret chamber. Uganda was still fortunate enough to escape the obloquy; and the fact that this obnoxious piece of legislation which so disgraced the Empire's fair name was identical with a law that had existed in Uganda for some years without comment continued to remain unnoticed.

Kenya, in fact, came in for all the blows. The reason was not far to seek. It was the presence of the settlers. They had become exceedingly unpopular among certain sections of the British public. They represented the capitalist serpent in the African garden of Eden. Everything that the Kenya Government did was put down, with more haste than justice, to their malign and subtle machinations.

Uganda, where missionary influence was predominant, was above reproach. Tanganyika, under unfettered bureaucratic control, sheltered from the harsh winds of criticism behind the mandate. Northern Rhodesia was protected from too much inquisitiveness by influential capitalist mining groups. Nyasaland was so remote that no one knew very much about it. But Kenya, easy and delightful to visit (the very fact that homesteads were scattered about the highlands made it possible for critics to find cheap and comfortable quarters from which to collect their data); settled mainly by "small men" and so unprotected by powerful financial interests; devoid of a rich mining industry; and too preoccupied with breaking in new country to defend itself, was an ideal target.

The settlers felt rather aggrieved. They could not understand why they should be so bitterly blamed for the actions of a government over which—as well they knew—they had no control. It was somewhat ironical that the sins of a government should be visited on a permanent opposition.

People in England condemned the employment of African labour as "exploitation of the native". It was a point of view that the colonists could not understand. It was not considered a crime for one man to work for another in England; why should it be so in Africa? The English cotton operative who worked, day in day out, long hours in the foetid, noisy spinning-room was considered lucky to have a job. *He* could not throw it up when the spirit moved him, unless he was willing to see his wife starving herself to give her family a meal, his children going ragged and hungry. He had to toil, with perhaps a fortnight's break a year, until he grew old and tired in this economic bondage. But the African who worked in the fields for a few months a year (his food, house and medicines provided free) for a wage which, small though it might be, did not need to be pitifully stretched to cover rents, rates, clothing and a bare living, and who then retired for several months' rest to his own plot of cultivation and his flocks, was being grossly exploited by the evil capitalist.

What magic, the colonist wondered, transformed the Englishman with a few hundred pounds of capital from an honest, hard-working and fair-minded citizen into a designing oppressive monster as soon as he abandoned England for the Kenya highlands? Why was Africa assumed to destroy at once the normal British individual's sense of justice? It all seemed very unfair, to the settler; he could never understand why—so long as the capitalist system survived—the employer of white labour should be a benefactor and the employer of black labour a beast.

It appeared strange, too, to the colonist that the most vehement denouncers of native grievances were usually members of Parliament representing the most poverty-stricken districts of British industrial cities. The average native—or at least those belonging to the wealthier tribes—lived in ease and luxury compared to the English or Scottish slum-dweller. It seemed to savour of hypocrisy that members of Parliament should devote so much time and indignation to the often exaggerated plight of people such as the Kikuyu, with an average of two acres of cultivation to a man; or the Masai, with 180 head of stock to each family, all with free land and housing, with employment waiting whenever they desired it, when so many of their own constituents were squeezed six or eight into a single lice-infested room, their children tuberculous and underfed, living a hand-to-mouth existence in the squalor of the slums.

9

At the end of 1919 Sir Edward Northey had the misfortune to lose an eye playing polo in Nairobi. He went home to England for treatment and discussed the labour question with the Secretary of State. Lord Milner supported his policy but felt that public opinion should be reassured.

The points about which I should like to be most specific [he wrote] are:
(1) That women and children are not employed away from their homes.
(2) That chiefs do not make the call upon them for labour an occasion for favouritism and oppression, and in particular that they do not attempt to put pressure upon men whose labour is wanted for the cultivation of their own land.
(3) That government officials must exercise vigilance to see that the provisions of the Masters' and Servants' ordinance, 1919, are fully observed.
I have therefore had a circular drafted which, while fully upholding the principle of the "Ainsworth circular", *i.e.* the discouragement of idleness, nevertheless makes the above points perfectly clear.

This circular was issued in July 1920. In August Lord Milner wrote a despatch, published as a white paper,[1] in which he supported Sir Edward Northey's policy and denied in strong terms the accusation that the Ainsworth circular sanctioned forced labour for private employers.

"There is no question", he wrote, "of force or compulsion, but only encouragement and advice through native chiefs and headmen." From his own experience, he added, he did not hesitate to accept the thesis that the native should be encouraged to work for the good of his own character and that it was better for young men to become wage-earners outside their reserves than idlers within them.

"In my opinion", he continued, "the Protectorate Govern-

[1] Cmd. 873 of 1920.

ment would be failing in its duty if it did not use all lawful and reasonable means to encourage the supply of labour for the settlers who have embarked on enterprises calculated to assist not only the Protectorate itself, but also this country and other parts of the Empire, by the production of raw materials which are in urgent demand."

The interests of the natives, he concluded, were amply protected by the Masters' and Servants' ordinance. "It would be hard to find a more comprehensive set of regulations to secure the well-being of natives employed outside their reserves," he remarked.

Lord Milner's despatch went some way towards reassuring public opinion. Controversy continued, however, for some years. Mr. Churchill, when he succeeded Lord Milner as Secretary of State in 1921, issued yet another despatch on the subject. In this he reiterated the principle, already acted upon, that the Government of Kenya would "avoid recourse to compulsory labour for government purposes except where absolutely necessary for essential services".[1]

On his instructions a further amendment to the Native Authority ordinance was introduced. This laid down that the previous consent of the Secretary of State must be obtained before any compulsory labour was called out. It was passed in 1922. The next year Uganda followed Kenya's lead and introduced a similar amendment to its ordinance.

Since that date paid compulsory labour for government purposes has only been called out in Kenya on one occasion. In 1925 sanction was given by the Secretary of State to recruit up to 4000 men for the building of the Uasin Gishu line and a smaller number for the Thika-Nyeri railway extension. In both cases the work was urgent, construction was being held up because labour was not forthcoming, and the country was being involved in heavy financial loss as a result. Compulsion was exercised among tribes which had hitherto supplied practically no labour and whose young men were making no effort to produce surplus of crops in the reserves.

Compulsion was used for three months only. The maximum number of compelled labourers at work was 1500 in one month on the Uasin Gishu line and 1300 on the Thika-

[1] Cmd. 1509 of 1921.

Nyeri extension, which ran almost wholly through a native reserve. No compulsory labour has been called out for government purposes since this occasion.

10

In spite of labour difficulties and the 1921 world-wide slump, Kenya began to recuperate from the set-backs of the war with all the speed and resilience of youth. But before she had passed the stage of convalescence another blow, crippling in its force, fell upon her—delivered this time by her rulers at the Colonial Office. This was known as the exchange settlement.

The story is that of the painful transformation of rupees, previously the unit of East African currency, into shillings. It is a complicated tale, but one which closely affected the colony's stability and which was severely to penalise the producers for many years to come.

The Indian rupee was established as the East African monetary unit when the British Government first took over the country. In those days trade channels flowed mainly east to India. But as white settlement developed trade swung gradually over to Britain and a natural desire arose to deal in pounds instead of in rupees.

At the outbreak of war this change had been contemplated and an Order-in-Council had been drawn up to effect it, but unfortunately this was shelved between 1914 and 1920. East African currency was regulated by an Order-in-Council passed in 1905 providing that one sovereign should be alternative legal tender for 15 rupees. So long, therefore, as the pound sterling was tied to gold, the value of the rupee in terms of sterling remained fixed at 1s. 4d. This was the basis on which all debts were contracted in East Africa. Money was borrowed, business conducted, schemes launched in the knowledge that a rupee was worth 1s. 4d.

Directly the war was over peculiar things started to happen. In the first place, Britain was off the gold standard, and a sovereign and a pound sterling had ceased to be one and the same thing. The fact, therefore, that a golden sovereign was legal tender for fifteen rupees no longer formed a link between British and East African currency. The bridge between the two was down.

At the end of the war the price of silver started to rise—slowly at first, then with mercurial speed. Behind this jump were world causes incomprehensible to East African producers and remote from their lives. America, for example, was buying up huge supplies of silver. But these obscure, unpredictable events affected the settler as directly as the rains or plant pests or the labour supply.

All through 1919 the value of the rupee in terms of sterling rose steadily. It left its old safe level of 1s. 4d. far behind, passed the 2s. mark and hovered for some time round about 2s. 4d. The result was that the producer who sold his goods in London and was paid in sterling received about half as many rupees as before.

His costs, meantime, remained the same. He had to sell almost twice as much coffee or maize to pay the interest on his overdraft.

The exchange also acted as a barrier against the introduction of new capital. A man who had a thousand pounds to invest found that instead of obtaining 15,000 rupees he could only get about 8500. The position hit many of the soldier settlers, who were just arriving with their barely adequate savings, very hard.

The exchange situation was highly embarrassing to the Government. A loan was urgently needed. Schemes for railways and piers were ready and waiting. But if the Government raised a £3,000,000 loan it would lose over £1,300,000 on exchange. The loan clearly had to be postponed. Uncertainty and confusion followed. It was evident that something had to be done.

Matters reached a crisis while Sir Edward Northey was in England early in 1920. The Governor of Uganda, Sir Robert Coryndon, was summoned home to join in the discussion. Lord Milner was in Egypt, and the question fell to the Under-Secretary, Mr. L. S. Amery, to decide.

11

Everyone agreed that the Protectorate must be switched over from the Indian to the English currency system as quickly as possible; the question was how to get it over the points with a minimum of jarring. The first step must clearly be to stabilise the rupee in terms of sterling in order that the change might be made. It was here that differences of opinion arose.

There were two schools of thought. One held that the rise in the sterling value of the rupee was permanent and was likely to grow steeper still. This school thought that East African currency should be stabilised at or near the existing rate—between 2s. and 2s. 4d. This would admittedly be hard on debtors, but it could be achieved without any violent dislocation of the money market.

The other school of thought held that stabilisation at a high rate would be both unfair to the debtor and a disaster to the country, since it would impoverish the producer on whom economic stability depended. This school advocated stabilisation at the rate at which all debts had been contracted—the normal rate of 1s. 4d.—in spite of the practical difficulties involved, and believed that the rupee would sooner or later return to the neighbourhood of its old level of 1s. 4d.

A highly technical argument raged throughout December 1919 and January 1920. It was known that Mr. Amery, supported by some of the Colonial Office officials and the head of the Crown Agents, was in favour of stabilisation at or near the current rate of exchange. Sir Edward Northey was strongly opposed to this course. In the meantime the exchange was fluctuating so violently that stabilisation was a matter of urgency.

Stabilisation became the burning question in East Africa. Producers were solidly aligned against conversion at 2s. or over. "It seems to me impossible", Delamere wrote, "that any government can destroy old-established contracts made at the rate fixed in the currency Order-in-Council." The bankers were believed to be in the opposite camp. As creditors they stood to gain enormously on paper, although in the long run they could not collect their interest if producers were forced into insolvency. Discussion raged. Everyone had an opinion to express, although few people concerned, either in East Africa or in London, could claim any knowledge of the subject. In 1920 currency was still a mystery that none but experts had dared to probe.

In London, the Governor fought the producers' battle with all the vigour at his command. He realised clearly how seriously the farmers would be injured by conversion at the higher rate. A settler currency expert, Mr. Grogan, came over to urge the case for conversion at 1s. 4d.

In January 1920 it became clear that Mr. Amery and his officials were in favour of conversion from rupees to sterling at the 2s. rate.

Sir Edward Northey presented his views to the Under-Secretary of State in terms that could hardly have been strengthened:

I am convinced, after most careful thought, that there are vital reasons why these proposals [stabilisation at 2s.] should not be adopted if the true interests of the Protectorate are to be safeguarded.

When the currency Order-in-Council, 1905, was framed establishing the sovereign as legal tender for fifteen rupees, the escape of the rupee from control was not for a moment anticipated. The obvious intention was that the rupee should remain permanently at one-fifteenth of a sovereign—the legal unit of value: on this understanding all local contracts were made. . . .

The rupee should have been kept at one-fifteenth of £1; this certainly would have been done if the consequence of not doing so had been foreseen: therefore the correct solution is to revert to the position that would have been established if correct action had been taken.

The florin proposal now before us is open to vitally serious objections. The rupee is to be stabilised at an inflated value, fifty per cent above the one-fifteenth which is the fractional value fixed by law and still employed in the Protectorate financial accounts. Such a stabilisation must arbitrarily and permanently sustain the cost of native labour, local produce, nominal services, and in general the cost of production and of living at such a greatly enhanced value that East African exports could not hold their own in the world's markets. Sisal as an industry would be doomed at once; it is doubtful whether any of the young industries of the country could last; they were not making a fifty per cent profit before the rupee rose: they are hanging on in hopes of stabilisation at one-fifteenth, which they have every right to expect.

. . . . .

The strongest local opposition to the scheme is a foregone conclusion: if it is introduced the pre-war settler will be ruined and the new settlers must fall with him; the local cost of production will be prohibitive and capital will be kept out of the country. The employer will know that his wages bill, and all local costs, will be permanently increased by fifty per cent: chaos must result, which will set back industry for years. If carried into effect this scheme must be put forward as the device of experts in England: no East African resident could support it, and I deeply and respectfully regret that I must oppose it.

That the scheme stands on an unsound basis is amply demonstrated by the extraordinary and anomalous suggestion that official salaries shall be paid at fifteen florins to the pound sterling: an official whose salary is £600 will receive £900! The alteration of the fractional relationship of the rupee to the pound can have no possible bearing on the value of an official's services as expressed in sterling: he does not become more valuable because the metallic value of silver has chanced to rise out of relation to all other values: but it is obvious that as he is now paid in rupees at fifteen to the £1 he will refuse to take only ten of the new rupees; for these reasons alone the scheme is unworkable.

In these emphatic words the Governor ranged himself at the head of the debtor-producer forces; but the Under-Secretary of State had joined the creditor-financier camp.

12

A decision was precipitated by an announcement from the Government of India that the value of the rupee was to be fixed at 2s. in gold. But a gold pound was at that time worth £1:7:8 in sterling. A rupee fixed at 2s. in gold was thus worth slightly over 2s. 9d. in sterling. A further sudden rise in the East African rupee was therefore inevitable.

The Under-Secretary of State and the Colonial Office acted at once to check this further rise, which they thought would be permanent. Their decision was taken, the Colonial

Office announced later, after the action of the Government of India made it clear "that the sterling value of the rupee could never (except for possible temporary fluctuations of exchange) fall below 2s. 9d. and was likely to remain for some appreciable time above it". Had this been so their action would have lightened the burden of the East African producer. But "never" is a rash word to use in monetary affairs. Wisdom after the event showed their judgment to be wrong and their action precipitate.

The decision to stabilise the East African rupee at 2s. was taken after a meeting between the Under-Secretary of State and the heads of the East African department of the Colonial Office, a representative of the Crown Agents, three bankers and the chairman of a London firm doing business in East Africa. Sir Edward Northey was not invited, no representative of producing interests was present, and no disinterested students of currency or experts on exchange were consulted.

Within six months of stabilisation at 2s. the Indian rupee had fallen to its original parity of 1s. 4d. It did not rise materially again and steadied down to 1s. 6d., where it has remained ever since. So the tide receded, leaving the East African rupee marooned high and dry at 2s.

All debts contracted by producers, all overdrafts out of which development was being financed, were increased—literally overnight—by 50 per cent. The settler who went to bed owing, say, £5000 woke up owing £7500. And the injustice was cumulative; it went on for ever. Not only did his overdraft suddenly expand to these monstrous proportions but he was condemned to go on paying interest (at 8 per cent) for the rest of his life on a fictitious £2500 which he had never borrowed. This amount he would have to squeeze out of his existing assets, for he had no £2500 worth of development to show for his inflated overdraft and to pay for his increased interest.

It was a crippling burden and it fell heaviest on those who had risked most. For Delamere it proved disastrous. Not only were his personal liabilities increased by about £20,000 (and the liabilities of many of the small companies in which he was interested increased *pari passu*) but he was compelled in future to find an extra £1600 a year to pay interest on a sum he had never borrowed.

The immediate effect of stabilisation was greatly to increase many of the costs of government and of production. Native labour received an automatic and universal rise of 50 per cent. The most remarkable position of all arose in regard to the Civil service. What Sir Edward Northey had described in his memorandum as the "extraordinary and anomalous suggestion"—that the salaries of officials should be paid at the rate of fifteen florins to the pound instead of at ten to the pound—was actually adopted.

All other salaries were adapted to the legalised rate of ten florins to the pound. Officials, alone, were presented with a bonus of five florins for every pound they were paid. The result was, obviously, to inflate enormously the costs of administration and to pave the way for the financial collapse which followed inevitably a year later.

As soon as the rupee was stabilised it was decided to introduce a new coin, the florin, to replace it. East African currency would thus be shifted on to a sterling basis and cut loose from the rupee. The eventual objective was the shilling. Florins of the same size as the English coins were minted and despatched to East Africa.

13

The rupee was stabilised in February 1920. But Mr. Amery's action did not end the story of the currency question.

Sir Edward Northey, on his return to the Protectorate, had the doubtful pleasure of seeing his prophesies proved right, the rupee falling and the chaos and even ruin that he had predicted coming to pass.

In face of the steeply falling prices of the post-war slump, producers found the extra handicap of drastic deflation to be even more crippling than had been anticipated. Labour, railway and ocean freights were raised against them by 50 per cent. Internal prices did not adjust themselves. For their produce in London they received ten florins to the pound, but this only purchased in East Africa as much as fifteen of the old rupees.

Towards the end of 1920 a strong demand to go back to the 1s. 4d. rupee arose. It was supported by Sir Edward Northey, who had never changed his position, but opposed by the banks and commercial houses. Since stabilisation they had made loans in florins; if they were paid back with an equal number of rupees they would lose money. The creditor, in fact, would be made to suffer to the same extent as the debtor had suffered when stabilisation at 2s. had been effected.

The interests of the farmers on the one hand and the banks and commercial men on the other had clearly parted company. Sir Edward Northey took the producers' part. He believed that reversion to the old rate of exchange—an "as you were" order—would bring costs of government back to normal and save the country from impending financial collapse. He was supported by the Governor of Uganda and by his own Executive Council, both of whom agreed that reversion to the 1s. 4d. rupee without compensation was the wisest course to take. In February 1921 he summoned a special meeting of the Legislative Council to debate the currency situation.

He naturally assumed that the unofficial members, representing the producers whose interests he was concerned to protect, would enthusiastically support his move to return to the 1s. 4d. rupee. For several months they had been agitating for this very action to be taken.

The Treasurer introduced a motion proposing that the country should revert to the old 1s. 4d. rupee. To the Governor's intense surprise it was opposed by all the unofficial members except one. (Delamere was not a member of the Council at that time.)

Their reason, they said, was that the "pledge" given by the Secretary of State in March 1920—that ten East African rupees or florins should be equal to one pound—must be honoured. The unofficial members stated that the breaking of this "pledge" would seriously injure East Africa's credit and do more harm than good by scaring capital away.

The truth was that the country's banking and commercial interests had won a victory over the producers. On the evening before the special session, a meeting had been held in Nairobi between the bankers and the elected members.

The bankers had used that old but almost invariably effective threat, that the proposed change would ruin the country's credit. They added that it would be necessary, if the florin's value was altered, to call in all overdrafts at once and to foreclose on all mortgages. This, they pointed out, would ruin the producers quickly and thoroughly. Their argument was, of course, a subtle form of blackmail. The producers lost their nerve and capitulated.

It was decided that the "pledge" must be honoured. The Treasurer's motion was defeated. A commission composed of local bankers, producers and business men was set up to consider the best means of introducing the shilling as quickly as possible.

The currency commission reported in record time that the florin should remain at the 2s. rate and that it should gradually be replaced by shillings as soon as they could be minted. The Colonial Office supported the bankers and the currency commission, and the last chance of undoing some of the harm that producers had suffered passed.

14

There remained only the introduction of the shilling. This had been the aim of the home Government since the beginning. It was hoped that a standard coin of lower value might do something towards reducing the inflated level of internal costs.

It has been suggested that the introduction of the shilling was a deliberate piece of deception engineered by the settlers to dupe the native. It is not clear, however, in what way the native suffered from it or—still less—how the settlers could have arranged it.

By the time that shillings were introduced the East African Currency Board, composed of Colonial Office and Crown Agents' officials sitting in London, was in complete control of East Africa's currency affairs. How the settlers managed to impose their supposed will on the Currency Board—which could hardly be credited with nourishing secret designs to defraud natives—has not been made clear.

The accusations were based on the size of the East African

shilling. It was a larger coin than its English counterpart. It was therefore suggested that the East African shilling was trying to disguise itself as a florin, or at least as something more valuable than an ordinary shilling.

The size was decided by the East African Currency Board because of the natural inability of the native to follow complicated currency changes.

The florin was, in the mind of the native and in the little store where he made his purchases, of exactly the same value as the 1s. 4d. rupee which it had replaced. And the new shilling was, to his simple mind, equivalent to the old half-rupee whose real value was only eightpence.

Had the new East African shilling been minted the same size as half-a-florin, nothing would have convinced the native that it was worth any more than the old half-rupee to which he was accustomed. He would have gone on believing it to be worth eightpence however much he was told that it was really worth one shilling.

The value of the shilling was midway between the rupee and the half-rupee. The obvious way to convey this to the native mind was to introduce a coin midway in size between the two coins whose value he already understood. The shilling was, in fact, worth three-quarters of a rupee; and so a coin three-quarters of the size of a rupee was minted.

The decision was thus a logical one made without intention to deceive. The native, in fact, gained rather than lost. His cents were redeemed at the rate of two shilling cents to one florin cent. This meant that the native made fourpence on every rupee's worth of cents. As regards his wages he emerged, in the end, all square from the currency muddle. The labourer who was paid six rupees a month in 1919 received six florins in 1920, and twelve shillings in 1921. His wages were thus automatically increased by 50 per cent. This bonus he did not retain.

By the time that shilling currency was introduced the depression of 1921 was in full swing. Commodity prices had fallen more abruptly and almost as far—though not with the same deadly permanence—as they were to fall nine years later. The settlers were forced to reduce costs or else go under. They could not afford, at this particular moment, to raise wages by one-half when all their competitors in the world's markets were indulging in an orgy of wage-cutting. The introduction of the shilling was also having the desired effect of reducing internal prices. Employers therefore took steps to restore the *status quo*, to return to the wage-level that had prevailed before the currency crisis had begun.

At a meeting of the Convention of Associations it was agreed to cut wages in all parts of the country by 33 per cent. This was put into force in June 1921. The labourer whose old rate of pay was six rupees thereafter received the same value, eight shillings, in the new currency. And so the native was back where he started from. The producer was not so fortunate. He gained a burden of debt that, thanks to the immortality of interest, he carries with him still.

CHAPTER XVII

RECONSTRUCTION
1920–1922

I

In one respect Delamere stood to gain from the exchange settlement. Money was owing to him from the sale of land at Njoro. Payments begun in rupees had legally to be completed in florins. But his gains were not nearly large enough to offset his losses, and in part they were dissipated by his generosity.

Plans for the subdivision of his 100,000 acres into small farms had been drawn up in 1914. Before the land could be split up, however, it had to be watered. A pipe-line to take water from the Rongai river across the plains was surveyed. Then came the war, and the scheme was postponed.

In 1918 Delamere found himself more than ever in need of money to carry on at Soysambu. He decided to sell the rest of his Njoro estate—about a third had already been disposed of in two large blocks—as soon as the war was over. The pipe-line was begun. Water was piped for sixteen miles and thirty-nine tanks were built at regular intervals so that homesteads could be dotted along it. The cost was considerable, about £12,000. The land was divided up into farms ranging from 500 to 3000 acres. Some were taken up in 1919. But the majority were not sold until after the rupee was stabilised, so that Delamere did not gain much, even on paper, from the settlement.

The farms were offered on easy terms and payment was spread over a long period of years. After the currency change Delamere let it be known that he would consider revision of the agreements made before stabilisation in all cases where purchasers found it hard to meet the artificially increased payments. Nearly all of the instalments due to him were reduced.

RECONSTRUCTION

The total purchase price of all the Njoro land sold between 1913 and 1924 amounted, on paper, to over £200,000. Paper sales, however, were a very different matter from cash receipts. Purchase prices were in many cases reduced not only on account of the currency muddle but as a result of the flax *débâcle*. The flax boom was at its height when a large part of the land was sold. Many of the new settlers who took up these Njoro farms went in for this unlucky crop. After the slump flax did not pay to harvest. Instalments on newly sold land dwindled and in a good many cases petered out altogether.

Delamere had a reputation for generosity to debtors. He added to it on this occasion. Many purchasers of his land who had legally forfeited their farms found that their instalments were waived for several years and then permanently reduced. As a result of this policy Delamere voluntarily relinquished about one-third of the money legally due to him from the Njoro sale. This was the equivalent of reducing the purchase price of all the land by about one pound an acre. Other instalments ceased with the second slump of 1930. And all the cash paid over for the farms was devoured by the hungry overdraft, insatiate as a sacred crocodile propitiated at intervals by offerings of human babies sacrificed to stave off its dreaded anger.

2

In February 1920 the first election held in the Protectorate took place. Delamere stood for the Rift Valley constituency and was returned unopposed.

In his first election manifesto he summarised his views on all the main political questions of the day.

The "amalgamation" of the three East African British-governed dependencies, Kenya, Uganda and Tanganyika, was one of them. Lord Milner's Under-Secretary, Mr. Amery, was known to be pressing forward the idea, feasible for the first time now that Germany's old colony had passed into British hands. Delamere opposed it. "I feel very strongly", he wrote, "that for the next few years this country should stand alone if it is to realise its ideals of civilisation and progress." Encouraging headway had been made towards the ultimate goal of self-government; if the colony was amalgamated with its neighbours "the European community here would be merged in an enormous native state over which it is unlikely that we should ever be given control".

"My policy", he concluded, "would be for this country to stand alone until we are a self-governing colony and have digested the problems of this country first." At the same time every effort should be made to link up economic policies and to co-ordinate services such as railways, posts and customs.

The "Asiatic question" was already threatening to tax with its complexity the statesmanship of the colony's rulers. Here again Delamere was definite in his views.

"It seems to me quite wrong that the home Government should allow the future position of the African to be prejudiced now by allowing the unchecked immigration of Asiatics", he said. "If we believe in our own civilisation we should make every effort to keep Africans free from the influence of Oriental civilisation until such time as they are fit to judge for themselves."

In the meantime, all minor government and other posts should be kept for educated Africans instead of being given to Asiatics. And, as a corollary, the African must be educated as quickly as possible to fill such posts. "Nothing, in my opinion, would reap so great a reward as the widespread teaching of the native in the skilled work of his hands."

Delamere anticipated, in this manifesto, a recommendation to be made fourteen years later by an official commission.[1] This was that special areas should be set aside where land could be leased on individual tenure to more advanced natives. "At present the more or less detribalised native has no place to go and live if he leaves his job", he wrote. "These gardens for detribalised natives should be free from tribal discipline and their owners should be encouraged to take part in native councils."

The manifesto made a special point of the need for the provision of a good education for the next generation of European colonists. "A first-rate education is needed to

[1] The Kenya Land commission, 1934.

produce judgment and balance in a ruling race", the author remarked. Every effort should be made to provide technical as well as general training. "I believe that technical education without general education produces a narrow unbalanced outlook, and that general education without technical education produces a man who, unless he has great force of character, will probably drift into one of the dead-end occupations of life."

The principle that all borrowed money should be spent on revenue-producing projects—notably on railways and harbours—was laid down as the basis of the elected leader's financial policy. "The control of finance by the legislative chamber of the country is a right that must be upheld to the uttermost", he added. "Financial action by the Secretary of State should begin and end in vetoing expenditure which would entail a grant-in-aid from the Imperial Treasury, the prevention of unfair taxation of natives, in seeing that this country fulfils its contracts, and in straightening out the exchange and the treaties. All other financial action should be transferred to the Legislative Council here. Every effort must be made to see that all financial problems are discussed openly and that they are not settled beforehand in confidential despatches."

As regards taxation Delamere believed that import duties should form the basis of the fiscal system in a young colony. They were "the most easily collected, the fairest and the most elastic" form of taxation. The clause in the treaty limiting all import duties to a maximum of 10 per cent should be abrogated, and protection given to promising agricultural industries after a full investigation by government. The natives, he added, "ought to get more than they do for the money they pay", particularly in better medical services. Education, also, should be expanded. "Technical education seems to provide a more useful native citizen, but it would be right to provide a measure of ordinary education for those who want it and show aptitude for it."

One further need for which Delamere put in a special word was the better organisation of the fight against both human and animal diseases. Inter-state co-operation, he said, was urgently required. "The Colonial Office has always been chiefly interested in international agreements for the preservation of game. No general effort has, so far as I know, been made to combat co-operatively the diseases of Africa throughout the continent."

"The chief duty of your representative, I am sure," the manifesto concluded, "is to help forward any policy which, by increasing the wealth and the population of the country, brings nearer self-government."

3

When the eleven elected members took their seats in a greatly swollen Legislative Council Delamere retained without question his position of unofficial leader. He was already becoming an institution. He had even become white-haired by now; his war-time illness had caused the change. The long locks flowing to his shoulders from beneath the spreading helmet gave him a patriarchal appearance which fitted well with his position. His vitality was as unlimited as ever; his mind was never more keen, his memory more useful a weapon nor his repartee more quick. He was a very sprightly patriarch.

Experience had equipped him with a battery of local knowledge and political acumen which was invaluable in his dealings with the official world. He had watched five Governors come and go and learnt much from the cavalcade. The old guard of officials who had known East Africa in the Company's days was fading away. Delamere knew the country better than anyone else, apart from these few survivors. He, almost alone among those who were active in the colony's public life, could see its history as a whole. Others, Governors and senior officials, came for a few years, took over the controls, and departed for Fiji or the Windward Islands, the Gold Coast or Guiana. They knew nothing of the past and had no personal concern for the future.

It was from this that he drew his power. Transient officials could not ignore him; he was disconcertingly liable to confound them with some telling fact or promise dug out from the well-stocked storehouse of an excellent memory. And his personal concern for the future supplied for his actions a background of sincerity and conviction which was inevitably lacking in an official.

This was the real difference between the settlers' and the Civil servants' approach to the country's problems. The colonial Civil servant could cheat nemesis round the Empire. By the time the effects of a mistaken policy were clearly seen he, as often as not, was far away from the disaster; and ultimately, however calamitous his errors of judgment, he would come safely to rest in the haven of pensioned ease. Not so the settler. He had to stay to reap the harvest sown by his departed rulers. He remained to pay the price of official blunders —or, no less, to reap the benefit of official sagacity—until his death; and his children inherited the debt. He, and his successors, had to foot the bill for costly projects planned by departed optimists in the Secretariat, to make up deficits on railway freight rates that crushed his competitive power in overseas markets. It was the settler's permanence, and his knowledge of facts based on experience, that gave him a political importance disproportionate to his numbers.

Delamere derived much of such influence as he exerted over Governors and government from the respect which they were bound to pay to his experience. The extent of that influence can never be measured. Delamere's enemies either exaggerated or minimised it. Those who exaggerated it did so to prove that all the sins of the Kenya Government were traceable to the underground machinations of the settlers, who "got at" Governors and officials and coerced them into acquiescence. Those who minimised his influence did so to prove that his abilities were greatly overrated, that his politics were "full of sound and fury, signifying nothing". Between the two poles stretches a wide territory, and Delamere's position can be fixed only by opinion. There are few factual bearings.

Much depended, of course, upon the Governor's attitude. He could either draw upon Delamere's fund of practical knowledge, or he could regard this knowledge as tainted and dangerous and reject it. He could, in other words, either use Delamere or avoid him.

4

On many matters Delamere's advice was of great value to the Government. It was easier to deal with a man of his calibre than with eleven discordant elected members. He was willing to help as well as to harry.

But he could be a dangerous opponent. He was always on the alert. Outwardly he was urbane, charming and courteous; ready, at any conference or interview, to voice an opinion in the most conciliatory, almost deprecating, fashion. But little escaped him; and at the first error of fact or flaw in argument he would pounce quickly, still with unruffled courtesy, his blue eyes twinkling as he puffed a large cigar, his head cocked on one side like a sparrow. On occasions he had a keen appreciation of the dramatic effect of sudden outbursts of temper, to be followed by a complete withdrawal and an apology so charmingly delivered that offence had to be forgotten.

During Sir Edward Northey's régime a system of what Delamere later christened "government by agreement" grew up. The phrase meant, broadly, that Government and settlers bound themselves to co-operate to the fullest possible extent. On the one hand, the Government would not introduce a controversial measure by springing it on the country without warning, steam-rolling it through Legislative Council with the official majority and rushing it into law without paying any attention to unofficial views. An important measure was, by agreement, outlined to the elected members before being introduced into Council so that they could express opinions and, if necessary, suggest modifications.

The elected members, on their side, undertook to support any measure once it had been passed and to urge their constituents to do so too. Any motion that they proposed to introduce into the Council was, similarly, discussed first with the Government, who either indicated that it would be accepted, suggested modifications, or prepared a reasoned refusal.

"Government by agreement" was carried further, probably, in Sir Edward Northey's day than at any later date. A free vote was allowed in Council on all matters except when instructions were received from the Secretary of State ordering the use of the official majority.

When Delamere's protests against government policy were entirely ignored his favourite gambit was to resign from the Council. He did so within six months of the first election.

This gesture was made to call attention to what he considered to be an arbitrary act of dictatorship on the part of the Colonial Office. They disallowed by cable the inclusion in the budget of receipts from railway rates after the estimates had been passed by the Legislative Council. Delamere declared that this was an infringement of the powers of the Council and that, if details of the budget were to be settled in Downing Street and sent to the colony as cabled orders, it was waste of time to have a local body to debate these matters at all. The Colonial Office ignored his protests. He therefore resigned from both the Legislative and the Executive Councils and retired to Soysambu to look after his sheep and cows.

5

They were badly in need of attention. The sheep were dying in thousands from heartwater. This disease, for which no cure was known, reduced the numbers of sheep on Soysambu from 23,000 in 1916 to 19,000 three years later. Altogether about 25,000 sheep and lambs died of heartwater during this period. The pastures became so poisoned with infection that only one remedy could prove effective —to move the sheep on to fresh land. For this purpose it was necessary to buy grazing in an undeveloped part of the colony. Delamere was forced to acquire more land, for the second time, in order to save the lives of his stock.

The best sheep lands in the country were the open downs of the Laikipia plateau. It was here that Delamere's first choice had lain in 1903. The pastures were dry and close-cropped, such as are favoured by merinos. Rivers were few and widely separated, so that the land could only be farmed in large blocks, and by men who had enough capital to stock it with thousands of sheep.

Delamere had purchased some land on Laikipia as long

ago as 1910 as the nucleus of a sheep ranch, but he had never had the money to develop it. He had also bought some land (about 20,000 acres) at Ndaragua on the slopes of the Aberdare mountains, half from Mr. Galbraith Cole and half from Mr. Thorne, who had found the farm too far away from the railway to make it pay. He therefore had a bolt-hole for his sheep when heartwater attacked them so venomously on Soysambu. In 1920 he sent them up over the escarpment and on to the plateau with his manager, Mr. E. C. Long, in charge.

They went first to the Ndaragua farm on the slopes of the Aberdares. It proved to be no safer than Soysambu. It was high (about 7800 feet), and three rivers flowed across it. The climate was cool and invigorating, but the grass was too long and lush for merinos. It was good land for dairy cattle, but unsuited to sheep. The name Ndaragua meant cedars, for the farm lay just below the cold, thick cedar forests clothing the higher ranges of the Aberdares—forests so cool that English bulbs, such as daffodils and hyacinths, have found themselves at home in gardens made by settlers along mountain streams on the outskirts. For the first few months the death-rate among the sheep at Ndaragua was at the rate of 85 per cent per annum. They were quickly moved on to the Laikipia plateau, further north.

The country here consisted of open, rolling downs. To the east the snow-cap of Mount Kenya rose out of a dark collar of forest above a massive shoulder of green foothills. The rocky escarpment towering above Lake Baringo bounded the plateau to the west, and northwards lay the Guaso Nyiro river, with the desert beyond. To the south the peaks of the Aberdares, linked by thickly forested shoulders where buffaloes grazed in steep ravines, drew their dark and jagged outline against the sky. In the forest rainbow trout lay under the fern-fringed banks of streams that cascaded down miniature rapids to the plains below. The Laikipia plateau was open and wind-swept, the grass short and sweet, the air dry and crisp. There was no forest, few trees but short bush-like "whistling thorns", so called because of the shrill swift note made by the wind as it cut through their leafless twisted branches. The depth and span of the sky seemed greater here, where flat horizons stretched unbroken by shadow-patterned hills, than in more mountainous country. Immense cumulus clouds, piled in massive contours and richly shaded from white to dark grey, passed all day in a stately cavalcade over the plain.

The northern part of this plateau was uninhabited. Part of it had been alienated to soldier-settlers. Most of these farms had never been taken up, for the waterless nature of the country made a small area, two or three thousand acres, an impossible unit. No natives had made use of it since the Masai moved south in 1912. The only occupants were herds of game—zebra and oryx, gazelle and eland—that grazed undisturbed over the open flats.

Delamere's sheep roved all over this unoccupied land. The grazing suited them and they thrived. The grass was burnt in front of them, so that they were always moving on to young, tender pastures and away from the land where they had shed their full-fed heartwater-infected ticks. After a stretch of country had been grazed over it was left alone until the ticks had perished from lack of a host from whom to suck their nourishment. Then it was burnt again, and the sheep came back on to clean land. In this way heartwater was stamped out and the death-rate reduced to less than 6 per cent. The sheep multiplied; others were bought; in a few years the flocks increased to over 40,000.

Other developments were in train elsewhere. Delamere decided to devote himself to two things, sheep and dairying. He believed that the time had come to concentrate on the dairy industry along New Zealand lines, with co-operative creameries and an export trade in butter.

He backed his opinion by buying (mainly out of overdraft) a first-class dairy-farm of 1600 acres at Naivasha. He paid a high price for the land, and began to stock it with pedigree Friesians and the best of his high-grade heifers from Soysambu. A consignment of expensive pedigree Friesian and Shorthorn bulls was shipped out from England in 1920 under the charge of an experienced cattle man. Everything on the new dairy-farm was to follow the most up-to-date and thorough lines. Milk records were to be kept, feeding scientifically regulated according to yield, lucerne to be grown under irrigation, breeding for butterfat to be practised, the land to be paddocked and rotational grazing adopted. It was to be a model dairy-farm. Delamere started laying plans for a co-operative creamery to follow.

Nor was Soysambu neglected. Immediately after the war part of the rocky Eburru mountains which bordered Soysambu to the west were acquired to supply water for yet another pipe-line. (This was the third.)

The first attempt to install it was a failure. A cedar flume five miles long was laid from the top of the hill to the land below; but it warped under the heat of the sun and a galvanised iron pipe-line had to be laid to replace it. After this was completed there were over thirty miles of pipe-line on Soysambu.

6

One of the central political questions of the 1920–1921 period was the future management of the railway. It was in need of drastic reorganisation. During the war renewals and betterment had gone by the board. Any profits went straight into the Treasury of the East Africa Protectorate and Uganda did not receive a penny, although receipts from carrying down her cotton crop were the largest item in the railways' revenue. And a system by which a financially hard-pressed Government pocketed all the profits was obviously not one that encouraged the lowering of rates.

In October 1920 an eminent railway engineer, Colonel Hammond, was sent out by the Colonial Office as special commissioner to draw up a reorganisation scheme. As a preliminary step railway finances were separated from those of the Protectorate. Since then all profits have been devoted first to improving the line, secondly to paying interest and thirdly to reducing rates.

Colonel Hammond's proposals were radical ones. The railway was to be detached entirely from the Protectorate Government, removed from all control by the legislatures of Kenya and Uganda, and placed under a council with an independent and permanent chairman brought out from England. No legislation affecting railways was to be introduced into Kenya or Uganda without the consent of the council. The property rights of the railway were to be vested in the council; and the chairman was to have the right to veto any of the council's decisions.

Delamere emerged from his political retirement to protest against the sweeping nature of these proposals. The principle that the railway should be run by a non-political body, independent of government control as regards administration, he endorsed. But the Hammond scheme implied, he said, relinquishing all control over the railway—the country's greatest asset and its only outlet—for ever. If and when the country attained self-government, it would find that it did not own, and could not control, its own railway.

There were other objections. The railway was an instrument of development as well as a system of transport. If local governments ceased to have any say in the framing of railway policy, then there would be no possibility of using rates to encourage struggling but essential young industries. Then, again, the first big loan of £5,000,000 (raised, unfortunately for the colony, at 6 per cent, at £95 and without a redemption clause) had just been sanctioned. It was to be floated on the colony's own credit. The Imperial Government were not to guarantee it. The greater part of this loan was to be spent on the Uasin Gishu railway, which was to be carried through to Uganda. Kenya, and Kenya alone, was responsible for the interest on the capital needed to build it. If Kenya surrendered all control over railway finance she would be in the position of a person who guarantees in perpetuity to foot the bill for all debts run up by an individual over whom he has no control and whose accounts he is not even allowed to scrutinise.

Sir Edward Northey also opposed the scheme. It "set up a second government in Kenya", he said. As a result of his arguments and of those advanced by the Legislative Council, a decision on the Hammond proposals was postponed.

A new general manager, Mr. C. L. (later Sir Christian) Felling, was brought up from South Africa to take charge. He was one of Sir Edward Northey's finds. The Governor telegraphed to General Smuts asking him to select a first-class man to rehabilitate a chaotic railway. Mr Felling was chosen. The Colonial Office were somewhat taken aback by this precipitate action; but the appointment was arranged before they had an opportunity to object. Mr. Felling, who took over control on January 1st, 1923, proved himself to be the most able general manager ever seen in East Africa and one of the outstanding railway organisers in the Empire.

7

The final reform of the railway was not completed until 1925. A scheme was drawn up by Mr. Felling three weeks after his arrival. It was discussed for two years and finally accepted almost as it stood. It differed in several respects and in one fundamental matter from the Hammond proposals.

Argument centred for some time round the question as to who should be the ultimate owner of the railway. The Hammond scheme awarded all the permanent assets to the council. Delamere felt very strongly that they should be ultimately vested in the government of the country in which the railway lay, either Kenya or Uganda. This view was endorsed by Mr. Felling, and he won his point. Under his final scheme—which was based on the amalgamation of the South African railways as laid down in the Act of Union—the control and management of the railways and harbours were vested in a High Commissioner for Transport to be administered on behalf of both Kenya and Uganda. But the ultimate ownership remained with the two countries; only the control was transferred.

A railway advisory council was set up under the High Commissioner, consisting of two official and two unofficial members from each country. The council's object was to be to provide the cheapest possible transport system so as to stimulate development. The estimates were to be laid before both Legislative Councils for criticism.

These principles were unanimously accepted by the elected members, provided that it was made clear that the colony could one day, if and when its constitution was changed, resume control of its railways and ports.

This definition of ultimate ownership was finally embodied in a clause worked out by Mr. Felling and Mr.

Hugh Martin, an able young man recently transferred from the Malayan Civil service and then promoted from a junior position in the Secretariat to the command of the Land office by Sir Edward Northey. The "Felling-Martin agreement", as this clause was known, was included in the Order-in-Council approved in August 1925 defining the new status of the railway.

While the future control of the railway was still under discussion, a start was made with the laying of the long-awaited line to open up the Uasin Gishu plateau and tap the rich cotton-producing districts of Uganda. The cotton crop could then be railed direct to Mombasa instead of, as at present, shipped to an inadequate harbour at Kisumu and unloaded by hand into railway freight cars.

After this line had been completed, some of the most extraordinary unfounded allegations ever made against an individual were advanced against Delamere. It was hinted in two books by retired Kenya Civil servants that he had, by some unspecified means, influenced the choice of the route so that the new line ran parallel to the old for fifty-five miles, in some places only ten miles away, in order to pass through part of his Njoro land.

The Uasin Gishu extension branched off from the original coast-to-Kisumu line at Nakuru. It then passed through the maize-producing districts of Rongai and lower Molo, climbed the Mau escarpment parallel but to the north of the old line, and proceeded across the Uasin Gishu plateau and into Uganda to the north of Lake Victoria.

It was suggested that the line should have followed a different route. It should (according to this theory) have left the old line fifty-three miles further on at a station called Mau Summit on top of the escarpment, and then turned north to join up with the route that was actually followed. This would have avoided a second expensive climb over the Mau. The line would have been about fifty miles shorter and a considerable sum of money (it was said) would have been saved.

Delamere's original Njoro land lay in the angle between the old line and the new. The old railway passed through a corner of it; the new one skirted the opposite boundary. The longer and more expensive route would, it was hinted, increase the value of Delamere's Njoro land; and this was the reason for its choice.

No proof of any sort was advanced in support of this suggestion (not unnaturally, since none existed) and it appears almost incredible that anyone should have seriously believed it. To bribe or otherwise coerce the Secretary of State for the Colonies, several senior officials at the Colonial Office, the Governor, Colonial Secretary and the entire Executive Council of Kenya, Colonel Hammond and several other independent engineers and surveyors, would have been a feat of which any man might have boasted. All these individuals considered in detail the merits of the two alternative lines and all agreed on the choice of the Nakuru route.

Delamere's motive in hatching such a Machiavellian plot was, moreover, a little obscure. When the final decision as to the routes was made in 1921 practically the whole of his Njoro land had already been sold. The new railway, therefore, hardly affected Delamere's assets.

8

The facts of the case, briefly, were these.

A railway to open up the Uasin Gishu plateau had been discussed in Sir Percy Girouard's time, when the possibility of starting it out of the first loan had been touched upon. Nakuru had always been recognised as the natural jumping-off place. A survey of a route from Nakuru to the north end of Lake Victoria had been undertaken before the war and the commission had reported in 1915. The matter had then lapsed until after the war, when it was considered by the Colonial Economic Development committee set up by Lord Milner in 1919.

While the question of the route was under discussion local engineers in the Public Works department suggested that it might be possible to take the line along the top of the escarpment from Mau Summit, thus avoiding the necessity of climbing the Mau twice over. Sir Edward Northey at first favoured this scheme. It was estimated to save about £900,000 over the alternative Nakuru route. A motion was introduced into the Legislative Council in July 1920 by Sir Charles Bowring, the Colonial Secretary, proposing that the Mau Summit route should be adopted. Delamere voted in its favour and the motion was carried unanimously.

But other considerations led the Government to change its mind. In the first place, the maize and wheat output of Rongai and lower Molo increased to such an extent that the branch line asked for by the farmers was fully justified by potential traffic. If the Mau route were adopted, therefore, a branch line would have to be built as well, and this would absorb most of the £900,000 of anticipated savings.

Then Colonel Hammond, as an independent expert, examined both routes and reported that the difficulties of taking a line along the top of the mountainous, thickly forested crest of the Mau were greater than had been realised by the local engineers. He pointed out that costs of working such a line would be much higher than those of the Nakuru route, owing to unevenness of alignment and to the fact that the route passed through barren country instead of through a productive area. A smaller capital outlay would therefore be offset by higher running costs.

Finally yet another expert, Colonel J. Kerr Robertson, was called in to give advice. (He was employed by a London firm who were appointed consulting engineers to the Colonial Office in connection with the Uasin Gishu railway.) The Government was reminded that the Uasin Gishu line was destined to become the main outlet for the Uganda cotton crop, and that the intention was eventually to extend it to the Belgian Congo. The gradients on the old line, where it climbed the Mau, were too steep to enable much extra traffic to be carried. Existing bridges and culverts were not strong enough to support heavier locomotives and wagons. If all the extra traffic from Uganda and the plateau was to come over this section between Mau Summit and Nakuru, fifty-three miles would have to be entirely realigned, gradients reduced by 1 per cent, and bridges rebuilt.

Armed with this new information, the Government calculated that the cost of relaying the Mau Summit-to-Nakuru section and of building a branch line to lower Molo as well would more than offset the saving to be made by taking the line from Mau Summit, instead of, as originally intended, from Nakuru.

The whole question was carefully investigated by the Economic Development committee of the Colonial Office, assisted by several railway experts, in the summer of 1921. The decision to revert to the Nakuru route was made in London and approved by the Secretary of State.[1] Work was begun the same autumn. The first big loan of £5,000,000 was floated in London in November 1921 to finance the new line and the harbour works.

The remarkable hints as to Delamere's mysterious influence on the Secretary of State, the Colonial Office and the local Government concerning their choice of route were first made in a book published in 1924. Delamere seriously considered taking action for libel against the author. He never minded what people said about his own motives—he was used to malicious interpretations of his actions—but he resented strongly the implication that the local Government was corrupt. But he was too preoccupied with affairs in Kenya to follow the matter up; and in any case the suggestions, unsupported as they were by any facts, were unlikely to carry much weight.

9

Delamere's absence from politics lasted for a year. In August 1921 he resumed his seat on the Legislative Council.

He had not been idle during his retirement. In the brief interlude he had formed a political organisation which he christened the Reform party.

The eleven elected members had been returned mainly on personal grounds. They had no common policy, no link save that of opposition. What was wanted, Delamere believed, was a positive programme which could be consistently urged upon the Government. Their only hope of getting anything done was to speak with one voice.

Delamere therefore drew up a complete programme and

---

[1] The Under-Secretary for the Colonies stated in the House, in reply to a question: "Colonel Robertson's report [recommending the Nakuru route] was supported by the general manager of the Uganda railway, by Colonel Hammond, and by the consulting engineers in this country as well as by the Governor of Kenya with the unanimous concurrence of his Executive Council".

launched the Reform party in May 1921. Its main plank was to be insistence on economy in costs of government in order to bring expenditure into line with what the country could afford. Several years later the Reform party was re-organised and renamed the Elected Members' organisation. In this form it survived the death of its founder.

The re-entry of the settlers' leader into politics synchronised with a severe financial crisis. In the month of his return the Governor sailed for a second visit to London. This time it was to discuss with the Colonial Office how a deficit of £412,000 could be met. Surplus balances were long since exhausted and the colony had a large overdraft at the Crown Agents.

Delamere and the other elected members had been consistently preaching economy since the war. Their entreaties had been ignored. The extravagance of the Government had, in the past two years, been startling in its prodigality and almost magnificent in its indifference to the obvious sequel.

The local Government was less to blame, in this case, than the Colonial Office. Much of the new expenditure had been forced upon it from home. Outgoings were bound to increase once the drastic pressure of the war, which squeezed all departments to the limit, was removed; but the colony was debarred by treaties over which it had no control from expanding its revenue to meet expenses by import duties. And at the same time the source of revenue on which it had chiefly (though no doubt wrongly) relied in the past—the railway—was removed, again by a higher authority. The local Treasury was therefore faced with an exceptionally difficult problem.

The financial record of 1920 and 1921 was nevertheless a deplorable one. By 1921 costs of administration had risen by about 350 per cent over the pre-war level. Total expenditure in 1913 was £600,000; in 1920 it was just under £2,000,000.

Worse still, the estimates for 1922 had climbed to the startling total of nearly £3,000,000—an increase of a million, or 50 per cent, in less than two years. The cost of running the country had now reached a figure over three times as great as its total exportable wealth. It was almost incredible that any government should have allowed such an economically hopeless position to arise. No country whose exports account for a very large proportion of its total trade can spend on the unproductive costs of keeping itself well governed more than three times as much as it receives for its exported goods, and still remain solvent.

By 1921 Kenya was spending on her costs of administration about half as much again as Southern Rhodesia, whose white population was four times as large and whose economic structure was balanced by a mining industry.[1]

The root of the trouble was that the Colonial Office, with its solid, thorough, English ideas of the functions of a government based on the home model, had from the first imposed too elaborate a form of administration on a rudimentary colony. Kenya was a pioneer country and all she could afford to support was a pioneer form of government. Native wealth consisted mainly of unmarketable cattle and destructive goats, and native exports of undersized, tick-punctured hides and a small quantity of low-priced grain. Indians contributed little productive wealth to the country. European wealth was derived solely from a group of (in 1921) 1339 farmers, some of them doing little more than winning their own living and most of them, owing to the war and to the exchange settlement, in debt to the banks.

It was true that these few farmers had managed to achieve a remarkably large amount of development. They were cultivating, for example, an average of 150 acres each besides all the pastoral land which they had reclaimed from veld. Between them they accounted for nearly all the exports. Two wholly European crops, coffee and sisal, made up for three-quarters of the total. In a single year (1921) European production of all crops increased by 30 per cent. But, even so, the settlers could not afford their share of the upkeep of such an elaborate system of government as the Colonial Office thought desirable and therefore forced upon the colony. It was calculated that in 1920 the tiny white population of 9000 people contributed in taxation about £800,000, or nearly

---

[1] In 1919 Southern Rhodesia's public expenditure (in round figures) was £1,000,000 and the value of her exports was £4,700,000. She therefore spent less than 25 per cent of what she received for exports. In the same year the East Africa Protectorate expenditure was £1,500,000 and her exports £1,100,000. She thus spent about 26 per cent more than she received for her exports.

half the total revenue. The Colonial Office held the view that, in the interests of the natives, a reasonably complete government machine must, at all costs, be maintained. This, of course, was arguable; but they omitted to lay a sound financial foundation for the machine, and it was therefore not surprising that the structure on which it rested cracked. They did not face the implications of the fact that, in the long run, every country must get the government it can afford, unless someone else is willing to pay for a more complex one. They gave Kenya an over-expensive government and took no steps to help the colony pay the bill.

"Countries which depend on agriculture have to have a very inexpensive government and a very low standard of living", Delamere summed it up.

10

Two examples of government extravagance were stressed by Delamere in a plea for economy uttered in Council in the autumn of 1921. One was the huge increase in expenditure on military forces. Before the war British East Africa's southern boundary, nearly 500 miles long, marched with the territory of a foreign power; and her military vote was £50,000. In 1921 that boundary was no longer foreign and the military estimates were £225,000—four times as large.

This was one of Delamere's favourite points of attack. He regarded military expenditure as a running sore draining away the country's financial strength. Productiveness was Delamere's yardstick by which he measured the merits of expenditure. He was always in favour, for example, of spending as much money as could be afforded on native health and education, for he regarded this as productive spending which would lead to a stronger, more skilled and intelligent native population. "As far as I am concerned", he once said in a debate on education, "I look upon education and medical services as insurance, and there has never been any intention on this side of the house to cut down those services except in so far as seeing that the country gets its money's worth. We call that productive expenditure."

But if ever there was unproductive, and therefore bad,

expenditure, it was this enormous lump sum that was extracted every year from the meagre revenue and apparently buried in the useless sand and volcanic lava of the northern frontier.

Kenya's army was stationed in this inaccessible desert for the sole purpose of keeping out Abyssinian slave raiders. Delamere believed that an unnecessarily large number of troops was maintained for this purpose. "It is a country of deserts, wells, and one river", he declared. "Any man sitting in the middle has his hands on the whole country. Nobody can go to these wells without being known."

He felt, also, that the holding of an international frontier was an imperial responsibility. The Imperial Government should either be prepared to help keep this boundary intact, or else they should allow the colony to reduce the load. They did neither. Repeated attempts to cut down military expenses were made by the local Government. Each time their efforts were blocked by an all-powerful authority at the Colonial Office called the Inspector-General. His word was law. Several times military reductions were passed by the Legislative Council, approved by the Government and submitted to the Inspector-General; in each case they were vetoed and the higher estimates retained. In these circumstances it was not always an easy matter for a country under strict Colonial Office rule to balance its budget.

When Abyssinia became a member of the League of Nations in 1923, Delamere said, the position became absurd. Here was a British colony spending an enormous sum of money (relative to its resources) every year in preventing subjects of one of Britain's co-equal partners in the League from murdering British subjects and carrying them off as slaves. All that was needed to complete the farce, Delamere added, was for Abyssinia to become a member of the Mandates Commission and as such a supervisor of Britain's administration of Tanganyika.

The money for this unproductive expenditure, it was further pointed out, came partly from the pockets of the more diligent and industrious of the native tribes who contributed most to the hut tax. Could it not be better spent, it was asked, in providing these tribes with agricultural instructors to show them how to grow better crops, with serum for their cattle, with technical schools to teach them trades, with medicines to relieve them of the diseases which lowered their vitality?

There was another direction in which Delamere maintained that the price of government could be reduced. This was in the cost of the Civil service.

Both the numbers of the Civil service and their rate of pay had soared, relatively, into the financial stratosphere since the war. A commissioner, Sir Alfred Lascelles, who had been sent out in 1919 to report on Civil service conditions had recommended an immediate increase of all salaries by 30 per cent or more. This had been put into force at once and at the same time the size of the service had been increased, also by about 30 per cent.

Delamere agreed that this rise was fully justified. But he did not admit that the further and entirely gratuitous increase of 50 per cent as a result of the exchange settlement was justified on any grounds whatsoever. This windfall for the Civil service, which was called a "local allowance", added an extra £300,000 a year to the colony's expenditure and was chiefly responsible for unbalancing the 1923 budget to such a decisive extent.

While all salaries had nearly doubled, some had multiplied themselves threefold or even more. Leave conditions, equally, were generous. In spite of the healthy climate prevailing in the majority of government stations, leave conditions in Kenya were uniform with those in countries such as Uganda and Tanganyika where, for the most part, the climate was tropical and often unhealthy. Officers received six months leave on full pay every two and a half years. In Ceylon and Malaya, both much richer and certainly not healthier countries than Kenya, leave every four years was the rule.

Delamere therefore urged that bureaucracy, with its alarmingly high rate of reproduction, should be restrained. "At present the money which should be building factories for meat canning and creameries and for putting more land under cultivation is being used to pay for an extravagant administration completely out of keeping with the finances of the country", he said.

These conditions formed the prelude to the appointment of the Bowring committee in March 1922 to recommend how expenditure might be reduced and production stimulated.

11

Sir Edward Northey returned at the end of 1921 with proposals to reduce the £412,000 deficit. The chief of these was to swell the revenue by an estimated £240,000 by raising the customs duties. The treaties binding Kenya to a limit of 10 per cent had been abrogated by the convention of St. Germain-en-Laye and a new tariff could now be drawn up. Expenditure was to be reduced by cutting down the local allowance by half.

The European population was unanimous in feeling that these proposals did not really meet the needs of the case. Increased taxation, they said, was not enough. Delamere suggested that the money to be collected from the new customs duties should be used for the relief of taxation—especially native taxation, for he pointed out that the hut tax was much too high—instead of for wiping out the deficit. The budget should be balanced by economies and not by new taxation.

The budget was sent back again by the Council and Sir Edward Northey imposed further cuts. He succeeded in paring £250,000 off the original estimate of £3,000,000 and in reducing the hut tax by one quarter.

Demands then arose for the appointment of a strong committee, on the lines of the "Geddes committee" then sitting in England, to suggest economies. The Convention of Associations sent a deputation to the Governor to press for an unofficial majority. The Governor supported this proposal and Mr. Churchill, who was then Secretary of State, concurred. The committee was appointed with the Colonial Secretary, Sir Charles Bowring, as chairman. Three elected members—Delamere, Mr. E. S. Grogan and Mr. J. E. Coney—represented the producers. Two nominees of the Associated Chamber of Commerce and one Indian Legislative Councillor made up the committee.

The committee was not confined to suggesting economy

cuts. It was officially called the "Economic and Finance committee" and it could, under its terms of reference, frame a broad economic policy for the country.

This was, in fact, what it set out to do. The remarkable thing about it was that most of its recommendations were immediately carried out. Procedure was modelled on that of the War Council. The committee met every morning and framed resolutions which were handed to the Governor the same afternoon. And he acted on them at once. Its success was mainly due to Sir Edward Northey's co-operation. There was no pigeon-holing of resolutions. In a day or two, very often the next day, a slip of paper would come back to the committee informing them of the action taken by the Governor. Within a few weeks many of the suggested measures had actually been enforced. The committee sat almost continuously from March to October and presented 125 resolutions to the Governor.

The War Council and the Bowring committee probably achieved more action in a short time than any other bodies have done in Kenya. It is significant that their origin and their composition were similar. In both cases the Governor of the day accepted non-official co-operation and virtually handed over the controversial questions to a body with an unofficial majority. Although these bodies were purely advisory it was understood that the advice would, so far as was possible, be genuinely carried out. In neither case was the advisory body cramped by narrow terms of reference, nor were its suggestions ignored.

12

The committee was instructed to suggest how imports might be reduced and exports fostered. (The balance of trade was too adverse for safety.) They had to decide which crops at present imported might be legitimately grown at home.

Their first recommendation was that the colony should concentrate on maize production. It was a crop that both natives and Europeans could grow. It was bulky and would provide traffic for the railway and it gave a heavier yield per acre in Kenya than in the principal maize exporting countries. And it was not an exacting crop as regards labour.

The committee suggested that a low flat-rate for export maize should be introduced on the railway to put the industry on its feet. This was put into effect and exports of maize increased rapidly as a result.

The committee next turned its attention to wheat. In spite of the War Council's efforts to encourage the industry, Kenya was still importing £135,000 worth of wheat annually. All this might be home-grown. The imposition of a 50 per cent duty on wheat and a 100 per cent duty on flour was recommended. These were condemned as excessive by the Secretary of State and finally a tariff of 30 per cent on both wheat and flour was imposed.

Kenya's adoption of a protective tariff on wheat provided an opportunity for another veiled attack on Delamere's good faith. In 1924 it was stated in a book on Kenya that " the Legislature imposed an *ad valorem* duty of 100 per cent on imported wheat and flour to protect an infant industry largely conducted on a single immense estate".[1] The implication was that the "single immense estate" belonged to Delamere.

This statement was untrue in every particular. The duty was 30 per cent, not 100. Delamere had not grown an acre of wheat since 1914, when Equator ranch was closed down. The largest grower in the country in 1922 produced less than 10 per cent of the total wheat output, the remaining 90 per cent being grown by a large number of small farmers mainly on the Uasin Gishu plateau.

Delamere's only connection with the wheat industry was through his flour mill, Unga Ltd. This company had never paid a dividend. To appease the shareholders Delamere had bought most of them out. By 1922 he owned about three-quarters of the shares. About a month before the protective duty was imposed he wrote to the manager of the mill, Mr. A. K. Constantine, saying that it was to be clearly understood that the duty was imposed for the benefit of the wheat-growers and not of the mill, and that the company must not take advantage of it to increase the price of flour.

[1] Norman Leys, *Kenya*.

If possible, he added, the price was to be lowered in anticipation of the reduction of milling costs which would result from an increased output.

These instructions were followed. The price of local flour was substantially reduced before the duty came into operation; and it has never since been so high as it was before the duty was imposed.

At the same time Delamere told the Governor in an interview that there would be no question of his deriving any personal profit from the duty. He had made up his mind, he said, to transfer his interest in the mill to the growers as soon as its finances were straightened out.

Mr. Constantine urged him to make this statement public in view of the innuendoes that were flying about. Characteristically, he refused. "H. E. is entitled to know", he said, "because I am on the Executive Council; and you, as manager of Unga Ltd., are entitled to know; but if certain people choose to misrepresent my actions I certainly shan't waste my time in defending myself. They can say what they like."

Unga Ltd. did not pay a single dividend after the duty was imposed, nor did Delamere make a penny out of it. His promise to hand the mill over to the wheat-growers was redeemed in 1926.

13

Other changes were made in Kenya's fiscal system by the Bowring committee. Such export duties as survived were abolished and railway rates on hides drastically reduced in the interests of native production. A measure of protection was given to rice, timber and butter. The new schedule of duties was reviewed by an independent tariff committee, modified in certain directions to meet Uganda's wishes, and passed into law in September 1922.

To balance this increase in indirect taxation, the income tax which had been imposed in 1920 was removed. It had not been a success. In the first year collection had been abandoned owing to difficulties in getting the machinery of assessment into working order. In the second year the Government, in one of its sudden bursts of optimism, estimated the yield at £328,000, although the total number of taxpayers was about 2500 Europeans and, at the most, 5000 Indians. The actual amount collected was £58,000.

The final task of the Bowring committee was to reduce expenditure still further by cuts in the working costs of the various departments. Each in turn was scrutinised and pruned. The result was to pare the 1922 estimates down from £2,000,000 (to which they had already been cut by the Government) to £1,500,000. Even more drastic economies were proposed for the following year.

By the time the 1923 budget came to be framed, however, Sir Edward Northey had been recalled and the Bowring committee dispersed. After 1922 times began to improve. Expenditure crept up once more and within two years the two million mark was reached again and passed.

Delamere was, throughout its sittings, one of the most active of the committee's members. For six months he deserted his farms in order to attend almost every meeting. He made quick dashes to Soysambu every week-end and spent his Sundays jolting round the estate in an old Ford to inspect progress. On Monday he would leave at dawn to motor to Nairobi in time for the morning meeting.

On all such committees he was well known for his impish, Puck-like humour. This characteristic saved the Bowring committee, on one occasion, from a possible collapse.

Like all committees, it had its under-currents of personal feeling and its bad days when no one would agree on anything. In the middle of its career a serious disagreement arose between two heads of departments. Discussion led to bitterness, resignations were threatened, and the committee seemed to be on the verge of disruption. The Governor was asked to attend in the hopes that he might find a compromise. He arrived, rather inclined to annoyance at the committee's inability to settle its own troubles.

"Well, gentlemen," he said, "what's all this about?" Delamere, acting as spokesman, started to explain. The Governor, displeased at being disturbed for, as it seemed to him, inadequate reasons, administered a sharp and military rebuke in terms likely to have the worst effect on Delamere's notoriously inflammable temper.

The rest of the committee looked on with great anxiety while their spokesman sat listening, silent and flushed with anger, to the tirade. An explosion appeared inevitable. Delamere would resign, others would follow, and the committee would come to an ignoble end.

The Governor finished his remarks and for a few seconds there was a dead silence. Everybody held their breath. Delamere, still in silence, pulled slowly out of his pocket a large, violently coloured bandana handkerchief. He held a corner in each hand and twirled it round two or three times on its axis. Then he clapped it round his head like a bonnet, peeped out from underneath the bandana flap, and solemnly winked at the Governor.

There was a suppressed yelp of laughter from one of the members and everyone else turned to stare at the offender. The Governor addressed himself to the chairman; and the tension was over. The members settled down again in peace and amity to continue the work of the committee, perhaps with the suspicion that Delamere's temper was not as uncontrollable as he often pretended.

CHAPTER XVIII

THE INDIAN QUESTION
1920–1923

I

KENYA's first years as a full-fledged colony were stormy ones. No sooner had financial collapse been averted than another crisis, brewing since 1920, came to a head. This was the Indian question.

No other problem which has ruffled the waters of Kenya's political life has as yet assumed the same importance. It lashed such powerful breakers into action that the small though sturdy boat of white settlement was all but swamped by the waves.

The controversy transcended Kenya's borders. It became an imperial issue of major significance. At one time it seemed almost as though the fate of India depended upon its outcome. It drove the handful of settlers to the verge of armed rebellion against the King's Government. It was earnestly considered by the Cabinet, the Viceroy, the Premier of South Africa, the British Parliament, the Indian Legislature and innumerable smaller fry. This obscure little colony suddenly found itself a battle-ground of imperial principle and the focus, for a short time, of imperial interest.

All through the history of East Africa, Indian political ambitions on the one hand and European demands for restriction of Indian immigration—which was unlimited—on the other cropped up at intervals. But Indian claims for political representation had no force behind them before 1914. Nine Indians out of ten took no interest in the subject. The tenth might belong to a political society in Nairobi or Mombasa but he was seldom a very enthusiastic member. On the whole the East African Indians were contented enough. It was not until nationalists from India took a hand in the matter that any real political feeling was created in the bosoms of the Indian store-keepers, clerks, stone-masons and other diligent but poorly educated people who made up East Africa's Indian population.

The necessary stimulus came soon after the war. India, the brain-centre, was stirred by the post-war spirit of self-determination, discontent and unrest. Kenya, the distant muscle, twitched in response.

Behind the Indian agitation in East Africa lay the revolt in India herself. The Montagu-Chelmsford reforms had given her a new position in the British Commonwealth; dominion status, like world prosperity in later years, was "just around the corner". England had called upon Indian soldiers for help against her European enemies in time of need; she could not turn round directly the danger was over and stigmatise the men who had served her as members of an inferior race. In her new-found assurance India could afford to support with greater vigour the political claims of her nationals in other parts of the Empire. And the British Government knew that to administer an African snub to a hypersensitive country which she had recently been at such pains to placate would give rise to violent accusations of injustice and even further complicate the Indian Government's immensely difficult task.

2

India fired the first shot at the Imperial Conference of 1918 by pressing for the removal of restrictions on immigration into the Dominions. She met with little success. The logical argument that Indians, as British subjects, should not be treated as though they were on a different footing from any other British subjects failed to convince the Dominions that the time had come to remove the barriers protecting their jealously guarded standards of living. British politicians might—and did—proclaim in all sincerity that race, colour and creed should never again be a bar to advancement to the highest positions in the Empire; but the Dominions continued to talk of the level of civilisation and the standard of living as the crucial tests of equality.

In July 1918 the Imperial Conference passed a resolution that:

It is an inherent function of the governments of the several communities of the British Commonwealth, including India, that each should enjoy complete control over the composition of its own population by means of restriction on immigration from any other communities.

So the Dominions bolted their already closed doors against India's surplus population. All that was left for the Government of India, in spite of its representation on equal terms in the councils of the Empire and on the League of Nations, was to hammer angrily on the panels when voices of protest against injustices were raised from those who had already penetrated to the other side.

Between 1919 and 1921 the treatment of Indians in South Africa again came to a head. The Transvaal had, for many years, been trying to check the constant influx of Indians from Natal. In 1919 the Government experimented with the policy of enforcing an old law, dating from 1908, which prohibited Asiatics from occupying land in proclaimed gold areas. There was a storm of protest, and in 1920 a commission, including Sir Benjamin Robertson (a member of the Viceroy's Council), was sent from India, with the concurrence of the Union Government, to investigate.

At the time when the status of Asiatics in East Africa was first seriously considered, therefore, India's experiences in the Dominions had made her particularly sensitive on the subject of the position of her nationals in other parts of the Empire.

Claims for political rights in the Protectorate were put forward by the Indians during and immediately after the war. The agitation soon gathered enough force to disturb the peace of mind of the Europeans. The session of Convention of Associations which met in January 1919 drew up a petition to the Governor requesting him to obtain from the Secretary of State a ruling that the position of Europeans, acting in trust for the native peoples, should not be prejudiced by giving the franchise to Asiatics, allowing them to acquire land in the highlands or permitting free immigration.

When Sir Edward Northey arrived early in 1919 he found

the Indian question a small weed just appearing in the East African garden; he was to leave it as a monstrous growth overrunning all the flower-beds. (Perhaps he might have felt more inclined to compare it with the paw-paw tree which is alleged to consume anyone who sleeps beneath its sheltering but carnivorous leaves.) Almost his first declaration caused it to sprout into a full-grown plant.

The announcement that the Europeans were to be allowed to elect their own representatives to the Legislative Council precipitated a demand from the Indians for equal privileges. Europeans and Indians, they said, should vote on equal terms, in the same constituencies and on a common roll.

3

In March 1919 a sharp counter-attack was launched by the Europeans in the form of the report of the Economic commission. On the subject of Indians it was blunt rather than tactful. The welfare of the native, it was stated, was affected more directly by the influence of the Asiatic than by any other factor; and the influence was a bad one.

Indians filled all the minor skilled posts and their presence, "organised as they are to keep the African out of every position which an Indian could occupy, deprives the African of all incentives to ambition and opportunities of advancement. . . . In every direction the sphere of the Indian in this country is not complemental but competitive with those of the European and the African."

After dealing with the economic side of the question, the commission rashly ventured on to the more delicate ground of the Indian's moral effect on the African. (The commission was, of course, referring only to the Indians found in Kenya —mainly of the lowest caste and type—and not to Indians in general.) "Physically, the Indian is not a wholesome influence because of his incurable repugnance to sanitation and hygiene", said the report. "In this respect the African is more civilised than the Indian, being naturally clean in his ways; but he is prone to follow the example of those around him."

The "moral depravity" of the Indian, the report went on,

VOL. II

was equally damaging to the African, who in his natural state was "innocent of the worst vices of the East. The Indian is an inciter to crime as well as to vice, since it is the opportunity afforded by the ever-ready Indian receiver which makes thieving easy."

The Empire's choice lay between "the vital interest of the African and the ambition of India".

The presence of the Indian in Africa was "quite obviously inimical to the moral and physical welfare and the economic advancement of the native". Should Indians be further encouraged, by lack of all immigration bars, to come to Africa?

"Our own view is that there can be no excuse for meting out to the African treatment to which India herself would never submit", the commission stated.

On economic grounds at any rate the admission of Indians to East Africa was a cardinal error of policy. The first result was the economic stagnation of the African. The error ought gradually to be rectified, so far as possible, by restricting fresh immigration and by partial repatriation.

"It is our firm conviction", the report continued, "that the justification of our occupation of this country lies in our ability to adapt the native to our own civilisation. If we further complicate this task by continuing to expose the African to the antagonistic influence of Asiatic, as distinct from European, philosophy, we shall be guilty of a breach of trust."

The publication of this report set a match to the powder of racial feeling. The Indian Association in Nairobi protested vigorously. At the same time the Indians reiterated their demand for equal representation with Europeans on the Legislative Council, no segregation in the townships, the right to hold land in the highlands and promotion to the highest ranks of the Civil service.

The Convention of Associations took alarm and wrote to the Governor calling his attention to the dangers to white settlement inherent in the Indians' claims. The Chief Secretary set their fears at rest. "His Excellency has no hesitation in affirming that universal suffrage for the Asiatics in this Protectorate on equality with the whites is out of the question", he replied in a letter to Convention.

The Indian Association received a similar answer. "The principle has been accepted at home", Sir Edward Northey told them, "that this country is primarily for European development, and whereas the interest of the Indian will not be lost sight of, in all respects the European must predominate."

"His Excellency believes", another official letter said, "that, though Indian interests should not be lost sight of, European interest must be paramount throughout the Protectorate." Within three years that famous word "paramount" was to be used (and by the Imperial Government) of native and not of European interests. This, in the long run, was probably the most far-reaching result of the Indian controversy.

4

The Indians, disgusted at their rebuff, sent a deputation to interview the Viceroy of India. Some of the statements made by the delegates gave rise to renewed alarm among the Europeans.

All the higher government appointments are absolutely closed to Indians of the highest education and ability [they complained], whereas in the adjoining colony of Portuguese East Africa, Portuguese Indian subjects hold the highest posts such as judges of the High Court and other heads of administrative departments.

Agitation continued to simmer throughout the year and in March 1920 a second Indian deputation sailed, this time to England to see the Secretary of State for the Colonies. It was introduced to Lord Milner by Lord Islington, a warm supporter of the Indian case. The principal claims put forward were for equal representation with Europeans on the Executive, Legislative and municipal councils; for rejection of the principle of segregation; for the throwing open of land in the highlands to Indians; for the right to unrestricted immigration (which they already had); and for the promotion of persons according to their ability and irrespective of race to the highest positions in the administration, police and army.

The European community contested all these claims. The

basic question was that of the franchise. In the census which took place in 1921 the population consisted of 9651 Europeans, 22,822 Indians and between two and a half and three million natives. Indians thus outnumbered Europeans by more than two to one. An equal franchise on a common roll would have meant (so the Europeans said) complete surrender to the Indians of the limited amount of political power so recently accorded to the white community. Europeans could have been out-voted up and down the country and nothing but Indian elected members returned to the Legislative Council.

This would have been the end, the colonists said, of white settlement in East Africa. Combined with unrestricted immigration, which would have allowed East Africa to become almost the sole outlet for India's surplus and impoverished population, accession to the Indians' demands would have been tantamount to delivering the young and struggling colony over lock, stock and barrel into the hands of India. White civilisation would be swamped in a brown enfranchised flood and the white settlers, not to mention the indigenous natives, politically butchered to make an Indian holiday.

The question of the right to acquire land in the highlands aroused, perhaps, the deepest feeling. Whatever might be said about the Indian's enterprise as a trader on the coast, he could not possibly claim to have been a pioneer in the highlands. Indians had been established along the coast-line for many generations before the British arrived, but until the railway had been driven across the waterless and hostile plains to Nairobi and beyond no Indians had, except for an occasional commercial foray, penetrated behind the ten-mile coastal strip. Indian coolies imported by the Government to lay rails were the first to travel inland. All the credit for the opening up of the highlands, the building of an agricultural industry, lay with the white man.

The settlers had always regarded the limited area of "white highlands" (a patch of only about 12,000 square miles of upland amid a sea of native reserves, plain and bush) as their own preserve. They had established their homes in this oasis of white endeavour and they were determined, at all costs, to defend them. And in any case the home Government, the settlers added, had given its word. Surely the published promise of a Secretary of State could not be broken to meet the wishes of a few Indian agitators? They took their stand, therefore, on the "Elgin pledge".[1]

There was, in fact, no legal bar against the acquisition of land by Indians. The Crown Lands ordinance of 1915, however, contained a clause which required the Governor's sanction for any transfer of land between members of different races. As a matter of administrative practice this was withheld where land within the area prescribed in the "Elgin pledge" was concerned. In this way the pledge was kept. Within the townships this veto was not generally exercised.

5

The Europeans felt almost as strongly on the subject of immigration. Since the war Indians had been entering Kenya in large numbers. There was little doubt that, if they were given full political rights in East Africa, they would pour over the ocean in their thousands to enter the only country in the world where they were admitted without restriction and were accorded full political equality with Europeans when they arrived.

And then there was the position of the African to consider. His well-wishers at home were fond of stating that East Africa was his country and that we held it only in trust. Had we, then, the right to allow unlimited numbers of an alien race, for whom he did not always entertain much respect, and who occupied jobs as skilled workmen and traders that he would otherwise be able to fill, to populate his country? The position seemed to the Europeans to be illogical. In the same breath people accused the white man of stealing the natives' land and enlarged on the iniquities of not allowing the brown man to acquire it. What was sauce for the white goose was not, apparently, sauce for the brown gander.

Behind all this lay a feeling of resentment that a brown wedge would be driven between black and white in Africa. The Africans were our responsibility; for good or ill we had

[1] Quoted on p. 209, Vol. I.

decided to impose our civilisation upon their savagery; and we had no right to share this responsibility with an Asiatic race quite inexperienced in colonisation and unqualified for the complex task of ruling a less enlightened people. The two systems—British and Indian—of government, of ethics, of religion, of law, did not and could not mix. Since we had taken it upon ourselves to undermine the native's pattern of existence and to substitute our own, we could not leave the job half done and let the Indian complete it. That would be a blatant shirking of responsibility and it would leave the native far worse off than before.

This was a point on which Delamere felt especially strongly. In a letter written several years later he said:

I am sure this is the great question of East Africa. Our people will either create a civilisation for all—themselves and the indigenous peoples—or in the far future the indigenous peoples may oust them—who knows? We have handed over countries before. Or, more likely, our people will contract to a limited highland area if the pressure from the indigenous peoples on their standard of life becomes too great. No man to-day knows what the ultimate future holds between ourselves and the indigenous peoples of Africa.

But allow an unchecked flow of Asiatic immigration into Africa, and a state of affairs is created which no man can control at all. The result is peaceful penetration into all the trades and craftsmanship that Africans are capable of carrying on in all parts of East Africa, and the fixing on African reserves of the social and family system of India.

There is no doubt that two fundamental results will follow:

(1) That the Englishman will be squeezed out or his standard of living lowered generally to Asiatic standards;

(2) That the native will not be able to compete with the Asiatic in work and trade. One of the most peculiar things in discussions on the future of Africa is that our enemies in East Africa and England never appear to object to Asiatic competition with natives.

If it is determined that unchecked immigration from India is to be allowed, then the British Government must understand that it really does mean the swamping of the European leader and creator of civilisation, and of the African who is trying to attain to a standard of competence where he can compete with the Indian. He cannot gain this standard in the face of unrestricted Indian competition.

In this view the settler community carried the bulk of missionary opinion with them. The Convention of Associations meeting held at the beginning of the agitation was the first to be attended by representatives of the Christian missions. Canon Leaky spoke strongly in favour of the resolutions protesting against Indian competition with Africans, and thought that any attempt to give the Indian equal rights in Kenya would be "highly detrimental to the African".

The leaders of the Church in East Africa ranged themselves solidly behind the white point of view in the years that followed. The Bishop of Mombasa, speaking at a mass meeting in Nairobi, said that "it would be fatal to give India the government here when our native races were beginning to realise that they had a future before them". The Bishop of Zanzibar wrote a letter opposing the Indian claims in very strong terms, principally on the grounds that the Indian had neither won nor deserved respect from the African. Canon Burns stated forcibly that the Indian had shown no regard for the uplift of the African and said that if Indian demands were granted the progress of the native would be retarded for fifty years. Settlers and missionaries found themselves in whole-hearted agreement.

6

In the spring of 1920 the Indian deputation, the India Office and the Indian Overseas Association presented their case to Lord Milner at the Colonial Office. Sir Edward Northey, who was in England at the time, opposed most of the Indian demands. The question was thoroughly thrashed out and Sir Edward Northey was able to take back with him to East Africa a despatch containing what was at that time believed to be a final decision. It was published in August 1920 in the *Official Gazette*. Lord Milner stated:

> I have hitherto held the view that . . . the time has not yet come for basing the representation of Indians in the Protectorate on the elective principle.
>
> I am, however, impressed both by the Indian representatives of East Africa and by the Secretary of State for India as to the importance which is attached by the Indians to the election of their members,

I have, therefore, decided that arrangements shall be made for the election of two Indian members to the Legislative Council on a special franchise.

On the subject of immigration the Europeans lost their case.

I could not countenance any restrictions which would place natives of India at a disadvantage as compared with other immigrants; . . . and there must be no bar to immigration of Indians.

On the other hand, Lord Milner upheld the Elgin pledge.

This decision, which applies only to agricultural land, has been reaffirmed by Secretaries of State subsequently; and I do not feel that I should be justified in reversing it.

It is clear that if the limited areas on which alone European settlers can live were thrown open to the competition of Asiatics, who are physically fit to settle in other areas from which Europeans are by nature excluded, there would be, taking the Protectorate as a whole, a virtual discrimination in favour of Asiatic as against European settlement. I cannot regard the Indian claim on this point as just or reasonable.

Other areas were, however, to be set aside for Indian settlement. Lord Milner also upheld the principle of segregation as being the best for all races on the grounds of sanitation and social convenience.

The Milner despatch was accepted, with some reluctance, by the Europeans. They objected to the ruling on immigration, but they agreed to the terms without further argument on the understanding that the matter was finally closed.

The Indians protested vigorously and refused to elect their two members to the Legislative Council. Nothing less than complete political equality with the whites would satisfy them.

By this time the Government of India had taken an active part in the controversy. When the Milner despatch appeared, Sir Benjamin Robertson was in Kenya on behalf of his Government looking into the Indian case. He was accompanied by a senior Civil servant, Mr. Corbett, who prepared a despatch on the Indian claims. This document was endorsed by the Government of India and passed on to the Colonial Office in October 1920.

The three main Indian demands—a common roll, no segregation, and the right to acquire land in the highlands—were strongly supported. These findings reawoke European fears, especially as the despatch openly admitted that, given the common roll, Indian voters might with better education and increase of wealth eventually outnumber the Europeans.

In the following January (1921), Lord Milner retired and Mr. Churchill inherited the controversy.

Soon after his arrival at the Colonial Office it became clear that the Milner despatch was not, after all, to be the last word. The first hint received by the colony that new proposals were being considered came in April, when all land sales were postponed. The significance of this was not lost upon the settlers. The "white highlands", their holy of holies, were being threatened.

In May Sir Edward Northey called a round table conference between Indian, European and Government representatives to try and arrive at a local agreement.

The Europeans' fear that India wanted Kenya, body and soul, as a population outlet, and that her present demands were only a prelude to the gradual squeezing out of white influence, was strengthened by the speeches of the Indian spokesmen.

> It might be asked [Mr. Mangaldass said] why Indians wanted land so particularly. India has an overcrowded population. She wants room for expansion. She looks for expansion in the British Empire, as she has every right to do. . . . Europeans can go to Canada, to Australia and to South Africa, and for Europeans to claim this colony as their special preserve is grossly unfair. We have been promised time after time that this country should be an Indian colony.

This was not an isolated hint. On a previous occasion the Kenya Indians' leader, Mr. Jeevanjee, had said:

> I would go so far as to advocate the annexation of this African territory [Kenya] to the Indian Empire, with provincial government under the Indian Viceroy, and let it be opened to us, and in a very few years it will be a second India.

7

The conference reached a deadlock and broke up. Convention, by now thoroughly alarmed, met in the following month. They formulated their "irreducible minimum" on which the Europeans took their stand. Its provisions for Indians were:

(1) Strictly controlled immigration at present, with a view to ultimate prohibition.

(2) Two nominated but not elected members on the Legislative Council.

(3) Segregation in residential areas and in commercial areas where possible.

(4) No further alienation of land to Indians in upland areas.

(5) Full recognition of existing Asiatic rights in property and security of tenure.

Shortly after the meeting at which these demands were formulated (and from which the Governor was driven forth by a heated reference to the settlers' "misguided childlike faith in the Government here") Sir Edward Northey sailed for England to discuss the financial situation. While he was in London the third report of the standing joint committee of both Houses of Parliament on Indian affairs was presented. It dealt with the Kenya question. The committee supported the views of the Government of India by a majority of one.

In Nairobi, in the meantime, the Convention's "irreducible minimum" was answered by a mass meeting of Indians held in July. "When we ask for our rights here", a speaker proclaimed, "the Convention of Associations show us their rifles." They passed with acclamation a resolution stating that Indians could only remain in the British Empire on conditions of perfect equality with Europeans both within and without India.

The weak spot in the Indians' case was the native question. However sound arguments for self-government in their own country might be, even the extremists found it hard to advance any convincing reasons why they should be given an equal voice with Europeans in the shaping of the future of nearly 3 million Africans, for whose destiny they had accepted no responsibility, especially in the face of the almost unanimous protests of the missionaries and the more educated chiefs. The Kikuyu elders, for example, took alarm and wrote a letter to the Governor strongly opposing the Indian claims.

As for Indians occupying positions of authority over us such as district Commissioners, etc., we wish to state that we have no confidence in them in view of their ways as we know them. We could not agree to such a thing, nor could we approve of their being given equal status with the Europeans in regard to anything affecting our affairs.

The native races as a whole had not advanced far enough to give any real opinion on the matter. Only two tribes, the Wakikuyu and the Bantu Kavirondo, out of more than twenty, possessed at that time even a small quota of educated members. These young mission-taught men were far from being representative of the chiefs and elders and the black masses, the blanketed conservatives who formed the bulk of the tribes.

Among the young educated Africans was one called Harry Thuku, secretary of a small political group called the Young Kikuyu Association, composed of partially educated and detribalised Wakikuyu. (He was subsequently deported for "conduct to the danger of peace and good order", and his arrest caused a riot in Nairobi.) A meeting of natives in Nairobi was organised by Harry Thuku and a series of resolutions passed supporting the Indians' claims. These were forwarded to the Prime Minister, the India Office and others as representing the native point of view.

These resolutions aroused surprise in Kenya. Enquiries were made. It was found that Harry Thuku and others had attended a tea-party given by one of the Indian leaders two days before the meeting and that an offer had been made to take a group of natives for a free trip to India in return for the support of the Young Kikuyu Association. The publication of Thuku's resolutions was immediately followed by a meeting of Kikuyu chiefs and elders presided over by Kinanjui, the paramount chief, at which Thuku was removed from his secretaryship and a contradictory set of resolutions, condemning the Indians' demands, was passed.

8

While feeling was stoking up in the colony on both sides Mr. Jeevanjee was in London pressing the Indian case on the Secretary of State. It was felt that a new decision was imminent. The Europeans' fears that Mr. Churchill intended to reverse Lord Milner's policy grew daily more pronounced. The temper of both parties in Kenya made mutual agreement out of the question. It was a time for action.

Pressure from the India Office was being tightened up, it was known, upon the Colonial Office. The settlers, even in their most effervescent moods, felt unable to counteract it single-handed. They resorted, therefore, to strategy.

Kenya Indians might look east across the ocean for their friends: the Europeans would look south across a continent. South Africa had faced the same problem that was confronting Kenya; she would understand. More than that, she might fear: for though she had locked her own doors, south and east, to Indian immigration, railways and roads had opened up a back door in the north which she could not afford to ignore. Africa was no longer a series of land-locked settlements, buffered by fever-ridden deserts and tangled jungles, where events and policies could shape themselves independently of distant neighbours; it was a single continent, linked from north to south by one sovereignty, and the policy evolved in one state would eventually, if gradually, have its repercussions on another. South Africa might be expected to look askance, therefore, at any action so opposed to her own policy as the full recognition of Indian political equality in British Africa. Perhaps she might use her influence in Downing Street to balance, to some extent, that of the India Office.

Her attitude towards her own Indian problem had been publicly reaffirmed only a few months before. The 1921 Imperial Conference had relented in its uncompromising views on Indian rights sufficiently to pass a resolution stating that:

> This Conference, while reaffirming that each community should enjoy complete control over the composition of its own population by means of restriction of immigration from any of the other com-

munities, recognises that there is an incongruity between the position of India as an equal member of the Empire and the existence of disabilities upon British Indians lawfully domiciled in some other parts of the Commonwealth, and that in the interests of the solidarity of the Empire it is desirable that the rights of such Indians to citizenship should be recognised.

South Africa, represented by General Smuts, added this rider:

The representatives of South Africa regret their inability to accept this resolution in view of the exceptional circumstances of the greater part of the Union.

The exceptional circumstances, of course, consisted of the fact that there actually was an Indian community already in the Union. In Canada, Australia and New Zealand combined there were 4500 Indians and 15 million whites. Those Dominions had no need to worry. It was easy to grant equal rights of citizenship when immigration was not restricted but prohibited. In Natal, where there were almost as many Indians as whites, the concession would have been a real one and South Africa was not prepared to make it.

General Smuts was still in power. In August 1921 a little mission of two settlers and the editor of the *East African Standard* sailed for South Africa to see him. From Salisbury to Pretoria they travelled on the same train as a deputation who were on their way to London to discuss the granting of self-government to Southern Rhodesia. The Kenya men talked to them with envy, wondering if they would live to travel along the same road. This was the first direct contact made with the southern colonies.

The Prime Minister of the Union declined to receive the deputation formally but agreed to meet its members for an exchange of views. The pilgrims from Kenya explained that they wanted advice and help. The question was really an African, not only a Kenyan, one. There were many South Africans, both Dutch and English, in Kenya. If the Government of India could intervene on behalf of Kenya Indians, General Smuts, with equal justification, could intervene on behalf of Kenya South Africans.

General Smuts was sympathetic. He said that he regarded

equatorial Africa as the natural hinterland of the south. He looked on the backbone of high country, running up the continent, as the stronghold of western civilisation in Africa. He advised caution but firmness, and constitutional resistance to every attempt to force from the white community concessions to Asiatic claims. The deputation came away with the conviction that they had won the genuine sympathy of a powerful ally, tempered by a passing hope that they had not been reduced to the position of "fascinated rabbits" by the Premier's magnetic charm.

9

In Nairobi, the Convention of Associations had not been idle. Their "misguided childlike faith" in the Government had been shattered by the jettisoning of the Milner settlement. They meant to safeguard their adopted country for the British race however much Britain's rulers seemed determined to discard it. They formed an embryonic cabinet, the Vigilance committee, to advise Convention on any action to be taken over the Indian question.

It consisted, at first, of five members, of whom Delamere was one. They met in secret. Their task was a difficult one. They had to map out a plan which would enable a handful of settlers, unrepresented in England and scattered in Kenya, to defeat the avowed intentions of the Government of India and to persuade the Colonial Office to reverse its policy.

In London, in the meantime, Sir Edward Northey had succeeded in convincing the Secretary of State that any attempt to force through an arbitrary settlement from home, without local consent, would lead to serious trouble. The Secretary of State for India, Mr. Montague, had taken the matter up personally and was urging the Indian claims on the Colonial Office. Mr. Churchill favoured a scheme based on the joint Parliamentary committee's report. The substance of what was to become the "Wood-Winterton agreement" was already taking shape.

Sir Edward Northey knew what this would mean. He had a copy of Convention's "irreducible minimum" in his pocket, he believed that the colonists were more in earnest than was realised in Whitehall, and he had no wish to be driven into enforcing government with machine-guns. His own views were directly opposed to those which were announced to the startled colony a year later. He made it clear that he would resign rather than enforce a decision which accepted the Indian terms.

Sir Edward Northey persuaded the Secretary of State to defer a settlement until he had returned to Kenya and made one more attempt to secure agreement there. He reached the colony in October and outlined to the leaders of both sides, in confidence, the main points in Mr. Churchill's scheme.

The home Government, Sir Edward Northey said, were determined to meet the Indians and a compromise was the best that could be hoped for. The Secretary of State for India had refused to regard Lord Elgin's pledge as binding and the Cabinet were backing him up. Even that issue had nearly been lost; but if the settlers would give way over the franchise they would get security in the highlands as a reward for docility.

As for the franchise, the Governor informed them that the Cabinet had definitely made up its mind. The Indians were going to get the common roll as soon as the present Legislative Council expired. In the meantime he had been instructed to appoint two additional Indians to the Legislature and one to the Executive Council. The common roll was to be qualified with an educational and property test which would allow about 10 per cent of the Indians to vote. It was further suggested that the total number of unofficial members should be reduced to eight, three of whom would be Indians. Segregation was to be abolished altogether.

In essence these proposals were much the same as those which were sent out just a year later as the Wood-Winterton plan. They differed mainly over immigration. The scheme which Sir Edward Northey brought back with him allowed for an educational barrier against Indian artisans and clerks likely to compete with Africans in the labour market; even this was abandoned in the Wood-Winterton despatch.

These proposals confirmed the Europeans' worst fears. Not only were the Indians to be given everything they asked for except (probably) the highlands, but a large slice was to be carved off the recently acquired privileges of the Europeans. The reduction in the number of their elected members from eleven to five would have been a shattering blow. Delamere protested that it was probably the only instance in imperial history where, once the principle of elective representation had been granted, a backward step had been proposed. The Europeans had done nothing to show themselves unworthy of their privileges. It seemed particularly unkind at a moment when India, in whose interest this cruel pruning hook was to be wielded, had received a solemn promise that she should go forward steadily towards the goal of self-government. It was hardly to be expected that the white community would agree to the Churchill proposals.

10

The Convention of Associations decided to send a deputation to England at once to lay their case before Mr. Churchill. Delamere and a soldier-settler from New Zealand were selected as delegates.

It was a question, Delamere said, of whether the future of Eastern Africa should be sacrificed on the altar of political expediency.

"People in England", he said, "apparently think that by handing Kenya over to be dominated by India they are doing something towards solving unrest in India." This was a fallacy. Capitulation to the Indians would encourage, and not stem, the movement towards self-determination in India. "I have never argued with a dangerous lunatic to gain time, but I feel rather like that at present", Delamere said. India's attempt to govern herself would at least be a legitimate experiment; "but to place these people in a position to govern others when they have never yet proved their capacity to govern themselves would probably be the most unstatesmanlike and wanton concession to clamour and the forces of disaffection in our history".

Delamere and his companion sailed at the beginning of December by way of South Africa with the idea of seeing General Smuts. But the Prime Minister was busy at a conference in Natal and could not be interviewed. Delamere had an attack of dysentery in Pretoria and only left his bed to board the *Arundel Castle* boat train.

This was his first visit to the Union. His idea that Kenya should be brought into closer touch with the south in order to break down her isolation as a white island marooned in a sea of black states took shape during the Indian question. Kenya looked south for support in a moment of crisis and Delamere believed that this tentative step should be followed up.

But the chain linking Kenya with the south, the ridge of white settlement of which General Smuts had talked, was not yet in existence. The immediate problem was to persuade a Dominion with troubles enough of her own to intervene with the Imperial Government in the interests of a remote and struggling colony.

Delamere gave his impressions of the position in a letter written on the way to England:

December, 1921
On board the *Arundel Castle*

I was very sorry that we did not see Smuts but it was quite impossible under the circumstances. I think he is very anxious not to press the Indian issue to the point because of the difficulties of the Imperial Government in India and the East. He is afraid that Natal could easily be stirred up on the question and this might force his hand, as if he outwardly showed any reluctance to tackle the question the Nationalists would use it for party purposes; therefore he does not want the matter raised.

It is quite evident that South Africa, having self-government, has the matter quite safe. They are proceeding with their voluntary repatriation. Any Indian who accepts voluntary repatriation is not able to come back again to South Africa. Indians have their ups and downs in business and whenever an Indian loses heart and accepts voluntary repatriation he is outed for good.

None can come in although white people apparently try to smuggle them in. In the train before us from Delagoa Bay to Johannesburg we were told that two Indians were found hidden in the little cellar in the dining coach, being smuggled in by a white man. Some 160,000 Indians or whatever it is against 1½ million whites in the Union, the whites increasing rapidly and the Indians hardly increasing at all, cannot create a serious difficulty, and from his own point of view it does seem wisest for Smuts not to mix himself up with our affairs openly.

He does however recognise the undesirability of having a semi-Asiatic state north of the Union, but I do not think he is willing to take any very strong steps to prevent it. . . . I think it is eminently desirable that we should not let anyone know how little support we may expect.

South Africa is evidently very much on our side in the matter and I do think that if things came to a head they would perhaps force the hand of their Government up to a point.

Delamere arrived in London in January, somewhat incongruously dressed in an old grease-stained British warm and a battered panama hat, and devoid of his luggage, which had got left behind at Genoa. He found Mr. Churchill more sympathetic than he had anticipated. The most important point gained by the deputation was the Secretary of State's admission that, as the colony had already taken the first steps toward self-government on the classic imperial model, its progress could not be indefinitely checked. Once this was accepted many things logically followed; the right to be consulted in questions vital to the country's future, for instance, and the right to regulate its immigration.

Mr. Churchill's answer to the deputation was given at the East African dinner held in London on January 27th, 1922. He made three promises.

We consider that we are pledged by undertakings given in the past to reserve the highlands of East Africa exclusively for European settlers, and we do not intend to depart from that pledge. And it must be taken as a matter which is definitely settled.

We shall apply broadly and comprehensively Mr. Rhodes' principle of equal rights for all civilised men. That means natives and Indians alike who reach and conform to well-marked European standards shall not be denied the fullest exercise and enjoyment of civic and political rights. The standard to be adopted is obviously a matter of the greatest importance, and is certainly a matter in which the European community have a right to be fully consulted.

We consider that the interests of the British settlers and the native population alike require that all future immigration of Indians should be strictly regulated. . . . We recognise that the laws relating to immigration and the administration of them, more than almost any other matter, must be a subject for the closest consultation between the official government and the existing residents in the country.

We do not contemplate any settlement or system which will prevent British East Africa—Kenya as it is now known—from becoming a characteristically and distinctively British colony, looking forward in the full fruition of time to responsible self-government.

These three definite and public assurances from the Secretary of State—and the last paragraph in particular, suggesting that self-government was no will-o'-the-wisp, but a legitimate goal—satisfied the deputation well. Mr. Churchill informed them that he was drawing up definite proposals and would refer them to Kenya for comment. The delegates returned feeling that some progress had been made and confident that the Colonial Office's next proposal would be modified in a favourable direction.

11

Then followed a long official silence. For nine months it was unbroken. It was shattered by a bombshell which reached the colony on September 5th, 1922. This was heralded, shortly before its arrival, by another bomb of a different kind, but charged, to a large extent, with the same Indian explosive.

On August 15th, 1922, Sir Edward Northey was suddenly recalled by telegram, without previous warning, on the ground that the circumstances which required the appointment of a military Governor no longer obtained. No other reason for his precipitate recall was given, nor was it explained what had caused the circumstances to change so swiftly that nothing less than an unheralded telegram would suffice to end his appointment. The inference that Sir Edward Northey had to go because it was proposed to force on the country a policy of which he was known to disapprove and which he had prophesied would lead to serious trouble was too strong to be resisted.

He left Government House within a fortnight. On September 1st Sir Robert Corydon came down from Uganda to take over control. "Have accepted Governorship of Kenya: no more peace", he wired to a friend.

Five days after the new Governor took over his duties the substance of the famous "Wood-Winterton agreement" was cabled out to Nairobi. It was not published until nearly a year later.

The proposals included a common electoral roll for all British subjects with a qualifying test so arranged as to enfranchise about 10 per cent of the Indian population. The seats were to be divided up among Indians and Europeans in the proportion of either four to seven, according to one plan (this was the favoured one) or four to eleven, according to another. Immigration was to be unrestricted. There was no sign of the Secretary of State's previous promise at the East African dinner that "all future immigration of Indians should be strictly regulated", although the Wood-Winterton plan was described in the cabled despatch from the Secretary of State as "a provisional agreement intended to meet difficulties in India without departing from the spirit of my previous pronouncements".

Segregation was to be abolished. On the question of the "white highlands" no final agreement was reached. The Colonial Office refused to make any change in the existing arrangement, but the India Office declined to accept this and reserved the right to reopen the question. The new electoral roll was come into force in time for the next general election.

The report had been drawn up in the summer by the two Under-Secretaries, the Hon. Edward Wood (later Lord Irwin) for the Colonies and Lord Winterton for India. They had met, attended by Civil servants, as a small inter-departmental committee to get the troublesome question out of the way. The terms of their report showed that the intensity of feeling, the high pitch of nervous tension, which had been reached in East Africa had not been fully realised in the even-keeled atmosphere of summer in Whitehall, with its pleasant hustle of going and coming on annual leave and its civilised background of shady trees and aquatic bird life in St. James's Park. The indignation with which the report was greeted came as a great surprise to its authors.

The Governor was told to consult his Executive Council and to "telegraph your observations as soon as possible, bearing in mind that the proposals constitute a nicely balanced agreement between the Secretaries of State for India and for the Colonies". Sir Robert Coryndon cabled back that the terms of the settlement were entirely unacceptable to the Europeans and probably could not be imposed except by force. He received a brief acknowledgment. This was followed by a three-months silence.

In November 1922 a change of government in England resulted in the departure of Mr. Churchill from the Colonial Office and the arrival of the Duke of Devonshire. Within three years, four different Secretaries of State had presided over the colonial Empire's destinies.

12

The Wood-Winterton plan aroused intense indignation in Kenya. Hopes raised by Mr. Churchill's statement at the East African dinner were rudely dashed, and bitterness followed. Ballot-box equality with a two-to-one majority of Indians plus unchecked immigration could hardly mean that Kenya was to develop as a "characteristically and distinctively British colony". That was one promise gone. Immigration was another; two out of three. And his assurance that the Indian settlement was a matter on which the Europeans had a right to be fully consulted was being ignored by his successors in a peculiarly high-handed way. The country, the colonists felt, had been thrown to extremist lions in the Indian arena. Persuasion had failed; the alternatives were surrender or resistance.

Over four months elapsed before the Colonial Office moved again. On January 10th a deputation of Indians arrived at Government House stating that the Governor had received a further secret despatch and demanding to be informed of its contents. The news had been cabled to them from their agents in London. They reached Government House before the despatch, which was actually brought to the Governor while he was receiving the deputation. It contained no new proposals but enlarged on some of the points in the Wood-Winterton plan and pressed the Governor to secure agreement to its terms.

The decisions reaffirmed in this despatch, in the view of the Europeans, made the Colonial Office's attitude lamentably clear. It was evidently approaching a settlement from the angle of satisfying the Government of India instead of from the angle of consideration for the colony's future. The belief that this attitude prevailed in Downing Street destroyed the colonists' confidence in their rulers' impartiality and convinced them that the case would be decided on a basis not of fairness but of fear, with an eye not to the future of Africa but to the pacification of India. It was this conviction that drove them to desperate and unwelcome measures.

One further decision was conveyed in this despatch. The life of the existing Legislative Council was to be prolonged for another year in order to allow a settlement to be reached before the next election. The announcement of this decision aroused the strongest feeling among the Europeans. They interpreted it to mean that, whatever happened, the common roll was to be arbitrarily introduced and some of their own rights taken away.

A bill to extend the life of the Council for another year was introduced and violently attacked by the elected members. Delamere described it as "a wanton and provocative action". "It is simply direct action on the part of the Secretary of State", he said. "There is no doubt that direct action breeds direct action. . . . I think this bill gives the people an example in direct action which they may follow."

This was the first open threat.

Meetings of protest were held all over the settled areas. A crowded assembly at Nakuru resolved, after a pyrotechnic display of speeches, that if the Indian claims were granted—

The community will take such action as they may consider proper and necessary to prevent any legislation with that object from taking effect;

That any action to be taken shall indicate in the clearest manner not only that the white community declines to be made a pawn in the game of Indian politics, but that in their internal politics they refuse to be over-ridden in their opinions by those at home who are obviously ignorant of, or indifferent to local conditions; and

That such action as may be taken shall be of a persuasive character as far as possible, physical pressure only being resorted to in so far as it may be required to show that the persuasion being exercised is intended to be acted upon.

Resolutions on the same lines were passed with acclamation by practically all the local associations. An impartial observer (an Indian Civil servant) who visited the colony at this time commented: "The whites are infuriated at the attempt to order their affairs from Simla *via* Downing Street. When I went to Nairobi I was astonished at the strength and universality of a grim determination not to submit to any such dictation. The old Bostonian spirit is abroad and must be taken very seriously. The terms laid down by Mr. Churchill in September will have to be very greatly modified or there will be civil war."

13

But indignation without organisation was a hollow expedient. Talk must give way to action. So the colonists set about the organisation of a rebel force. It was to be an original kind of rebellion, paralleled only by the situation in Ulster in 1914—a rebellion which aimed, not at breaking away from the Empire, but at remaining in it.

The Vigilance committee had, for some time past, been quietly organising an emergency military and political machine. The country was divided up into districts and in each area a "connecting link" was selected to act as liaison with the Vigilance committee. Plans were explained verbally to the "links" so that few incriminating documents would be found if the leaders were arrested. In each district a census of rifles, ammunition, cars, petrol supplies and horses was taken. Plans of mobilisation were worked out to the last detail.

The colonists, though ludicrously small in numbers, were strong in military experience. There was hardly a man among them who had not seen active service within the last six years. There were many who had served with the East African forces and who knew all there was to be known about campaigning under local conditions. There were the thousand or so ex-soldier settlers.

At that time the proportion of ex-soldiers among Kenya's population was probably higher than in any other country in the world. There was a number of generals and other senior officers among these ex-soldiers; and when a plan of action had been sketched in outline it was decided to hand the military organisation over to two or three of these experienced commanders. These men had first of all to be persuaded to risk the loss of their pensions, and perhaps even of their farms. They had also to satisfy their consciences that the cause which they were asked to forward justified their undertaking to engage in open rebellion against the local representatives of a Government they had served actively throughout their lives.

The question was broached by Delamere and some of his colleagues one Sunday morning, soon after the terms of the Wood-Winterton agreement became known, at the Norfolk hotel. The soldiers hesitated. The discussion went on all day. At last, late in the afternoon, the most senior of the officers brought his fist down on the table and exclaimed: "I feel we ought to do it!" The others, convinced by his enthusiasm, followed his lead.

Thereafter the actual organisation of the rising passed into military hands. Plans were drawn up to seize, by surprise raids, the railway and the postal and telegraphic systems. Trained telegraphists were detailed to take over immediately the signal was given with the intention of broadcasting messages all over the Empire stating the colonists' case and appealing to the home and Dominion publics for support. The Governor was to be kidnapped and taken to a lonely farm some sixty miles from Nairobi, where a guard had been detailed to look after him. (His comfort was carefully considered; his place of detention was selected on account of the excellent trout fishing available close by.)

At no time was it proposed to use any physical violence against Indians. The majority of them had little or no idea of what was going on; the question had got far out of the depth of the average local store-keeper. Indian masons and carpenters continued to work for European employers without ill-feeling on either side, although settlers tried as far as possible to replace Indian artisans with such trained natives as were available. The most drastic measure proposed in the event of trouble was the shipping of all Indians in the Nairobi bazaar in a series of special trains to Mombasa, where, once the rising had broken out, the British navy would presumably be able to look after them.

The Vigilance committee concentrated mainly on propaganda. They had to convince their followers as well as their opponents that they were in earnest. Most of the settlers did not enter at all light-heartedly into what was, after all, a seditious organisation. The war had not been over long enough for them to welcome the prospect of anything in the shape of another one. Many of them, like the senior officers, had pensions at stake. The visiting Indian Civil servant quoted above commented: "Numbers of senior, many of them distinguished, retired officers are ready to sacrifice their pensions upon which they are wholly dependent to fight for a principle. They have seen what a handful of determined Europeans with a knowledge of the country were able to do under von Lettow Vorbeck in German East Africa. The danger is not to be laughed away. Their attitude may appear comic to Londoners: not so in Nakuru."

14

Members of the Vigilance committee stumped the country addressing secret district meetings. Lists were prepared containing the names of those who were prepared to come out and the names (few in number) of those who could not be relied upon. Covenants were signed undertaking not to sell or lease any land in the highlands to Indians. These documents, together with other incriminating papers, were buried, for at one time the leaders lived in daily expectation of arrest and deportation. A series of secret sub-committees was formed, so that if one lot of leaders was arrested another batch would be ready to step into their places.

A notable feature of the rebellion was its intense loyalty to the Crown. The situation was, constitutionally speaking, very confused. The settlers held that they were preparing to rebel only against short-sighted ministers who were betraying the true interests of the King and the Empire. They had exhausted all pacific methods of protest. They had therefore no alternative but to resist these ministers by force, and so, theoretically, to defy the Crown. But Kenya settlers were more at home with practice than with theory and practically, they believed, their loyalty was proving itself greater than that of the misguided ministers. They adopted the motto "For King and Kenya" and generally ended their rebel councils of war with an enthusiastic rendering of "God save the King".

The home Government, the potential rebels felt, would be placed in an awkward position if and when the rising came. They felt confident that the officers of the K.A.R. and most of the police would resign their commissions rather than order black troops to fire on their countrymen. They believed that administrative officers would remain at their posts and continue to discharge their normal duties.

If the rising was successful the Government would have to send troops from England or from India. Public opinion, it was hoped, would swing in the colonists' favour if Indian troops were used to attack a small band of white settlers, many of them ex-officers who, five years ago, had been leading British soldiers into action in France and German East Africa—especially when the rebels, however illogically, proclaimed themselves ardently loyal to King and Empire.

By the same token they believed that English troops would be sent against them only in the last resort. The ships whose officers and men periodically visited the highlands for big-game shooting and football matches could, it was true, easily blockade Mombasa harbour; but that was some 350 miles away, with a desert in between, and the country was self-supporting in the essentials of life.

And, in the background, was South Africa. No one knew how far she would have come to the rescue if the appeal had been made; but there was little doubt in which direction her sympathies lay. If the home Government called out troops to enforce the Indian decision upon a desperate country there might be music to face in Pretoria as well as in London. Opinion in England was indifferent through lack of information; but if a bill for military operations were presented the public would wake up, and its reactions on waking were an unknown factor.

The outburst of atmospherics relayed home by the Governor at last convinced the Colonial Office that their proposals could not be enforced without serious trouble. Sir Robert Coryndon was summoned to London to confer, and European and Indian delegates were officially selected to lay their respective cases before the Secretary of State.

CHAPTER XIX

DEPUTATION TO DOWNING STREET
1923

I

THE European delegation was led by Delamere. With him went Mr. C. K. Archer, chairman of the Convention of Associations; Mr. T. A. Wood, representing the commercial community; the Rev. J. W. Arthur, head of the Church of Scotland Mission; and Mr. P. C. Green, representing the European Workers' Association, the Labour organisation in Nairobi. They were joined in London by Major W. M. Crowdy.

The Indian delegation from Kenya was composed of Mr. M. A. Desai, editor of the Indian paper in Nairobi; Mr. A. M. Jeevanjee; Mr. B. S. Varma; and Mr. Husseinbhai S. Virjee. They sailed by way of Bombay with the intention of interviewing Mr. Gandhi. This they failed to do, although he sent them messages of sympathy; but they were able to secure the support of a prominent missionary, the Rev. C. F. Andrews, who had visited East Africa in 1920. Mr. Andrews accompanied the delegation to England. Here they were joined by two representatives of the Government of India, the Right Hon. V. S. Srinivasa Sastri and Sir Benjamin Robertson, both members of the Viceroy's Council.

Sir Robert Coryndon sailed with the European delegation on March 26th. Sir Charles Bowring took charge of the colony in his absence. The Governor did not leave Kenya with an altogether easy mind. The Europeans were in a highly inflammable mood. Before he sailed a truce between government and settlers was arranged by Sir Robert Coryndon, who was well acquainted with the structure of the rebel army. Convention pledged itself to do nothing to prejudice the issue while the delegates were at home, but to do all in their power to discourage and prevent "direct action".

They gave a final growl, however, to show that they still meant business. A resolution was passed, just before the Governor sailed, affirming their unswerving loyalty to the King and their determination to uphold the Empire, but stipulating that if the settlers were forced into taking "any action prejudicial to His Majesty's peace and abhorrent and ruinous to themselves" the responsibility would rest solely on "the ill-considered advice of His Majesty's ministers".

This was direct and open defiance. It was received with pained surprise in England. A threat of armed resistance in the Empire is a sufficiently rare occurrence to excite some interest, and the Indian problem in Kenya began to figure in the news. Hardly anyone, apart from a few politicians and bishops and the members of the Aborigines Protection Society, had heard of Kenya. Articles with maps explaining roughly where it was began to appear in the papers and several questions were asked in the House.

In India a resolution was passed in Congress calling on the British Government to protect innocent and unarmed Indians in Nairobi and up-country who were being threatened by armed settlers and going in fear of their lives. This resolution won much publicity in the House of Commons and Indians in Kenya sent home nervous telegrams. There was, in fact, no danger of any assaults on individual Indians by the settlers. One of the most remarkable features of the crisis was the lack of personal enmity between the races. There was not even an isolated incident of physical violence towards an Indian on the part of a European.

2

Delamere and his team left in a "to the last man and the last penny" atmosphere. The deputation had definite instructions to accept no compromise. They had a prodigious fight before them. The Wood-Winterton agreement had been accepted by the Cabinet and confirmed unequivocally by the new Secretary of State. The Government of India stood absolutely firm and the Viceroy was known to attach the greatest importance to a settlement in favour of the Indians. Public opinion in England, in a conciliatory frame of mind, was not unnaturally more inclined to conciliate the Indian Empire than a handful of settlers in a remote colony of which hardly anyone had heard. For over two years the Europeans had been advancing arguments only to see them brushed aside; and there was little to add. Against the colonists was pitted the Cabinet's decision, Colonial Office timidity and all the weight of the Government of India; behind them lay only an apparently rather ludicrous threat of force and the misty shadow of South Africa.

For the next three months Delamere fought the stiffest and perhaps the most crucial fight of his political career. If the Europeans were right in their interpretation of Indian demands, then the whole future of East Africa as an outpost of white civilisation, a pivotal point in a continent where history was only just beginning, hinged upon the success of the settlers' deputation. For if they lost their case and if East Africa became—as the settlers believed it would then become—a projection of India overseas, the northernmost link in the chain of white settlement stretching from the Cape to the borders of Abyssinia would be smashed forever. Kenya, instead of establishing itself as a rallying-point of British endeavour in Africa and developing perhaps into the nucleus of a new dominion, would become a funnel through which an Asiatic flood would pour into Africa and filter down the eastern territories, lapping against the foundations of a western political and economic system which were even now being tentatively laid.

Full equality of citizenship for Indians was a noble and a just sentiment, well in keeping with England's post-war mood. But it meant, if Delamere was right, so much more than, on the surface, it implied. Carried to its conclusion in East Africa it would ultimately mean domination, not equality. The same fear that prompted every self-governing country in the Empire to put up impregnable barriers against Asiatics—the fear, amounting to a certainty, that a more prolific race on a lower economic level would gradually drive out the race with a higher standard of living—lay at the root of the settlers' protests. The admission of Indians to equal rights would mean the end of British colonisation and the ruin of the settlers. If the deputation failed, all the progress of the last twenty years would, so they believed, be ground to pieces between the upper and nether millstones of post-war anti-imperialism and the fear of Indian unrest.

Delamere resolved to appeal not only to the Secretary of State but beyond him to the British public, who must ultimately, through Parliament, sanction or reject the settlement. In this he had to overcome the minor difficulty of hostility and the major one of indifference. Few people cared for Kenya's troubles. There was no powerful group of financial interests behind the scenes to bring pressure to bear in the right quarters. And the British public was not going to lose its sleep over the fate of a handful of farmers.

The only chance was to rouse it over the principle involved, and in particular over its responsibilities towards the native population.

3

The deputation set about creating an interest in a methodical way. That they succeeded so well was largely due to Delamere's readiness to devote his private means to the cause. He was always a believer in creating an atmosphere. There was to be nothing apologetic about the atmosphere surrounding the delegation. It was to be one of giving, not of asking.

The first step was to provide a suitable background. To this end he took a house in Grosvenor Place at his own expense and had it equipped, before his arrival, with a carefully selected staff, including a first-class cook.

To this lavish setting came, on a cold and wet March night, a disreputable, huddled group who announced themselves to a sceptical butler as the principals of the piece. Delamere, in an old torn coat, a hairy khaki shirt and a tie protruding from under one ear, had some difficulty in convincing the butler that he was indeed the aristocratic tenant of the house. The rest of the delegation, one in a disintegrating burberry on which red mud from the coffee nursery mingled with grease from the farm engine, did little to raise the tone of the bedraggled party.

The greatest surprise of all were the two shivering Somalis who had accompanied their master and who were believed for some time by the butler to be Delamere's sons. They rapidly descended in the social scale. On the first evening they were referred to as "the young African gentlemen" and on the following day (the butler being a Yorkshireman) as "thim lads".

The delegation set about at once to enlist the support of the press. Innumerable luncheons and dinners were held in Grosvenor Place, articles written and interviews given. The "Kenya question" began to figure prominently in the press.

The Bishop of Uganda started the ball rolling with a letter to *The Times* supporting the European point of view. He intervened on the grounds that the settlement, though not of immediate concern to Uganda, was of primary importance to the future of the African. He held that segregation was a natural and convenient arrangement carrying with it no necessary implication of racial inferiority.

The confining of Europeans to their own quarters in Chinese towns, the exclusion of Europeans from certain towns in Nigeria, the exclusion of European settlers from native reserves in Kenya itself in no case carries with it any stigma of inferiority.

When two races differ widely in language, habit and tradition it is better, from the point of view of either, that they should occupy separate areas. . . . Indians not only observe rigidly the principles of segregation in their own caste system in India, but themselves demand in East Africa that Africans should be segregated from the Indian community. Segregation between European and Indians, is, however, condemned as being inconsistent with the status of complete equality.

Since Indians had as yet gained no experience in democratic self-government—far less in the guidance of races less advanced than themselves—it would be premature, the Bishop suggested, to associate them as trustees in the government of Africans. "No claim for Indians in Africa", he said, "can be put forward which cannot with far greater force be advanced for Africans in their own country." Indians, the Bishop continued, "have so far shown little evidence of any aptitude or desire to teach or uplift the native races. Their 300 years of intercourse with them on the coast have left singularly little mark on the native population."

They had, he added, no responsibility for East Africa. If there was a deficit, Britain made it up; if there was a rising, British forces put it down. India could not claim privileges without earning the right to hold them.

Finally, he concluded, India did undeniably belong to a different civilisation from our own. "It is not necessary to assume that it is a lower civilisation. It is more ancient than ours; in some respects it may be better; but it is essentially different. It would be impossible for representatives of two completely different civilisations conjointly to administer African races alien to both."

4

Delamere and Mr. Srinivasa Sastri, the principal spokesman for the Indian delegation, made full statements to the press. There were wide discrepancies not only in their opinions but in their facts. (Mr. Sastri had, at that time, never visited East Africa and had to take his facts on trust from the Kenya Indians and the Rev. C. F. Andrews.) The following examples—two among many—taken from press articles and interviews show how wide a choice of evidence on this issue was offered to the public:

Mr. Sastri

Long before the British ever came there, we had established our connections and built up our business. In fact, the Britisher came there in order to protect our interests, and it was because of our influence with the secular powers already established in these parts that the British established a Protectorate and then converted it into a Crown colony. It was all for our benefit in the first instance. (June 2nd, 1923.)

Lord Delamere

The Indians in Kenya followed where the white man trod. They never pioneered Kenya. They financed and provided arms for the slave trade and the irony of the situation is that we have destroyed the Arab power which held the coast because of the slave trade, and now we are discussing whether the people who financed them, even after the British Government had forbidden slavery, should take an equal part

We admit the dominant rights of the native. We recognise his claim to education and development. But it is from the Indians, not the whites, that he is getting it. It is the Indian who learns his language and teaches him trades. (April 30th, 1923.)

with us in the government of Kenya. (May 25th, 1923.)

It is a fact that so long as British Indians are allowed into the minor posts in the Kenya Government service no African will get in there.

Africans in other parts of Africa are able to work as stonemasons, carpenters and so on, but in Kenya the Indians will not allow Africans to work alongside them, and if a European builder wants to employ native skilled labour he is immediately boycotted by the Indians and strikes are fomented against him. (May 25th, 1923.)

The controversy continued in a fervid atmosphere. Mr. Sastri proclaimed, as he stepped off the boat on arrival: "If we are rebuffed in this matter, I will not undertake to predict what will happen in India". The Rev. C. F. Andrews went further: "If there is to be restriction on immigration in Kenya it will mean that India goes out of the Empire. That is the view, not merely of Indians, but of practically every type of Englishman in India."

"You mean discriminatory restrictions?" asked a *Daily News* reporter. "No," replied Mr. Andrews, "any restrictions." Mr. Sastri clinched this view with a statement at a reception in his honour in London. "Failure on the part of the British Government to do justice on the present occasion", he said, "would be regarded as a deliberate and final verdict concerning the position of Indians in the Empire."

No doubt was left that this was to be a test case. The challenge was taken up. The Kenya David stepped out pugnaciously to meet the Indian Goliath.

After a month of intensive propaganda, the delegation succeeded in winning a good deal of sympathy for their cause. There was, of course, a bitter section which pointed to Kenya as the last stronghold of rusty nineteenth-century imperialism and to the settlers as fanatical racial bigots. This group opposed the settlers' claim to have any say in the government of the colony and advocated the confiscation of such powers as they already had. Misconceptions of every sort appeared daily, ranging from the crude confusion of East with South Africa to subtler misstatements such as those printed in the *New Statesman:*

"It is doubtful whether European women and children can live even in the highlands. The Council should be nominated and Kenya should be governed from Whitehall. Kenya is not solvent. Almost inevitably it will default next year and have to be subsidised by the Imperial Government." (In the following year revenue exceeded expenditure by over £250,000.)

But on the whole there was more sympathy than antagonism in the press and—so far as could be gauged—among the public.

5

The Duke of Devonshire received the deputation on April 24th. Delamere opened his case by asking for a definite statement of Indian demands from both the Kenya Indians and the Government of India. An official list of demands had never been seen by the Europeans, and the Indians had shifted their ground so often that it was difficult to know the exact extent of their claims.

His request met with no response. The Europeans were never officially acquainted with the Indian demands. They were left to gather them mainly from an article inspired by Mr. Sastri in *The Times* and from such reports as reached them of the meetings held between the Indian spokesmen, the Duke of Devonshire and Lord Peel, the Secretary of State for India. Then they pieced together the Indian case as best they could and answered it point by point.

It was based upon the claim to complete equality of status with Europeans by virtue of a common citizenship of the Empire. In support of this Mr. Sastri quoted a list of proclamations by sovereigns and statesmen, beginning with a pronouncement made by Queen Victoria in 1858. The Indians also advanced four particular points to justify their claim to special treatment in Kenya.

The first was that of priority of occupation. Indians had been well established in East Africa, they said, for 300 years before the British arrived. So much the worse for their claim to be pioneers, the Europeans retorted. They had lived only along the coast-line, on sufferance, under Arab and then Portuguese rule, and their principal contribution to the uplift of the African had been the financing of the slave trade. David Livingstone was quoted: "But for the goods, arms and ammunition advanced by the *banians*, no Arab could go inland to slave. It is by their money that the slave trade is carried on."

In 1900 there were no Indians in any province of what is now Kenya Colony except those working on the railway. They came in only as indentured coolies, protected always by an armed British guard. "At one moment at Tsavo", Delamere added, "man-eating lions nearly sent the whole lot back to India, and it was only with the greatest difficulty that they were persuaded to go through a country where the sport of the young African warrior was to kill lions with the spear. Later they established small shops under the shadow of the protected administrative stations. How do these things establish their claim as pioneers of Kenya?"

The next Indian claim was based upon their war services. They had helped to keep the Protectorate for the Empire, they affirmed, and to conquer the German colony. The Europeans did not deny that troops from India had fought bravely in the campaign. Since the Indians raised the matter, however, they did draw attention to the war record of the local Indians who were in the country when war broke out. This read: killed, nil; wounded, nil; died of wounds, nil; executed for treachery, five. They compared this record with a casualty list of nearly 50,000 killed, wounded and died on active service among the natives.

Another claim was that Indians were doing a great deal to enlighten the African by teaching him useful trades. The Europeans asserted that the exact opposite was the case. There were no schools for natives run by Indians although not only Government and missionaries but settlers ran many small African schools. They quoted cases where Indian artisans had gone on strike because trained Africans had been engaged to work alongside them.

The fourth Indian claim was that Indians paid most of the taxation and so ought to have the greatest say in the way the money was spent. Government figures for 1922, however, showed that Europeans paid more than two and a half times as much as the Indians although their numbers were only half as great.

6

The principal concessions asked by the Indians were five in number.

The first demand was for the franchise on a common instead of a communal roll. The common roll was defined by the Secretary of State as a system whereby "European and Indian voters with identical qualifications vote for a candidate of either race and in the same constituency". The communal method was that "Europeans vote for a European candidate in a European constituency, and Indians vote for an Indian candidate in an Indian constituency, the qualifications not being necessarily identical and the constituencies being necessarily different".

The strongest objection to the common roll advanced by the Europeans was the implication it would entail in regard to native policy. The colonists implored the Imperial Government not to prejudice the whole political future of the African by committing Kenya, out of anxiety to placate the Indians, to a line of development—a common roll for everyone who could pass an elementary education test— which might well prove to be an unwise one.

Students of African affairs had expressed the gravest doubts as to whether the system of democracy as practised in certain advanced European countries, with its paraphernalia of ballot-boxes, elections and political parties, was suited to the mentality and traditions of the African. Already democracy was falling into disrepute among most of the countries which had adopted it. Was it, then, wise and fair to commit the African to it, without further consideration, as a side issue of another problem? Statesmanship demanded that the native issue should be kept clear. The grant of a common roll in a racially mixed country would inevitably confuse it, perhaps disastrously.

The Indians, all along, had agreed to an educational test enfranchising 10 per cent of their community, should they be accorded the common roll. The Europeans objected to this. In the first place, they said, the proportion of Indians in Kenya who had attained even a low standard of literacy and general education was not nearly as high as 10 per cent. In India itself only about $2\frac{1}{2}$ per cent of the population had got on to the voters' roll, and there was probably a higher proportion of educated Indians in India than in Kenya.

There was another, and more fundamental, objection. So long as only two or three thousand Indians were entitled to vote the Europeans would be in a majority. But once admit the principle and what guarantee was there that this 10 per cent would not be altered, that the test would not be lowered and even, eventually, abolished? Once the Indians got their foot in the door, the colonists said, it was only a matter of time before they pushed it open to its fullest extent.

The Indians denied this vigorously. There would be no question of the educational test being lowered, they said.

Then the Europeans produced a trump card. Mr. G. L. Corbett, the assistant secretary to the Government of India, who had visited Kenya with Sir Benjamin Robertson in 1920, had forwarded his comments on Mr. Churchill's proposals to the Indian Government in the following year. The despatch was headed "Secret". It came into the hands of the Indians in Nairobi and the Europeans obtained a copy through a missionary. The relevant part read:

> Provided the principle of the common roll is maintained, I personally do not regard the precise qualification for the franchise as of vital importance. However high the qualifications may be now, it may be regarded as certain that they will be lowered later.

That, the Europeans claimed, exploded the oft-repeated Indian assurance that there could be no question of lowering any test. When an eminent Civil servant says that a thing "may be regarded as certain", the possibility of its happening cannot be dismissed as absurd. The "Corbett secret note" was an effective piece of ammunition.

7

The next point was immigration. The root of the matter lay in the type of Indian coming into Kenya. The British public was apt to think of Indians in terms of county cricketers, rajahs in Rolls-Royces, studious undergraduates or bearded, warlike Sikhs. Unfortunately there were none of these in Kenya. Indian supporters accused the settlers of entrenching themselves behind the old and discredited colour bar. But it was not a question of colour, the Europeans replied. It was a question of civilisation and of standards of living. If the Duke of Devonshire could see a typical row of Indian *dukas* in a Kenya township he would understand their feelings better. Dirt, smells, flies, disregard of sanitation; swarming, squalling children packed into back rooms, crawling over filthy floors; traders haggling with natives over a handful of salt or a blanket and defrauding them, only too often, of a few cents; a few even organising gangs of youthful native housebreakers; this was the picture that the Europeans felt obliged to paint. It was a prejudiced one, of course, but they felt that it was necessary as a corrective.

Educated Indians who visited Kenya looked on their expatriated countrymen no more favourably and some had spoken with scorn of the East African Indians' political claims. Mr. Sastri, the leading spirit of the Indian delegation, had never set foot in Kenya. The only Indians that most Colonial Office officials had seen were charming and cultivated gentlemen, like Mr. Sastri himself, that any country would be glad to welcome.

Many of the Kenya Indians were Untouchables. Of these, the rest of their countrymen believed: "Their abodes shall be out of towns; their property shall consist of dogs and asses; their ornaments shall be rusty iron; their clothes shall be those left by the dead; they shall wander from place to place; no respectable man shall have intercourse with them". Yet it was for these people, bred for generations in the contempt of their fellows, that more fortunate Indians were claiming equality with the European. Outcast in India, they were to govern in Africa. The colonists questioned the sincerity of leaders who based their demands on the pure doctrine of democracy while refusing to regard an Untouchable as a fellow human being. Mr. Sastri, they pointed out, himself belonged to a high caste whose members would in no circumstances agree to live in the same street as an Untouchable. Why, then, should he urge with such eloquence that Europeans should be made to live cheek-by-jowl with families whom he, a fellow-countryman, would never consent to shake hands with, whose mere shadow would defile his food?

The question of immigration led on naturally to that of segregation. The Indians protested that they were not normally allowed to buy residential plots in European sections of the towns. This they regarded as a stigma of racial inferiority. Delamere replied that there were only two possible policies, in the long run, in a country of mixed races. One was complete fusion and the emergence of a new race. The other was social segregation. You could not have social intermixing without admitting the corollary of intermarriage.

Either policy might be right; the point was, which was practicable. In Kenya there could be no question, for the time being at any rate, of intermarriage between English and Indian. Neither race would tolerate it. Admitting this, you must also admit social segregation. It was not a question of racial inferiority, but of incompatibility. Neither European nor Indian mothers would like their children to play together in the next-door garden or to go to the same school. Whatever the merits of the theory, a gulf of religion, habit and ideals ruled out the practice of intermixture. "The points of contact", Delamere said, "are the points of friction."

A further Indian claim, for the grant of the municipal franchise in Nairobi on a common roll, was resisted by the colonists on the same grounds as they opposed the general franchise. The remaining Indian demand was for the right to buy land in the highlands.

8

Mere blunt opposition to the Indian claims was a negative attitude for the Europeans to take up. The Colonial Office asked for constructive suggestions for a settlement and the delegation then put up a series of definite proposals to the Secretary of State.

They covered far wider ground than the Indian question. They were, in effect, Delamere's skeleton framework for a new Kenya constitution, boiled down into seven separate proposals.

The first of these was that the native reserves should be finally demarcated and then removed entirely from the jurisdiction of the Legislative Council. These native lands should be held in trust for their inhabitants by the Governor, who should be directly responsible to the Secretary of State.

The second point was that, in the event of a further step being taken towards European self-government, native affairs should be a reserved subject dealt with, through the Governor, solely by the Secretary of State, who would thus be able to retain entire control over such matters as native taxation and labour policy.

These two proposals were intended to clear the way for further constitutional advance for the Europeans. The third suggestion was that the colonists should be granted an unofficial elected majority on the Legislative Council within the next five years.

In the fourth place, a law should be passed at once to control immigration. Restrictions should be framed on an economic basis and should aim at excluding immigrants likely to compete directly with Africans in the labour market.

The fifth condition laid down that Indians already in the colony should have the right to purchase land anywhere (apart from the reserves) except in the white highlands, and should have an area of land set aside for them, if they so desired it, from which Europeans would be excluded.

Segregation of races in the residential areas of townships was the sixth point.

The last proposal dealt with representation on the Legislative Council. The Indians should be allotted two seats to which they should elect members on a communal roll. This was the most that could be conceded, Delamere said, in view of the native complication. If Indians were admitted to a common roll with Europeans then nothing could prevent Arabs and semi-educated natives claiming the same privileges; and elementary education tests were "not in fact true tests as to capacity to govern". Policy should be directed rather to encouraging and building up native councils in the reserves to manage native affairs. These councils might ultimately combine to send African members to represent native interests on the Legislative Council. In the meantime, an unofficial European should be nominated to the Council to voice the native viewpoint.

This memorandum of Delamere's contained the first concrete demand from the colonists for the grant of self-government within a measurable time. It was made largely in self-defence. For while the Indian problem was in the melting-pot discussions suddenly took, to the settlers, an ominous turn.

The Indians had not been in England many weeks before they realised that things were not going as smoothly as they had anticipated. Public opinion was disappointing. The argument that Indians had no justification for demanding a say in the government of natives had carried great weight, and the Indians had reluctantly to recognise that for this reason, if for no other, they were in danger of defeat on the crucial question of the common roll.

They, therefore, shifted their ground. They reasoned that equality could be obtained by scaling down the Europeans' political privileges as well as by scaling up their own. They started an agitation for the removal of the Europeans' right to elect representatives to the Legislative Council.

The strongest possible pressure was brought to bear on the Duke of Devonshire and his advisers by the Indian delegation to adopt this alternative solution. The Colonial Office looked with some favour on the proposal. A solution on these lines would strengthen their own direct control over Kenya's affairs and dispose finally of a troublesome and vociferous opposition.

Delamere and his team thus found themselves attacked sharply in the flank. They were in imminent danger of a more crushing defeat than they had ever suspected could overcome them. There were now two fights at once to be carried on, against Indian expansion and against their own contraction. Their demand for self-government was in the nature of a counter-attack.

9

They presented their proposals early in June. From that moment they found the Colonial Office doubly reticent. Only from outside sources could they gather what was going on.

They heard disquieting rumours that the colony's future as a white man's country was likely to be prejudiced by the application to East Africa of the so-called "West Coast policy" of which the Under-Secretary of State, Mr. Ormsby-Gore, was a strong advocate. It was said that the Imperial Government intended to extricate itself from the difficulty by declaring that the trusteeship of the native devolved on the Government of Great Britain alone and not on the British people as a whole, and that neither Indians nor settlers were to have any political rights. The colonists grew alarmed. They had rubbed the magic lamp of native interests, but the Djinn who suddenly materialised before them was an unprepossessing monster with a nasty look, not at all the obedient servant they had hoped to see.

After the white paper containing the settlement was issued, Delamere was accused by some of his followers of having made a strategical blunder in stressing the native aspect of the case. It was true that neither Delamere nor his colleagues foresaw where their emphasis on native interests would lead. Even if they had, however, it seems certain that on no other grounds could they have won their case.

June passed, and still no decision had been reached. There were indications as to the probable terms. At a meeting with the permanent Under-Secretary of State the delegation was told that the questions of the white highlands and segregation were "definitely out of the way". From the context they took this to mean that both had been decided in their favour. It was not until the white paper was in their hands that they discovered that the second of these points had gone against them.

In July, rumours that the Cabinet had decided to settle the matter by removing the colonists' existing political powers and declaring the country a black territory, in which neither whites nor browns had any future, became more persistent. In an effort to avert catastrophe Delamere wrote to the Secretary of State informing him that, if the Government's decision "sold the pass" as regards the future development of Kenya as a British colony, the colonists would appeal to South Africa to lay the matter before the Imperial Conference due to meet that autumn.

The colonists had one piece of good fortune. This was the attitude taken up by their Governor.

Sir Robert Coryndon was by training an African administrator. He was born in Africa and marched with Rhodes' pioneer column when it occupied Mashonaland; he was British resident in Barotseland when he was twenty-seven, and administrator of north-western Rhodesia when he was thirty. He won a high reputation in Swaziland, Basutoland and Uganda as a just and progressive Governor. All his active life had been spent in native territories. He could claim to understand the needs and aspirations of the African as well as any man in the colonial service.

With a lifelong experience of Africa behind him he could not fail to look at the problem from an African standpoint. His conclusions on Indian immigration coincided to some extent with those of the colonists. As Governor he was bound to maintain a strict impartiality and to bury his own opinions in the silence of discretion. Only once did he let out an inkling of his views. It was just before he left Nairobi for the London discussions. The atmosphere was at its most tense. He had summoned the settler leaders to obtain from them a promise to abstain from "direct action" while he was away. They had agreed, and they asked him as a man who had carried British administration into savage parts of Africa and who cared much for the future of the colony under his charge, to prevent, if he could, the sacrifice of Kenya's interests to those of Indian politics. "Gentlemen," he replied, "you may remember that I am South African born."

The Secretary of State and his advisers could not altogether ignore Sir Robert Coryndon's opinion. The position was, in fact, a little awkward. The previous Governor had disagreed with the Colonial Office and had made it clear that he could not carry out their proposals. He had been dismissed. It so happened that his successor had similar views. He, also, expressed reluctance to enforce a decision wholly in the Indians' favour. And the Colonial Office could not very well quarrel openly with two Governors over the same question in a single year.

There were, in all probability, two main factors which finally influenced the Cabinet in their decision to refuse the Indian demand for a common roll and to leave the settlers in possession of their existing political rights. One was the fear of armed rebellion in Kenya; the other was the attitude of the Governor. Behind these was the background of limited but effective public sympathy which the colonists' delegation had succeeded in arousing.

10

Until a few days before the draft settlement was approved by the Cabinet, four seats on the Legislative Council were allocated to the Indians. The Viceroy, however, protested by cable, and on the day before the Cabinet considered the draft two more seats were added to the Indian quota. Counterpressure was brought to bear by Sir Robert Coryndon and others, and at the last moment one seat was knocked off again. Thus the final number of five seats was settled and Cabinet approval given.

The Kenya delegation received a copy of the white paper on July 24th, about thirty-six hours before it was laid on the table of the House of Commons. It was too late to press for the alteration of any of the wording.

The delegation discussed the terms of the white paper throughout the afternoon and into the night. The question was: should they accept it in the face of their instructions not to agree to any whittling down of the "irreducible minimum", or should they refuse, and take the responsibility of precipitating the carefully nurtured and now fully ripe rebellion in Kenya?

The terms of the settlement were briefly as follows:

Five Indian members were to be elected to the Legislative Council on a communal roll. The Europeans were to keep their eleven elected members. There was also to be an Arab elected member and one unofficial to represent native interests. The colonists' proposals for a greater measure of self-government were flatly turned down. "His Majesty's Government", the white paper said, "cannot but regard the grant of responsible self-government as out of the question within any period of time which need now be taken into consideration."

Elections to the Nairobi municipal council were to be on a communal basis.

The policy of segregation in townships was to be abandoned.

The virtual, though not legal, reservation of alienated land in the highlands for Europeans was to be maintained.

As regards immigration the white paper stated that they could not agree to any racial discrimination in Kenya. But it was evident that "some further control over immigration in the economic interests of the natives of Kenya is required". The Governor was therefore to be instructed to "explore the matter further on his return to the colony and, in concert with the Governor of Uganda, to submit proposals to the Secretary of State giving effect to that amount of control of immigration which the economic needs of the natives of both territories require".

The most pregnant paragraph of the white paper did not relate to the Indian question at all. It was at first overlooked by the delegates, but they noticed it the next morning and were not a little taken aback at its tone.

Primarily, Kenya is an African territory, and H.M. Government think it necessary definitely to record their considered opinion that the interests of the African natives must be paramount, and that if and when those interests and the interests of the immigrant races should conflict, the former should prevail. . . .

In the administration of Kenya H.M. Government regard themselves as exercising a trust on behalf of the African population, and they are unable to delegate or share this trust, the object of which may be defined as the protection and advancement of the native races.

These sentences were destined to be quoted and argued about and twisted and explained many times in the succeeding years. The 1923 white paper, fruit of the Indian problem, contained the seeds of another and perhaps as difficult a controversy.

The words which were sandwiched in between these two statements were less often quoted, but in fairness they should be considered in their context. They pinned down a pledge and contained some solace for the colonists:

> Obviously the interests of the other communities, European, Indian and Arab, must generally be safeguarded. Whatever the circumstances in which members of these communities have entered Kenya, there will be no drastic action or reversal of measures already introduced, such as may have been contemplated in some quarters, the result of which might be to destroy or impair the existing interests of those who have already settled in Kenya.

The settlers had won their case over white highlands and over the common roll. They had lost over segregation. The doubtful point was immigration. *Prima facie*, they had lost at least half the battle; but much depended on the way in which the promise to tighten up the regulations in the economic interests of the African was kept. Immigration was therefore the pivotal point.

11

There was no time to sound the colony's views before accepting or rejecting the terms. The members of the delegation knew that the white paper would not be popular in Kenya. What they did not know was whether the settlers would be willing to swallow it.

For their own part the delegation realised that acceptance was essential. Their first action, after the settlement was disclosed, was to find out what attitude the Indians were going to take up. They were left in no doubt. The Indians were furiously indignant and proclaimed that a great injustice had been done. Their delegation cabled to the Government of India saying that the decision was unacceptable on all points except segregation. They added that it was "couched in language grossly offensive to Indians and must inevitably create the impression that the white races are determined to reduce Indians in Africa to a position of utter humiliation".

Their attitude was the determining factor in the Europeans' decision to accept the terms and to claim them as a victory. The only alternative was open defiance. The success of a rising must depend largely on the amount of sympathy the rebels could arouse in England. They would get no sympathy at all after the white paper. It was looked on as a fair settlement, generous to the settlers.

On July 25th they sent a message to the Colonial Office accepting the terms, subject to a protest at the excessive number of Indian seats. Having accepted, it was vital to carry the settlers with them. But the Vigilance committee was restive. A telegram arrived from Nairobi on July 25th reading:

Vigilance unanimously consider country will not accept terms published, but will endeavour to restrain feeling pending your further news.

The delegation replied by cable explaining their position.

The first accurate information of the terms given us was in the white paper handed to us by the Colonial Office very shortly before publication. It being impossible to effect any alteration we decided to accept personally and express the hope that the colony would endorse our acceptance.

The following considerations prompted this decision:

(1) If no acceptance, we lose the great advantage of the Cabinet decision on main constitutional and imperial issues, and return the controversy into the melting pot, resulting in the loss in future of the public opinion to which we have appealed, and which considers the white paper constitutes a European victory.

(2) It definitely establishes that Indians have no part in the government of East Africa, which is a British trusteeship.

(3) The Cabinet decision definitely transfers details of immigration and the scheme to effect practical segregation to the Kenya Legislative Council and the influence of local opinion, removing it from the arena of English politics.

(4) It is essential to claim a victory in order to restore confidence in the colony in the future. Large sums reported to be waiting invest-

ment in Kenya pending a settlement. Should the differences continue the capital will stop away.

We think nothing in the decision prevents progression to self-government, which can be better fought as another issue later. Indians and Opposition furious. Convinced that delegation acted in the right way by acceptance. . . . Hope the colony will claim the settlement as a victory and restore confidence in Kenya.

To this the Vigilance committee returned:

Fear it will be impossible to induce country to claim a victory, but can probably postpone any definite expression of opinion either way if we can announce that you will be returning immediately to explain.

The delegation passed an anxious three days in London. The English press had proclaimed the white paper as a settlers' victory. Delamere and his team feared that the effect would be spoilt by rash and fiery repudiations—even, perhaps, by some isolated outburst of "direct action" which would fire the train of open resistance throughout the colony. Should that occur, all the sympathy that had been so laboriously won would vanish in a day.

The deputation spent the week-end of July 27th in considerable nervousness and in ignorance of the colony's decision. On Monday, July 28th, another urgent cable was despatched:

General Smuts advised a short time ago to accept the terms if the main principles were secure. The High Commissioner for South Africa thinks Kenya would be wise to accept.

Having regard to pressure from India resulting in weakness in the Imperial Cabinet, we urge Kenya to accept on conditions similar to ours, or to reserve decision pending the return of the delegation. Best to attract new settlers and consolidate position regarding immigration.

If Kenya accepts we can claim that we have placed a very favourable interpretation on doubtful passages in the white paper while the Indian ' refusal indicates a similar interpretation.

12

The deputation in Grosvenor Place were not the only people who were feeling uneasy. Colonial Office officials were not at all sure which way the Kenya cat was going to jump. At this juncture a peculiar coincidence occurred. On Friday, July 25th, the day after the terms of the white paper had been cabled to Kenya, a telegram was received in the Colonial Office from a highly placed Kenya official connected with the colony's military forces.

It conveyed the brief and urgent message: "Assistance". A puzzled clerk took it to the head of his department. They examined it anxiously and took it to the permanent Under-Secretary. Could it mean, they wondered, that the settlers had broken loose, repudiated their promise to take no "direct action" while the Governor was away, and risen in revolt? Had their rebel organisation decided to reject the settlement and strike swiftly and dramatically?

The Colonial Office grew a little uneasy. A telegram was hastily despatched to the acting Governor asking him to report immediately on the state of the country and on the settlers' reactions to the white paper.

Throughout the Saturday they waited anxiously for a reply. None came. They began to feel that something serious was wrong. That night two more telegrams went off, one to the Governor of Tanganyika and one to the Resident in Zanzibar, asking them to find out whether there was anything wrong in Kenya and to report urgently. On Sunday morning the replies arrived. Both said that it was impossible to establish telegraphic communication with Kenya owing to dislocation of the cable service. Kenya was cut off from the world.

By now the Colonial Office was genuinely alarmed. They had not taken the settlers' rebellion really seriously; now it seemed that the worst had happened. The telegraph lines had evidently been cut; the acting Governor might by now have been kidnapped. There was little rest for the permanent officials that week-end.

On Sunday morning Sir Robert Coryndon's sleep was disturbed at his house in the country by a telephone call from the Colonial Office. Had he heard what was going on in Kenya? He knew no more than they did. The Sunday morning rest of the settlers' deputation was then interrupted. The delegates were requested to go round to Downing Street immediately. Surprised and sleepy, they agreed. They were still in ignorance of the frenzied fluttering of Downing Street dovecotes; but something unusual, they realised, was on foot. They decided to say little, ask no questions, and let the Civil servants do the talking.

The permanent Under-Secretary was exceedingly polite. He asked Delamere if a reply had been received to the cable sent on Thursday night disclosing the terms of the white paper. Not yet, Delamere replied. Had he any idea, then, of the line which the settlers were likely to take up? They would resent strongly, Delamere thought, the sacrifice of segregation and, in particular, the absence of any safeguards regarding immigration. They attached a great deal of importance to that.

Did Lord Delamere think that there was any further way in which the Government could reassure the settlers as to its good faith and anxiety to promote the best interests of the colony? Delamere saw his chance. No need to worry about what lay behind this remarkable Sunday morning shower of manna from hitherto ungenerous heavens. "I think that if the Secretary of State were to cable a reassurance to the colony that the Government really means to bring in a new immigration law and to enforce stiffer tests", he replied, "it would have a considerable effect in quieting misgivings out there."

The permanent Under-Secretary accepted his suggestion at once and, while the delegation remained in the room, he secured the assurance, by telephone, of the Secretary of State that the undertaking to restrict immigration in the economic interests of the natives would be implemented as soon as Sir Robert Coryndon returned to Kenya. A cable to the acting Governor was then drafted, with Delamere's assistance, while the settlers struggled to conceal their surprise. The cable was despatched at once. It ran as follows:

As doubts may exist as to the early intentions of H.M.'s Government as regards immigration, I consider it desirable you should know that the Governor has definite instructions to take immediate action on his return to implement the decision of H.M.'s Government in the memorandum; and you should communicate this to the persons interested, including the Convention of Associations.

The permanent officials prayed fervently that the cable would be in time to check the trouble.

On the next day, the Monday, a wire came through from the acting Governor. The Vigilance committee was in session, it said, considering the terms. Everything was quiet; there had been no trouble.

The explanation was not discovered until several months later. It was as follows.

An arrangement had been made, some time before, between the Kenya military official who had sent the cable and a friend in the Colonial Office to the effect that if the estimates for his department were attacked by critics in Kenya, the soldier would cable the single word "Assistance" to his ally in Downing Street.

In the excitement of the Indian question this arrangement had been forgotten. By another curious coincidence, a storm had chosen that week-end to dislocate the cable line between Dar-es-Salaam, Zanzibar and Mombasa. And the acting Governor of Kenya, unaware of apprehensions in Downing Street, had allowed himself two or three days to find out the facts about the settlers' attitude towards the white paper before replying to the Secretary of State.

By Monday morning the rebellion scare was over; but the immigration cable had been despatched.

13

In the colony itself acceptance of the white paper had been, for three or four days, a matter of touch and go.

The Vigilance committee had not had an easy task keeping the more hot-headed members of its army in order while the delegation argued in London. There had been more than one scare of "direct action" while negotiations were dragging on. The colony was very much on edge. Possibly the exceptionally heavy rain during April and May was a factor which helped to keep it quiet and law-abiding. Torrential cloudbursts and immense floods cut off one district from another, and isolated farms for weeks at a time. Military manœuvres would have been difficult with bridges turned into rivers and every *vlei* a lake. It was better weather for shooting ducks than imperial or Indian troops. Vigilance committee members who had to get into Nairobi for regular meetings had often to wade, walk and even swim part of the way.

The biennial Nairobi race meeting began on Thursday, July 24th. There was an air of suppressed excitement in the capital. Messengers bearing cables and telegrams hurried between the Vigilance committee's headquarters and the racecourse. A summary of the settlement was published in a special edition of the *Official Gazette* on the morning of July 25th.

The first reaction of settler opinion was one of hostility to its terms.

On Monday, July 28th, a full meeting of the Vigilance committee and "links" from all districts sat in secret throughout the day. The general feeling was that the country had been committed in advance by its deputation. It could not go back on their acceptance of the terms. But a motion for immediate acceptance of the white paper was rejected by 16 votes to 7.

Moderate opinion strengthened in the weeks that intervened between the meeting and the return of the delegates. By the time Delamere and his colleagues landed, on September 1st, dreams of resistance to the decision had faded. Shortly after the return of the delegates the terms of the settlement were accepted by a full meeting of Convention.

The East African Indians denounced the settlement as a "gross betrayal." A campaign of non-co-operation was organised and payment of taxes resisted. (This policy was not relinquished until 1925.) Indians refused to vote at the next election and no members were returned to the Legislative Council for several years. The full number was not elected until 1931.

The feeling in India was more violent still. "The announcement of the Government's decision", *The Times* correspondent cabled, "has opened the floodgates of rhetoric and abuse to an extent to which it is difficult to find a parallel in recent years." A boycott of "all men and things colonial" was proposed. The phrase "gross betrayal" was in every newspaper; threats to leave the Empire filled the air.

Mr. Sastri, in London, was but little more temperate. In an inflammatory speech at the Hotel Cecil he said that "acquiescence was impossible" and talked about "betrayal". Interviewed by Reuter, he condemned the settlement as a profound humiliation and a deep affront to India, and remarked: "The India Office and the Government of India have been pushed aside, not for the first time, before the advancing spirit of South Africa . . . in fact the people of India are no longer equal partners in the British Commonwealth, but unredeemed helots in a Boer Empire".

Possibly he overrated the influence of South Africa. General Smuts did not intervene at all during the negotiations. After the settlement he congratulated the delegation and said that they had done better than he had anticipated, and at the Imperial Conference of 1923 he expressed profound sympathy with Kenya. India, he said, had pressed her case beyond the limits of prudence and wisdom.

The Indian crisis was over; but there remained the "implementing" of the Secretary of State's promise to tighten up the immigration law. On his return to Kenya Sir Robert Coryndon followed out his instructions and prepared, in consultation with the Governor of Uganda, a new law providing for a simple educational test for all comers.

By the time it was drafted another change of government had taken place in England. The Labour party had come into power, with Mr. J. H. Thomas as Secretary of State for the Colonies. The new immigration law was never put into force, the Imperial Government's written promise never implemented.

CHAPTER XX

SPOTLIGHT ON KENYA
1923–1924

I

WHILE Delamere was in England in 1923 he delivered his maiden speech in the House of Lords. It had nothing to do with the Indian question. It was a protest against the Imperial Government's decision to reverse the usual order of progress in Africa and to pull up a railway.

The line in question was a branch ninety miles long running from Voi on the Uganda railway to Kahé, a station on the German-built railway running from the port of Tanga to the highlands of Kilimanjaro. It was a military line, laid in 1915 to enable British troops and supplies to be moved to the German border. Now that the German colony was under British rule the Government proposed to sever this adventitious link between Kenya and Tanganyika Territory.

As in so many other East African questions, the root of the matter went deeper than the surface of railway economics. The whole question of the federation of the East African territories, soon to become a major political issue, cast its shadow before it over the Voi-Kahé argument.

The little branch railway tapped part of the fertile, coffee-producing highlands of Mount Kilimanjaro. After the war the produce of this area started to find its way out to the sea along the ex-military line to the port of Kilindini instead of, as before, to the port of Tanga. The distance to Kilindini was slightly less and the port facilities were far superior to those at Tanga.

The administration of the mandated territory complained that they could not make the Tanga line pay if all the Kilimanjaro coffee traffic was decoyed away. So the idea of uprooting the parvenu military line was broached. The Tanganyika settlers opposed this suggestion, for the Kilindini route was a cheaper and more efficient outlet for their produce. General Hammond went into the question thoroughly when he visited East Africa in 1920. He recommended that the Voi-Kahé line should be retained and part of it relaid, and that the Tanga line should be picked up.

Sir Horace Byatt, Governor of Tanganyika, objected to these proposals. He complained that if General Hammond's plan was accepted the port of Tanga would be sacrificed on the altar of Kilindini interests. He felt that this was contrary to the spirit of the mandate and considered that Tanga should be developed and made into a bigger and better harbour.

The matter dragged on unsettled for two years. The Colonial Office were unable to make up their mind. After a prolonged silence they announced by telegram early in 1923 that they had turned down General Hammond's proposals and accepted Sir Horace Byatt's. The Voi-Kahé line was to be pulled up. Orders were issued to close the branch at once.

This sudden decision stung Mr. Felling into protest. Why, he asked, spend more British taxpayers' money on developing a third big port on the East African coast? The economic thing to do was to concentrate on two main harbours, Dar-es-Salaam and Kilindini; there was no justification for a third. It would be wanton waste to dissipate the money available for port improvement by equipping a redundant and geographically bad harbour to compete with a more efficient one. The arguments used by the Secretary of State might have been sound had Tanganyika and Kenya still belonged to different Powers; but when they were both part of one Empire they should be regarded as partners and not as rivals. The right way to get round the difficulty, he said, was to have joint control of the two railway systems and a Governor-General over the two countries.

His proposals, in fact, involved some form of federation. This was the first time the issue thrust itself directly into practical politics.

2

The Voi-Kahé line was closed in April 1923. Public opinion at once started to bubble. The East African Chamber of Commerce, the *East African Standard* and the Tanganyika settlers voiced loud complaints. Why, asked the Convention in Nairobi, had the legislature not been consulted in a matter so close to the interests of the whole country?

When Sir Robert Coryndon went to England in 1923 he had urged the Duke of Devonshire to revise his decision. To pick up the Voi-Kahé line, he said, would be "strongly against the interests of East Africa as a whole". The Secretary of State submitted the proposals of the Governor of Kenya to the Governor of Tanganyika. Sir Horace Byatt opposed them and they were rejected.

It was at this stage that Delamere laid the situation before the House of Lords. He was exceedingly nervous at his *début*, and although the material was well prepared and clearly arranged his delivery was halting and weak. He explained that when the Anglo-German border was first considered, Kilimanjaro was to have been British; but the German Emperor made a personal appeal for the mountain because of his interest in the flora and fauna of the region (where the climate ranges almost from the tropical to the arctic); and the British Government agreed to his direct request.

After outlining the history of the construction of the two railways Delamere added that when Britain took over German East Africa after the war:

> Kilimanjaro was served by two railways to the sea, one 220 miles long running to the old German port of Tanga, and one a little shorter, down the Uganda railway to the port of Mombasa. Accordingly the problem which faced us was whether Mombasa or Tanga was the port to be used for handling the products of the area around Kilimanjaro, and which railway was to be removed and which left.
>
> I confess that there did not appear to me to be any doubt whatever as to which was the right port for Kilimanjaro. Tanga was a difficult port to develop and very large sums of money would be required to make it into a modern port. . . . On the other hand, Kilindini, the

port of Mombasa, is a very fine natural harbour and it already has two wharves. In addition there are at present being built at the cost of about £1,250,000 two more large deep-water berths; so that it would appear on the surface that this is the right port to use. . . .

From a political point of view, I submit that this decision [to pull up the branch] runs counter to the policy of His Majesty's Government in that region, which has always been to try, by linking up the customs, railways, telegraphs and post offices of these different territories, ultimately to bring them together in some form of federation.

The Duke of Devonshire replied to Delamere's plea for the Voi-Kahé branch, but he refused to spare its life. It would cost, he said, half a million pounds to put the military line into working order and it could never pay its way.

This figure was afterwards demonstrated to be a gross over-estimate. The line was in fact reconditioned at a cost of £30,000.

In spite of the Duke's discouraging reply the Kenya Government did in the end get their way. Sir Robert Coryndon's tact was mainly responsible. Soon after his return to East Africa he went down to Dar-es-Salaam to see Sir Horace Byatt and succeeded in talking him over. The Kenya Government bought the line from the War Office for £70,000, and after a few years of Mr. Felling's management it was paying its way. Later, it became the first section of any railway in East or South Africa to be operated entirely by African station-masters, engine-drivers and signallers.

3

The Voi-Kahé argument focussed attention for a time on the Kilimanjaro area and its future. In climate, soil and geographic conditions generally it was very much like the Kenya highlands. Over half the white settler population of Tanganyika was concentrated on the fertile slopes of the mountain, most of them growing coffee. In sympathies and interests these settlers had more in common with Kenya than with the mandated territory. They sent their produce out by Kilindini, went to Nairobi for their shopping, sent their children to Kenya for education.

These considerations led Delamere to start, in 1924, a

movement to detach the Kilimanjaro region from Tanganyika and attach it to Kenya. His idea was to consolidate the more closely settled parts of Eastern Africa into one administrative unit. He suggested that the area should be awarded to the colony as compensation for the 36,740 square miles of its own territory which was taken from it as a result of the war.

Kenya was the only member of the British Empire—indeed the only country whose people fought on the side of the Allies—to lose territory instead of gaining it after the struggle. The whole of Jubaland, including the undeveloped but potentially valuable basin of the Juba river, was handed over to Italy by the Imperial Government as part of the price of her entry into the war.

It could not be claimed that Jubaland had ever proved of much material value to Kenya. It had cost a good deal to police, and only produced a small revenue from an ivory tax. Still, it was an asset; and if at any future time money became as easy to raise for development as for warfare it might (so experts said) have been turned into an exceedingly productive area. All along the Juba river stretched flats which might, with irrigation, be made into immense cotton or rice plantations.

But it was more the manner in which Kenya was shorn of its dormant north-eastern province than the actual loss that offended the feelings of the white population. Jubaland had been promised to Italy in 1915 and yet Kenya had never been consulted or even told of the agreement. The first that was heard of it by the public was an announcement in the papers in July 1924 that a treaty had been signed in London ceding the province to Mussolini's Government. Even the Sultan of Zanzibar, to whom the coastal belt of Jubaland nominally belonged—he only leased it to the British—was not informed beforehand that his property was to be given away.

It was remarked in Nairobi that in spite of the great emphasis placed by the home Government on the rights of the natives, and in face of the declaration that "the interests of the natives must be paramount", no attempt had been made to find out the wishes of the Herti and Ogaden Somalis who occupied the area in regard to their future government.

Had their interests honestly been regarded as paramount, it was suggested, they might at least have been consulted before being handed over to a foreign Power as fixtures thrown in with the land. The actions of the home Government appeared to be inconsistent with its declarations.

Delamere led the chorus of protests against Kenya's soil being used as a counter in the game of war debts. He used this territorial amputation as an argument in favour of territorial grafting. Let Kenya have Kilimanjaro instead, he said: a mountain for a river. He took a quick trip to Arusha, and soon afterwards a petition was sent to the King by planters in the district, praying that they might be placed under the Kenya Government. They complained that uncertainty as to the future of Tanganyika was scaring capital away and holding up development. "One settler", Delamere commented, "has already taken the precaution of marrying a German wife."

Delamere's project was doomed from the start. Neither the Tanganyika Government nor the Mandates' commission would have considered it, had it been laid before them.

4

Early in the summer of 1924 Delamere injured his neck again during a fracas in which he became involved (through no fault of his own) after a dinner at Nakuru. He had to spend another three months on his back. By this time he was living a few miles outside Nairobi. Loresho, at Kabete, was the first permanent, solid house in which he had ever made his home in Kenya. The story of its origin is typical.

Shortly after the war he bought 400 acres of good coffee land near Nairobi. Coffee, he felt, had become so important to Kenya that he ought to learn something about the industry at first hand. The idea of building a house there arose on the morning that he left Nairobi for England in 1921. He was having breakfast with his manager before catching a train to the coast. Suddenly he remarked:

"Please have a house ready for me at Kabete when I come back. I want it built of stone, designed like this——" and he seized a menu card and sketched a rough plan on the back.

"Yes, but what about the money?" said the manager, looking dubiously at the plan. "A house like that will cost several thousand pounds."

"Well, borrow it," Delamere replied, dismissing the matter abruptly. The manager started on the house and Delamere moved into it as soon as he returned. It was a rambling stone building with a cool, broad veranda, standing on the summit of a ridge and looking towards distant ranks of other such ridges which stretched, one behind the other, into the horizon. The dark greens of near-by summits merged into blues and purples in the far distance; beyond lay a belt of thick indigenous forest.

Each ridge was separated from its neighbour by a steep valley and the sides of the slopes were red with rich, deep loam, where the finest coffee or native crops could be grown. At the bottom of each valley a tiny stream wound its way, beneath sheltering floppy leaves of banana trees, from the cold forests of Mount Kenya to join the Tana river on the sun-baked plains below. After clambering down so deep a valley it was a surprise to find no broad-flowing torrent at the bottom; they were pretentious streamlets to demand the elaborate settings of a full-grown river.

Far away the peak of Mount Kenya rose suddenly above the landscape. It stood out most clearly in the early morning when the air was so clean and fresh that every breath seemed to leave a mark upon it, like the imprint of a footstep on a sheet of trackless snow. At such times the peak appeared almost to float in the lightness of the atmosphere, the massiveness of its shoulders disguised by distance. Later in the day, billows of cloud would pass in slow convolutions across its outline, smothering the mountain in their white embrace.

In these surroundings Delamere recovered slowly from his injury, accessible to all his colleagues. Loresho became a popular meeting-place for the many officials and colonists who wanted to consult or to do business with him. Sir Robert Coryndon held meetings of Executive Council there so that Delamere could attend, lying on a sofa. It was a gesture of courtesy which the unofficial members appreciated.

5

During the summer that Delamere was laid up he found himself abruptly propelled into a spot-light of controversy and publicity in regard to his land dealings. The House of Commons developed an intense interest in every detail of his transactions. Wild and unfounded allegations were made, so prominently that the Imperial Government felt impelled to publish two white papers devoted to a defence of Delamere's honesty and good faith.[1]

The first of these command papers dealt with what became known as the "Ndaragua exchange". The facts were as follows:

After Delamere's sheep had been moved off his Ndaragua land they roamed over unoccupied farms on the Laikipia plateau under the charge of their manager, Mr. E. C. Long. He became a sort of pirate shepherd, raiding grazing wherever it seemed good and was not being used by somebody else. Nearly all the land over which the sheep were herded had been included in the ex-soldier settlement scheme, but had never been taken up because at least three-quarters of it were waterless. Farms of several thousand acres could be bought at this time for £50 apiece. The only way in which this land could be developed was to farm it in a single big unit, so that sheep could be driven long distances from one river to the next.

While his sheep were scattered over a vast no-man's-land, Delamere's property at Ndaragua was lying idle. It was excellent land but he had no money available to develop it. He was in the position, therefore, of owning about 20,000 homeless sheep and about the same number of idle acres. The possibility of exchanging Ndaragua for a Laikipia sheep-run naturally arose.

The suggestion came in the first place from the Commissioner for Lands. During a tour of the district Mr. Martin pointed out to Mr. Long that his sheep could not continue to roam over unclaimed country for ever. He suggested that Delamere might like to give up his Ndaragua land and take

[1] Cmd. 2500 of 1925 and Cmd. 2629 of 1926.

some of the abandoned soldier-settlement farms, now lying derelict, instead.

Delamere was in England when the matter was discussed. His manager, however, welcomed Mr. Martin's suggestion and negotiations followed between the Government and Mr. Long. The terms finally agreed upon were that Delamere should receive 63,000 acres of sheep land in recompense for his surrender of 21,400 acres at Ndaragua.

The controversy which followed was another example of the confusion which must sometimes arise when technical agricultural questions in Africa are considered by urban-minded politicians, inevitably ignorant of ranching conditions and living 6000 miles away from the country they are governing. It was widely suggested in England that the exchange was a ramp, and that Delamere was guilty of sharp practice in securing from the Government three acres for every one he surrendered.

The ratio was not, in actual fact, an over-generous one. The essential point was that the Ndaragua land was agricultural and the Laikipia land was suitable only for sheep. In any country in the world sheep land is worth a great deal less than dairying plus agricultural land. In Kenya this was particularly so, because sheep had not yet been conclusively proved to be a sound proposition.

The Commissioner for Lands was anxious to make the exchange, because Ndaragua could be divided into small farms which could be sold for more than three times as much per acre as the Laikipia land. Further, by chopping up Ndaragua into small farms the Government would secure from it double the annual rent that they at present received, because the rentals would be based on the Crown Lands ordinance of 1915, whereas Delamere held the land on the easier terms of the 1902 ordinance. And, in addition, the Government would be drawing rent for 63,000 acres of Laikipia which would otherwise be returning nothing to the Treasury.

There were no complications of native rights. Laikipia had been unoccupied since 1890, except for the brief interval between 1904 and 1912 when Masai had been moved there. Questions asked in the House of Commons on the subject of the exchange showed how slender a basis of knowledge sometimes supported a Parliamentary agitation. It was suggested for, example, that the 63,000 acres was being stolen from the Masai. "If the natives do not agree to the exchange shall we send a bombing expedition there?" Mr. Lansbury demanded. The local Government did send an expedition there, under orders from the Secretary of State, to find out if there were any natives at all. They reported that there were none of any tribe, save for a few herds employed by Europeans.

Delamere had had no idea that any objection would be taken to the proposal. As soon as the outcry began he suggested that the whole transaction should be dropped.

"Lord Delamere has written offering to withdraw from the deal if the Government is able to dispose of the area to other applicants in smaller blocks", Sir Robert Coryndon announced in Council. The Governor, believing that the exchange was to the advantage of the country, refused the offer.

After a good deal of further discussion the transfer went through. Delamere then spent another £18,000 in buying farms with river frontage so as to be able to water this exchange land by means of a pipe-line. In a few years there were upwards of 30,000 sheep on the place and the pipeline had been installed. Another unproductive waterless block of land had been turned to useful account.

6

The white paper on the "Delamere exchange" did not, however, assuage the interest of Parliament and sections of its electors in Delamere's land transactions. A second white paper followed shortly afterwards. This was published to refute the statement quoted in a book on Kenya that Delamere obtained his land illegally by a process known as "dummying".

"Dummying", said the command paper, "appears to be a somewhat loose term . . . in any case the suggestion of underhand dealing and evasion of law can be taken as a common element in any definition."

In less ambiguous terms, dummying may be described as follows: a man who wished to obtain more land than the Government were willing to sell or to grant to one individual, persuaded a friend to apply or to bid for a farm. (Under the Crown Lands ordinance of 1902 he had to apply direct to the Government; under the 1915 ordinance he had to bid at public auction.) Then the man who was dummying bought the land from the obliging dummy for a low and previously agreed price. Another method of dummying was to apply for land in the name of a relation in England who had no intention of taking it up.

Dummying was, in short, a simple method of getting round land laws framed to prevent one man from obtaining more than one grant of land.

In point of fact there was a very fine dividing line between buying land in the ordinary way from its owner and buying it from dummies. Men with sufficient capital to develop a large area of land inevitably tended to accumulate more land than men with little or no capital. Often it was necessary for their scheme of development to obtain a particular slice of land—an adjoining farm, for example, with a river frontage that would save their stock several miles of daily walking to water—and if they could not get it direct from the Government they did so in roundabout ways. Dummying was a fairly common practice in the early days, and was considered no more dishonourable than obtaining whisky from a bootlegger in New York before prohibition repeal.

The Government had two weapons with which it could extract the evil sting out of dummying—the clause in the Crown Lands ordinance requiring the Governor's sanction for all land transfers, and the stringent development conditions. If a man did not develop his land and could not prove that he had spent a specified amount of money on it, then it could be taken away from him altogether.

The dummying charge against Delamere was first made by a fellow-settler, Mr. Robert Chamberlain, in a letter to the *East African Standard*, written in 1920 but referring to events of ten or fifteen years before. Delamere and Mr. Chamberlain were political opponents of long standing who disagreed on almost every issue of importance. They had often attacked each other's views. Mr. Chamberlain's letter was a new move in a game that had been going on for nearly twenty years.

Delamere did not bother to answer it at the time. Mr. Chamberlain was notoriously hot-tempered, and Delamere considered it a waste of time to engage in personalities.

The substance of the letter was the accusation that Delamere had used his position as a public man to amass land. "As long as the Land office would yield juice, his Lordship was there with insatiable powers of suction", it said. No concrete examples of dummying, however, were given.

In 1924 part of this letter was published in a book written by a doctor who had retired from the Kenya medical service in 1918—Dr. Leys. Permission to quote from the letter was never asked. Mr. Chamberlain was dismayed to find his remarks reproduced in a context which gave them a far more damaging significance than he had ever intended. Only those parts of the letter most derogatory to Delamere were quoted. This gave a false impression.

Delamere himself would not have bothered to refute the charges repeated by Dr. Leys. But the accusations were as much against the Government as against the settlers. Every transfer of land had been ratified by the Government, so that the administration must have connived at the evasion of their own laws if the dummying allegations were true.

Mr. Amery had become Secretary of State by the time the charges came to the Colonial Office's notice. He ordered a full report from the Kenya Government. All Delamere's records and papers and relevant Land office files were sifted to get at the facts. The conclusions reached by the Commissioner for Lands and endorsed by the Governor were as follows:[1]

I find that genuine value was paid in each case to the vendor [of land bought by Delamere] after the grant had been made, and in each case with the full knowledge of the Government.

I further find that not only is there no evidence that Lord Delamere put up men of straw to obtain grants on the strength of financial

[1] The quotations which follow are taken from the white paper Cmd. 2629 of 1926.

guarantees supplied by himself, but that there is positive evidence in the private books of his agents to show that when once so approached he refused to do so.

In every single case of these purchases the prior consent of the Government was asked for and obtained before grants were issued, and, as already stated, Government may be considered to have been a party with full knowledge.

Not only were prices up to 5s. an acre paid in these very early pioneer days by Lord Delamere for these Rift Valley farms, but it would hardly be too much to state that these values were largely of his own creation, as the result of his own prior efforts and expenditure up to 1906–07 in the Valley of approximately £60,000.

. . . .

I can certify that in any district in which Lord Delamere holds land he develops land, and that no such district is not greatly benefiting from his activities.

It would not, I think, be too much to add that no better settler ever spent his all in such a difficult colony as this, and that any suggestion of underhand dealing in respect of his land or any other transactions with Government is not only cruel and malicious but conveys the precise opposite of the plainly evident truth.

7

Delamere was more interested in immediate action than in justifying actions that belonged to the past. Numerous projects had been held up while the Indian question filled the stage. Now that it was out of the way they were crying for attention.

There was, for example, the setting up of a training college for African artisans. This had always been a pet scheme of Delamere's, and in 1924 he succeeded in persuading the Government to adopt it.

The college was a by-product of the Indian question. It grew directly out of a body called the European and African Trades Organisation which was started early in 1923, mainly by Delamere, its first chairman.

The original purpose of this organisation was to enforce a boycott against Indian artisans. Delamere believed that the only ultimate way to solve the Indian problem as he wanted to see it solved was to make Kenya economically less attractive to Indian immigrants. The first step in effecting this was to enable Africans to take the place of Indians. The principal aim of the European and African Trades Organisation was to act as an employment bureau to place African skilled workers and also Europeans. One of its other objects was to encourage the opening of European and African stores and trading centres in the reserves. Funds were guaranteed by Delamere and Sir Northrup McMillan. The organisation met with an immediate success. The Kikuyu chiefs gave their support and several became members.

When the white paper of 1923 extinguished the Indian controversy the boycott was no longer needed as a political weapon. But Delamere believed that the employment of African skilled workers should still be steadily encouraged. He set out to win Sir Robert Coryndon's support for his plans.

In May 1924 the Government agreed to adopt a scheme for a native industrial training depôt suggested by the European and African Trades Organisation. This depôt was built at Kabete in the same year. It has since proved itself to be a most valuable institute, turning out every year well-trained and educated Africans who, at any rate until the depression, were eagerly snapped up by employers.

Delamere took a keen personal interest in all the details. "It is Lord Delamere's and my own considered opinion", the secretary wrote to the Government, "that an improved ration should be issued to all pupils, the object being to improve physique and, at the same time, to give them a taste for better food, which, combined with better housing conditions and cleanliness, will incline them towards living under better conditions when they leave the depôt."

Delamere's organisation also lent money to Africans who were anxious to set up as petty traders in the reserves. It interested itself in native markets and drew up a scheme for regulating them by the establishment of auctions. It did not close down until the end of 1927, after achieving much constructive work and finding jobs for numerous Europeans and Africans.

8

Another new departure in native education to which Delamere gave his strongest support was the setting up of a "Jeanes" school, also at Kabete, for the training of native teachers.

The idea, in this case, came from one of the first of a long series of commissions which visited Kenya. This, the Phelps-Stokes commission, consisted of American experts on negro education and advancement led by Dr. Jesse Jones. One of the members was the well-known West African native leader, Dr. Aggrey. Its object was to investigate conditions of African education in Kenya.

After an extensive tour the members issued a report largely endorsing a point of view which Delamere had for many years been pressing on the Government. The commission was absolutely impartial. Its members were known throughout the liberal world as crusaders for negro and African advancement. No one could say that the settlers had influenced them: and they echoed, in many passages of their report, almost the very words that had been uttered by the settlers' leader.

The gist of their findings was that education had, in the past, proceeded along lines too narrow and stereotyped to lay a sound foundation for African enlightenment. There was too much indigestible "book-learning" and not enough training in self-help, handicrafts and science.

Although all native society was based upon agriculture and stock-rearing, practically no attempt had been made to teach young Africans an elementary idea of the scientific theories which lay behind the growth of plants or the nutrition of animals; nor had they been taught anything of the practice of better farming and husbandry. A native youth was far more likely to know the names of Henry VIII.'s wives and the date of the battle of Hastings than to have any inkling of the laws of plant nutrition on which the improvement of soil fertility depends or the principles of heredity on which the grading-up of flocks and herds is based. He might know the names of the capital cities of Europe but be quite ignorant of crafts such as carpentry or building or shoemaking, which were not only more useful but which provided him with scope to use his own brains and initiative, and with an outlet for his constructive abilities.

A further objection to the random methods that had been followed in the past was that they made little attempt to graft western ideas on to existing African stock. They were inclined to root out the indigenous tree altogether and start afresh. Any latent buds of culture that might be lurking were destroyed, instead of being fostered and then trained in a more civilised direction. Education was apt to result in the storing of a collection of more or less useless facts in the mind, without order or sequence, rather than in a gradual and unbroken development of the mind itself along its natural lines. The system—or lack of it—was calaculated to turn out a somewhat muddled parrot; it did not tend to develop judgment and balance.

Then, again no common educational policy for East Africa as a whole had been hammered out.

Education was unco-ordinated, scrappy and subject only to very loose government control. It was almost entirely in the hands of the missions, which naturally varied widely in their methods, their aims and their skill.

The Phelps-Stokes commission advocated a greater measure of practical and technical education which would enable the native not only to earn more money and so raise his standard of living, but to develop his creative impulses through craftsmanship. "Teach them to use their hands", Dr. Aggrey urged, repeatedly; give them some outlet for self-expression so that the educated native does not merely become a discontented, mentally dyspeptic and not very efficient clerk—too good, in his own opinion, to live again among his own people.

Delamere invited the members of the commission to stay when they were touring Kenya and found them more than usually congenial guests. He regarded their report as a landmark in the colony's development and their criticisms of native education—which carried considerable weight in England—as one of the most valuable contributions yet made to the working out of a post-war East African policy.

The concrete result of the commission's visit was the

founding of the Jeanes school at Kabete. Its function was to take native teachers and their wives from mission, farm and "bush" schools and to give them a three years' course of training in matters such as handicrafts, hygiene and dramatics, as well as in more academic subjects. Each teacher and his wife and family were provided with a self-contained house with its own little garden. The students were trained in co-operative enterprises—the organisation of their own stores, banks, debating societies and so on.

The object of the system (which was started first among the negroes in the southern states of America) was to train Africans as leaders in rural community life rather than purely as school teachers. Each successful student was to become, on going back to a native reserve, a focus of civilisation and an example to the people in whose midst he was to live.

The Jeanes school at Kabete was the first to be established in Eastern Africa. It became an important influence in native education and attracted teachers from Uganda and Tanganyika as well as from Kenya.

9

By the middle of 1924 Delamere had recovered from his neck injury, although his health was still poor. One day in July he invited a friend, the South African Trade Commissioner (Colonel Turner) to lunch and said: "I want you to come with me to South Africa next week". They left Nairobi three days later.

Ever since the attempt had been made to secure support from South Africa over the Indian question, Delamere had been playing with the idea of cementing the rather nebulous connection between the southern focus of white settlement in Africa and the younger eastern outpost. He was anxious to arouse the interest of the Union and of Rhodesia in Kenya's problems and to make them East Africa-conscious. He believed, with General Smuts, that the white backbone running up through the eastern segment of this vast black continent must at all costs be strengthened. He still remained a champion of the Rhodes ideal. Did not Rhodes' statue itself convey a perpetual message to South Africans to think continentally, pointing for ever northwards with a hand outstretched from Cape Town and bearing the inscription "Your hinterland is here"?

On this matter of establishing a closer connection with the south Delamere did not secure unanimous support from his settler followers. There were two schools of thought. There was Delamere's, which held that, however widely Kenya's future policy might differ from South Africa's, an essential unity existed between the aims and problems of two communities of European stock transplanted into African soil, although one might seem as stout and strong as the baobab, the other appear as fragile and slender as the young acacia. This unity, he held, should be solidified in every expedient way.

The other school of thought believed that the difference in native policy as pursued in East and in South Africa was too wide to be bridged. In East Africa the Union's attempt, which some considered to be doomed to tragic failure, to prevent the African from rising to a level of economic equality with the European could never be imitated. To establish a liaison with the southern Dominion, this school of thought maintained, would be a grave political blunder.

The Union's native policy was deeply distrusted by many of Kenya's critics, who were always on the watch to detect manifestations of the same spirit working in East Africa. To forge a link between the colonists of Kenya and the rulers of white South Africa would be to give force to these critics' contention—which the settlers strongly denied—that Kenya, given its head, would follow the Union's lead on matters of native policy. Steer clear of South Africa, therefore, this argument ran: Kenya has her own destiny to work out, a different one from that to which the south is committed; a destiny, perhaps, of racial co-operation and not of racial dominance.

But to establish closer contact with the south was not necessarily to imitate southern policies. There could be no doubt but that much could be learnt from a first-hand study of the Union's problems, from her mistakes as well as from her successes. Delamere decided to go and see for himself.

Another reason for his visit was the fact that a change of government had just taken place in the Union. Delamere wanted to find out what attitude the new Premier, General Hertzog, was likely to adopt towards East African affairs. He wanted also to establish contact with the first prime minister of Southern Rhodesia (Sir James Coghlan) and the other Rhodesian leaders who had, two years before, led their country (with a white population four times as large as that of Kenya) triumphantly through the golden gates and into the Zion of self-government.

10

At Durban Delamere abandoned the style of hair-dressing he had followed for nearly twenty years. He was pursued all over the city by small boys, enthralled with his flowing locks. He was better than a king beaver. At last he grew tired of his retinue and decided to have a haircut. "A bob, please", he said to the barber as he sat down to have his mane removed. After this he never grew his hair long again.

In Cape Town he interviewed the Premier and General Smuts. Both were friendly and both remarked that South Africa was well disposed towards Kenya. General Smuts reiterated his opinion that the native could only make real progress in close contact with a European community.

This was Delamere's first meeting with Smuts. He had always admired the South African leader as a statesman; now he fell under his spell as a man.

From the Union, Delamere and Colonel Turner went on to Salisbury. They called on the Premier and on several ministers and endeavoured to persuade them that the policies shaping themselves in the north were of close concern to the south. The influence of northern policies would spread downwards as a stain of oil creeps gradually over a wooden floor.

Delamere's trip to the south marked his first excursion from the narrow platform of Kenya politics on to the larger stage of British Africa. It was the start of another phase in his career. He was adopting a new rôle—that of the prophet of anti-parochialism.

Delamere, like all able politicians, was sensitive to the tremors of approaching events. He could pick up the first vibrations emitted by a wave of public opinion. Already he saw that the linking up of East Africa, perhaps into one unit, was to become the next big issue in local politics. He wanted to gain the goodwill and co-operation of the south. At any moment moral support from that quarter might be needed. This, his first attempt to establish closer contact between the colonists of Kenya and Rhodesia, prepared the ground for his next active step in East African politics—the holding of an unofficial inter-colonial conference.

After Salisbury, Livingstone. Here he had several talks with Mr. L. F. Moore, leader of the unofficial members of the Northern Rhodesian Legislative Council. The settlers were jubilant at the transfer of their colony from Chartered Company control to the Colonial Office. "God help them," said Delamere, "that frame of mind won't last long." He went, reluctantly, to see the falls, but he was feeling ill and disliked them thoroughly. He only stayed a few minutes and then retreated, remarking that they were altogether too vast and unmanageable and made him feel too small. His bad health had not improved his temper. While he was in Salisbury he bought a watch which annoyed him by failing to keep good time. In a fit of rage he threw it on the ground and jumped on it until it was smashed into fragments.

Delamere returned to Cape Town to intercept the new Secretary of State for the Colonies, Mr. J. H. Thomas, who was visiting South Africa. He travelled on the same steamer as Mr. Thomas from Cape Town to Durban and had a long discussion on East African affairs. In September 1924 he returned to Kenya.

CHAPTER XXI

TANGANYIKA INTERLUDE
1924–1926

I

DELAMERE reached Kenya a few months before the arrival of the East Africa commission, a scouting party of three members of Parliament, one of each political complexion, sent by the Imperial Government to report on the problems and needs of the five East African territories.

This commission was originally intended as a first step towards the federation of the British dependencies in East Africa. It had its origin in a motion introduced into Parliament by Sir Sydney Henn in April 1924, suggesting that the time for federation was ripe and that a commission should be sent to investigate the best method of bringing it about. The debate on the motion was the first occasion on which East African federation was publicly discussed in England.

The idea had a natural growth. The amalgamation of the East Africa Protectorate and Uganda had been considered several times before 1914, but nothing had been done. After the war the whole of East Africa, from Lake Albert and the Juba river in the north to the Rovuma and the Zambesi in the south, was in British hands. North of Rhodesia this vast expanse of British territory, undeveloped save for a few infinitesimal patches, stretched to the upper waters of the Nile. The distance was some sixteen hundred miles in a straight line from Livingstone on the Zambesi to Nimule on the Nile. East Africa had a coast-line of 800 miles, an internal boundary of over 6000 miles. Its area, over a million square miles, was nearly as large as that of British India. Its population was only about 12 millions; India's, 300 millions.

East Africa, regarded as a unit, was immense, rich with

unexplored possibilities, yet dormant as a wintering bear. What latent powers might it not develop when awakened by the insistent proddings of European enterprise and inventiveness?

Five separate and distinct countries lay within these straggling borders, all under British rule. The boundaries followed no natural geographic or ethnological lines. They marched unheedingly through native villages, lakes, bush, pastures, cultivation, forests, deserts, mountains and the rest. They were purely arbitrary. The cost of maintaining five separate governments, each with expensive headquarters and each working along its own independent lines (and often jealously) at problems which concerned them all; each building its own railways regardless of where its neighbours' lines might go, developing its own ports heedless of the needs of the coast-line as a whole, seeking cures for human and animal diseases in ignorance of progress made over the border; the cost of all this duplication of effort must, it seemed, involve a high proportion of waste. And, apart from the question of cost, there was the question of wisdom: whether it was wise to pursue perhaps five different policies in one section of Africa when the conditions which those policies were designed to meet and to shape were much the same.

These considerations could not fail to come to the fore when German East Africa passed into British hands. The idea of some form of administrative federation was first discussed by a Cabinet committee which considered the future of the conquered German colonies before the end of the war. Both General Smuts and Mr. Amery were anxious to see German East Africa joined up with its two British neighbours. As a result, a special clause was inserted in the terms of the mandate under which Britain was to administer the ex-German colony. This provision was designed to dispose beforehand of any objections that might be raised should the Imperial Government wish to include Tanganyika in a future federation. It ran as follows:

The Mandatory shall be authorised to constitute the territory into a customs, fiscal and administrative union or federation with the adjacent territories under his own sovereignty or control, provided always that the measures adopted to that end do not infringe the provisions of this mandate.

This left the way clear for the Imperial Government to act. In 1919 the Governors of Kenya, Uganda and Tanganyika were instructed by Lord Milner to study the possibilities of closer co-ordination between their territories and to sketch out a plan for effecting it.

2

Had this post-war scheme been vigorously pushed, it is possible that some form of fusion might have been achieved before objections had had time to crystallise. Lord Milner, however, was involved in difficulties in Egypt and was too busy to give close attention to East Africa. Then the Indian question arose and all other issues were eclipsed.

When Sir Sydney Henn raised the question in 1924, federation had been temporarily shelved. But it was not dead. Mr. J. H. Thomas readily agreed to the appointment of a small commission to inquire into its possibilities.

When the terms of reference of this commission came to be decided, however, other matters of greater apparent urgency had again pushed federation into the background.

Chief among these was the question of native policy. The bitter attacks launched against the Kenya Government had focussed a good deal of public attention on the whole problem of what was to be done about the African—his education, his health, his future, whether it was right to make him work for others, how he could be best governed, and so on—not only in Kenya but in East Africa as a whole. And then there was the equally pressing question of development. Kenya was about to raise a second big loan and much private British capital was looking in that direction. But the Imperial Government had only a hazy idea as to what the potentialities of East Africa really were. How much could be produced there in future? Was native or European production the soundest line of development? Where ought new railways to run? These and many other questions were badly in need of an answer.

Federation was not even mentioned, in the end, in the terms of reference of the East Africa commission. Instead, four questions were singled out for particular study. These were: economic development; the social condition of the natives; the treatment of native labour; and the incidence of native taxation.

The commission was appointed by Mr. J. H. Thomas in May 1924. The three chosen individuals were a Conservative, the Hon. W. G. Ormsby-Gore, the chairman; a Liberal, Mr. F. C. Linfield; and a Labour member, Major A. G. Church.

The trouble about commissions, Delamere considered, was that they were apt to be too closely guarded by the Government, who arranged their itinerary and provided all their information. Commissioners, like tourists in Russia, were sometimes shown only what governments wanted them to see. Delamere determined that the envoys of Parliament should be given ample opportunity to hear the unofficial as well as the official point of view. He collected several colleagues and engaged himself as unofficial chauffeur to the commission, placing his and his companions' cars at its disposal. The Government was short of motor transport and was grateful for his offer.

Delamere had just bought a new car, a bright yellow Packard, of which he was very proud. It was acquired in a typical manner. Delamere was, as usual, short of cash; but he had to get a new car. The bank refused to enlarge his overdraft on the existing security. Then he remembered that he still had an undeveloped forest farm which had not yet been mortgaged, near the top of Mau. He wrote instructions to his manager from South Africa to buy a car, remarking, "You can give the bank the security of that farm on the Mau, the one they haven't got yet".

During the commission's visit his hospitality was at its most lavish. While the members were in Nairobi he asked them to dinner at Muthaiga club. Then he sent out sheafs of telegrams to innumerable settlers and friends within reach, ordering more than asking them to dine. It was almost a royal command. Over eighty people sat down to the dinner as his guests.

3

The chairman of the commission experienced, during his East African tour, a conversion almost Pauline in its completeness. He had hitherto been opposed to the policy of white settlement. Two years before he had stated in the House of Commons: "I personally regret the history of the colony and would like to have seen the development of Kenya proceeding on precisely the same lines as the development of the Gold Coast and Nigeria. . . . White settlement . . . will be an economic failure. The settlers are very nearly ruined now, and in five years' time they are likely to be absolutely ruined." After his tour he became one of the most enthusiastic supporters of enlightened white settlement and of the good character of the settlers.

Major Church, the Labour member, was also converted from a hostile to a friendly attitude. He wrote a book after his tour and devoted a chapter to Delamere's activities.[1] "Part politician, part *poseur*, part Puck, but the greater part patriot", he described the settlers' leader. In a speech that would have horrified most of his colleagues he declared:

> The settlers in Kenya are doing their best by the soil and they are setting an example to a somewhat feeble, degenerate and indolent people in regard to cultivation. . . . I have been astonished by the way in which the settlers, at great expense to themselves, are carrying out experiments for the betterment of their crops and their protection against disease. . . .
>
> We are sentimentalists with regard to the African and if the white settler can prove that he can stand the climate, stand the sun and rear his children on Kenya soil, then it will be to the advantage of the world to encourage white settlement.

In their official report[2] the commissioners were hardly less emphatic in their praises of the colonists:

> The chief characteristics of the Kenya settlers are their community pride, their love of the country and their collective determination to make white settlement in the highlands a real success. We found that the settlers were determined to make Kenya their permanent home

[1] Major A. G. Church, D.S.O., *East Africa—A New Dominion*.
[2] Cmd. 2387 of 1925.

and the home of their children and their children's children. There is no question of just making money in order to have enough to live elsewhere. Settlers of such type are not wanted by the existing community.

The settlers whom we met never lost an opportunity of impressing upon us their faith in the future of the highlands as a white man's country. They aspire to build up in those highlands a distinctive type of British civilisation which has neither a South African nor a West African character. The ideal expressed by them to us is based on a more complete inter-relation and co-operation between the European and the African than exists in either the south or the west of the continent. . . .

In the case of Kenya there has been too little recognition of the good that has been accomplished and too much emphasis on the mistakes. We wish to record our opinion that Kenya has been fortunate in the type of settler she has attracted. In fact, few of Britain's oversea colonies at their commencement have attracted a better type. They are men and women of energy and goodwill.

A lack of proportion had hitherto distorted the vision of many of Kenya's critics. Now, for the first time, the colony was subjected to a careful, impartial scrutiny, judged as a young and still undeveloped member of a group of East African territories by standards that were colonial and not Utopian. It came well out of the test.

4

The keynote of the Ormsby-Gore report was its acceptance of the so-called "dual policy". For many years the colony had been feeling its way towards some such foundation for its future progress. Sir Robert Coryndon crystallised the idea and adapted the phrase from Lugard's "dual mandate".

The dual policy has been defined as the "complementary development of non-native and native production". Its implications go deeper. It entails the holding of an even balance between European and African interests. Under the dual policy it is the Government's task to see that neither race is favoured at the expense of the other; that both go forward side by side. Agricultural production must be encouraged equally in the reserves and in alienated areas; railways planned with the view to serving native areas equally with white ones; medical and educational votes fairly allocated among African and European claimants.

Later, in 1926, Mr. Amery defined it in these terms:

> By the dual policy is meant a policy which recognises our trusteeship towards the native population—whom we found on the spot and whom it is our duty to bring forward and develop in every possible way—but also our trusteeship to humanity at large for the fullest development of these territories and towards those in particular of our own race who have undertaken the task of helping forward that development.

Since the appearance of the 1923 white paper there had been much discussion on the meaning of "trusteeship" for the native races. No one disputed the general conception that the more advanced races must watch over the interests of backward peoples under their control and guide them towards a higher level of material and intellectual living. There was, however, one important point which had not been definitely cleared up by the Imperial Government. Where, exactly, did the trust lie; with the British race as a whole, including its representatives in Africa, or with the British Parliament alone?

The settlers felt very strongly that the trust devolved upon the whole British race and that they, as the members of it in closest touch with the native, shared it equally with people in England. It was wrong and also impracticable, they said, to interpret trusteeship in such a way as to make voters from a Birmingham factory or a Brighton tea-shop responsible for deciding the fate of Africans and at the same time to deny to colonists who lived among the natives, spoke their language and knew their wants, any voice in shaping of policy. The colonists (they argued) were there to stay; and whatever the Imperial Government might do or say, the relationship between Europeans and Africans would ultimately be determined in the main not by speeches at Westminster but by actions on the 2000 farms already parcelled out in Kenya. It was from the settler, the official and the missionary that the native gained his knowledge of European civilisation, and to the settler, the official and the missionary that he looked for practical guidance. The colonists had a right to share the trust and to be given some say in its execution.

The Ormsby-Gore commission considered the question and arrived at much the same conclusion as that already reached by the settlers.

This duty [trusteeship] has been regarded in the past as the special function of the agents of the Imperial Government and of the missionaries. But such a limitation is neither possible nor desirable. Britain will not be judged at the bar of history by the work of these two alone; the trusteeship lies really upon the shoulders of every man and woman of European race in Africa. It is in very truth a white man's burden, and all Europeans in Africa must share in the work.

In order to face these responsibilities certain misconceptions have got to be removed. The first is that the interests of non-native and native must necessarily conflict. In order to be pro-native it is not necessary to be anti-white. To be in favour of white settlement in such portions of Africa as are climatically suitable for European homes it is not necessary to be anti-native.

This conception of trusteeship as the function of the race and not only of the British Parliament was generally accepted after the publication of the Ormsby-Gore report. Policy in Kenya proceeded fairly consistently on this assumption for six years until the interpretation was abruptly reversed by Lord Passfield in 1930.

5

By the end of 1924 Kenya had made a remarkably quick recovery from the combined effects of the post-war slump and the uncertainty of the Indian question. The colony displayed all the powers of rapid recuperation common to youth. Political troubles had receded. Capital was flowing in. Prices were rising. New settlers were arriving. The revenue was mounting steadily. All seemed to be going well.

The budget, for the first time, showed a surplus, after paying off a floating debt of £190,000. The tonnage handled at the port of Kilindini, both inward and outward bound, was twice as large in 1924 as in 1922. Exports were leaping upwards. In 1924 they increased by 70 per cent over the preceding year. The acreage under maize was doubled in two years. Sisal, wheat and sugar were being planted up rapidly; tea production and dairying were getting under way. In 1924 the average area of land cultivated by each European occupier was over 200 acres.

The railway was doing well. Traffic had doubled since 1922 and yet the total working costs had been reduced. Under brilliant management it was yielding fat profits. The new extension was opened in 1924 to Eldoret, the capital of the Uasin Gishu plateau; it was being carried through nearly to the borders of Uganda under the second loan. From there (at Turbo) it was being taken on into the cotton-producing areas of eastern Uganda by a special £3,500,000 loan, free of interest for five years, made by the Imperial Government for the development of cotton-growing in the Empire. (Kenya never asked for a share of this loan. The first that was known of the matter was an announcement made in Legislative Council that the money had been placed to the colony's credit with the Crown Agents. The elected members were somewhat taken aback and objected strongly to a loan for which the colony had never asked, and on which it would have to pay interest as soon as the five years was up, being forced upon it.)

Out of this money the railway was carried on through prosperous cotton-growing country in eastern Uganda until it established connection by rail and boat with the headwaters of the Nile. One day, Mr. Felling hoped, it would go on into the Belgian Congo and tap the potentially great mineral-producing areas of Kivu and the northern Congo. Before he died he had thrown out a feeler to the northeastern corner of the Congo by establishing a regular boat and lorry service from the terminus of the Kenya and Uganda railway to the Belgian side of Lake Albert.

In Sir Robert Coryndon Kenya had found a rare specimen, a Governor who was popular with everyone. The settlers liked him for his easy, unaffected manners and his enthusiasm for the colony's development. (He used to call it "the power-house of East Africa".) His own officials trusted and respected him. He was tactful enough not to fight with too much asperity his masters at the Colonial Office. And, finally, his policy of encouraging native production met with approval from the influential group of onlookers in England who held a self-awarded brief for native interests.

6

Such a policy for the development of the reserves was overdue. In questions of native progress an African government has to give the lead; it must combat apathy and conservatism before it can secure action. Until 1924 the Kenya Government had lacked funds and driving force sufficient to launch a comprehensive scheme. The time of the agricultural department had been taken up mainly with experimenting on European crops.

To a large extent this was inevitable. East Africa was always growing out of its revenue. The problem was to keep pace by increasing production. This was easier and quicker to do with European rather than with native agriculture. With the settler there was no barrier of suspicion and tradition to overcome. In the case of the native it was often impossible to persuade him to adopt better farming methods until general education had spread sufficiently to loosen the rigidity of his prejudices.

But now that the colony was becoming a little more prosperous, more money was devoted to native agriculture. Free seed was issued, a school of dairying opened in the Masai reserve, and a scheme started for the training of native instructors at the agricultural laboratories near Nairobi. Efforts were made to persuade natives to use ploughs instead of hoes, to build rat-proof granaries, to dry their hides in the shade instead of in the sun, to castrate inferior male stock, to grow European vegetables and other crops as well as maize and millet, and so on.

In native politics, as well as in agriculture, Sir Robert Coryndon caused the local government to take the lead. A measure of self-government was accorded to the tribes through the setting up of local native councils in each of the reserves.

Kenya's difficulty in regard to native self-government had always been the lack of a foundation of chieftainship on which to build. "There were few either hereditary or created chiefs of any real power or influence over their people", Sir Robert Coryndon stated. For twenty years the Government had been building this foundation by creating new chiefs and strengthening existing ones. By now the stones were firmly bedded and it was time to lay the first course.

The object of local native councils was to act as a link between chiefs and people and to provide an outlet for the political ambitions of the more educated and intelligent young men. These councils were to be a training ground for the development of responsibility among native leaders. The councils were given powers to impose a levy on the inhabitants of the districts they controlled out of which such work as the building of hospitals and dispensaries, the founding of schools, afforestation, experiments in agriculture, the issue of improved seed, the building of bridges and so forth could be financed. (In a few years a school costing £10,000 had been built by one of these councils, European engineers employed by another to build roads, and staffs of native instructors maintained by most of them to teach the ignorant how to plough and fertilise their land.)

The bill establishing these councils was introduced by the chief Native Commissioner and seconded by Delamere. He agreed warmly with the principle of separate but parallel development of local self-government for blacks and for whites—"two systems of development along somewhat different lines running on different planes".

This bill did, in fact, give to the natives more advanced privileges than had been accorded to the Europeans. The colonists did not yet possess the right, now conferred on the natives, of raising local rates and controlling their expenditure.

7

Early in 1925 Sir Robert Coryndon died suddenly, following an operation. His death was a blow to the colony. He had possessed the invaluable gift of reconciling opposing factions and of getting things done.

His successor, Sir Edward Grigg, came to Kenya as the prophet of federation. He had had an unusual training for a Governorship—journalist, soldier, private secretary to Mr. Lloyd George, Liberal member of Parliament. He was appointed by Mr. Amery, who became Secretary of State for the Colonies in 1924.

Mr. Amery had cherished the federation idea for some years and now that he was in a position to do so he intended to push it through. When the Governorship of Kenya became vacant, therefore, he selected to fill it a man who shared his ideas, whose imagination could grasp the vision of a new East African dominion, whose knowledge of politics could provide material for the framing of new constitutions and whose energy and ambition could be relied upon to carry a scheme to its conclusion.

Delamere had opposed federation when it was first mooted after the war. "My policy would be for this country to stand alone until we are a self-governing colony", he had written in 1920. But in the last few years he had changed his mind. He had come to the conclusion that federation was inevitable; that it was a matter of imperial policy. It had, he saw, many advantages. To oppose it would be useless; the right line was to welcome it but at the same time to ensure, so far as was possible, that the colonists' ideals were not swamped in a political merger with two so-called "black states", nor their future sacrificed to an extreme doctrine of native paramountcy.

Delamere, therefore, came down on the side of federation. In this he was in advance of his followers. Most of them were distrustful. They were afraid; afraid that the weight of the native state to the west and the mandated territory to the south—countries where European colonisation was either climatically impossible or politically discouraged—would crush white settlement to death. It was no easy task for Delamere to entice his followers after him along the path to closer union.

Sir Edward comes here at what I believe to be a psychological moment in the history of Kenya, when this country of ours has the chance, if we give it to her, of becoming the centre of thought and opinion in Eastern Africa [he told an audience at Nakuru shortly after the new Governor's arrival].

She has gone through a great deal of the period necessary for the consolidation of her own resources. She is now faced with the parting of the ways.

The question before us now is: are we going to remain an isolated island of civilisation surrounded by a sea of policies over which we have no control, or are we going to follow our destiny and try and use our centre of civilisation to influence the trend of events in the countries which lie between us and the great British communities in the south?

No one can force the question as to which country is going to be the centre of political influence in Eastern Africa in the future. It is on the knees of the gods, and it depends on the influence which any of these countries can exert on the rest as to where the centre of influence will lie. . . .

Kenya has a long start in civilised population, in railway development and in all things which go to build up a modern state, and she would be false to her destiny if she did not radiate her civilising influence southward to meet the civilising influences radiating northward from Rhodesia. . . .

We must, I submit, give up thinking only of Kenya as an isolated unit. We must believe that our safety as a civilised unit depends on the extension of our influence southwards, and any wavering now in our attitude towards an intercolonial policy may have the most disastrous effects on Kenya in the future.

Delamere did not ask the colonists to go blindly into federation. He had already evolved the idea of asking for "safeguards"—of using the colonists' agreement to closer union to obtain sufficient political power to enable them to resist the swamping that they so much dreaded. An unofficial majority on the Legislative Council, Delamere decided, was to be the price of the settlers' co-operation in an East African federation.

If federation was to come about, Delamere reasoned, there would have to be a federal capital. East Africa certainly would not be able to afford another Canberra. The headquarters would have to be in some existing city. Nairobi, in Delamere's view, was the obvious place; it was the most central, healthy, civilised and accessible of the three East African capitals. And the Governor-General envisaged as the head of a federated state would need a residence worthy of his position.

These thoughts were in Delamere's mind when the question of extending the small Government House in Nairobi came up in 1924. In spite of his views on economy he took the lead in urging in Legislative Council that a large and imposing new building should be erected in Nairobi and another in Mombasa at a combined cost of £80,000, to be found out of the £5 million loan. He supported a proposal that Mr. (now Sir Herbert) Baker, the creator of modern South African architecture, should be invited to the country to design it.

He was opposed by most of the other unofficial members, who considered the sum disproportionately extravagant, but he beat down opposition. A resolution of protest was passed by a mass meeting of his constituents in Nakuru, but he played his usual card and threatened resignation if their attitude was not modified. Sir Edward Grigg arrived while the discussion was in progress and supported the proposal. So Delamere got his way. The £80,000 was agreed and in due course two fine Government Houses, designed by Baker and Hoogterp, were built.

8

For some time Delamere had been turning over in his mind the idea of bringing the white settlers in the five East African dependencies into closer touch with one another. The great distances between one pocket of colonists and the next had kept them apart in sympathies as well as in the flesh. (Not more than 20,000 non-official Europeans were scattered over a territory one-third the size of the United States.)

Now, more than ever before, it seemed to him essential that they should exchange ideas, learn of each other's problems and come to some understanding among themselves. East Africa was on the verge of great changes. Only by presenting an unbroken front could the colonists make their opinions heard. A concerted shout from the throats of the united colonists of East Africa might penetrate the official ear-drum where the separate pipings of settlers from

Kenya and Tanganyika, planters from Nyasaland and Uganda, would be ignored.

The East African Governors, on the recommendation of the Ormsby-Gore commission, were to meet in conference to discuss their common problems. Why should not representatives of the unofficials do the same?

So the idea of holding an unofficial conference took shape. Both the idea and its execution were entirely Delamere's. No one else among the East African colonists would have had the imagination, the initiative, the means and the ambition to carry it through. The holding of the first conference was a triumph of organisation and a tribute to Delamere's personal prestige.

He selected a deserted mission house at Tukuyu, a small post in the southern highlands of Tanganyika about 300 miles beyond Iringa, as the meeting-place. Tukuyu was over 1000 miles alike from Nairobi and from Livingstone. The nearest railway station, Dodoma, was about 450 miles away. The very convening of such a gathering, held in a part of the continent that could only have been reached a couple of years before by a specially equipped expedition taking months from base to base, was something of a landmark in the opening up of Africa.

The great north road was open now from the Nile to Broken Hill. It was still an adventure to traverse it. The road itself was a track partially cleared of tree-stumps and in places suspended dangerously over crocodile-infested rivers by means of flimsy wooden bridges. At other times it plunged sharply into the torrent and clambered out over muddy banks on the other side. Here and there the young bush which sprung up with tropical rapidity choked its passage so that only an eye well trained to pierce the disguises in which African roads are apt to conceal themselves could have followed its route. "Straight on for a hundred miles and then turn to the right" were the only directions that the Northern Rhodesian delegates could secure when they started for Tukuyu, having railed their cars from Livingstone to Broken Hill.

Nor were there petrol pumps or hotels to be found along this primitive arterial road. All the arrangements for fuel supply were made by Delamere. Lorry-loads of petrol and oil were sent to Iringa and smaller dumps were placed near the Tanganyika-Rhodesia border. Southern Tanganyika was then so inaccessible that petrol there cost 7s. a gallon. Delamere even sent an agent with a spare car to meet the Rhodesian delegates south of Abercorn, and another detachment of cars to Lake Nyasa to collect the Nyasaland delegates who came by boat to the northern end of the lake.

All this Delamere paid for out of his own pocket. The conference cost him about £1600.

9

Transport was only one aspect of the organisation required to assemble this spectacular bush conference. There was also the problem of housing and feeding the delegates and their wives at the isolated mission house nearly 800 miles from the nearest shopping centre, Dar-es-Salaam.

The Rungwe mission was a tumble-down brick house built round a central lawn. The walls had been partly pulled down by troops during the war to make ovens for camp kitchens. Delamere had grass huts run up for bedrooms and tables and chairs specially made for the occasion at Iringa. (Most of the chairs failed to arrive but there were plenty of packing-cases to use instead.) Glass, cutlery, camp beds and canned provisions were bought in Nairobi, shipped to Dar-es-Salaam and transported to Tukuyu in a fleet of lorries.

The arrangements worked perfectly. On the appointed day the delegates arrived; three from Northern Rhodesia, led by Mr. L. F. Moore; two from Nyasaland, five from Tanganyika and three from Kenya.[1] They were charmed alike with their welcome and their surroundings. The country round Tukuyu was volcanic and behind the old mission house the forested mass of an extinct crater rose to 10,000 feet. The brilliant petals of flowering creepers here and there splashed the dark foliage of the forest's edges with colour. Alpine

[1] The delegates were as follows:—*Northern Rhodesia*: L. F. Moore, F. G. Clarke, T. M. Michlam; *Nyasaland*: Col. Sanders, C. Burbery Seale; *Tanganyika*: J. Stuart Wells, F. Billinge, R. Ullyate, G. H. Hewer, Maxton Mailer; *Kenya*: Lord Delamere, Lord Francis Scott, H. F. Ward. Uganda was not represented. The hon. secretary was Col. A. Fawcus.

strawberries grew along the shaded banks of streams, reddening for the birds. The air was cool and invigorating (this climate was too damp for maize to ripen), the country rolling and fertile. It was a perfect setting for an African political holiday.

Before the conference opened there had been a good deal of talk in Nyasaland and Rhodesia about "domination from the north". Delamere, it was said, was finding the Kenya platform too small for him. His desire to hold the limelight had prompted him to seek a wider scope and all East Africa was to be used as a stage for his ambition. He coveted Rhodes' mantle in the east. But Nyasaland and Northern Rhodesia, the European population averred, were no pet dogs to run obediently to Delamere's whistle. They wanted no patronage or dictation from Kenya settlers or from the ambitious peer who led them.

Several of the delegates, therefore, arrived at the conference in a rather antagonistic frame of mind. "I'm glad you've come", Delamere said to one of the Northern Rhodesian representatives as he climbed, weary and jolted, from his car. "I don't know why the devil I did", the Rhodesian snapped back. "Come in and have a drink", Delamere answered, falling back on his usual remedy. "Thanks", was the reply, "I'll have a glass of water."

This was a discouraging start. Delamere was a great believer in the political value of champagne. It created, he thought, the right atmosphere of friendliness in which to get business done. He had laid in a supply at Tukuyu and it was served in tumblers and tin mugs. It played its part on the first evening in smoothing the ruffled feelings of the Rhodesian and Nyasaland delegates, and by the following morning hostilities had vanished and general good-will taken their place.

The conference opened on October 10th, 1925. It had no formal agenda and only one rule of procedure: that every resolution forwarded to the various governments was to be unanimous. Delamere was chairman. He followed the method that he had come to use at all meetings over which he presided: to let everyone else speak first. He called on each member in turn and then, when everyone had had their say, put forward his own ideas in a conciliatory manner, answering and smoothing away objections. With these tactics his views were generally accepted.

The subjects of discussion were mostly practical matters affecting development of the territories. Resolutions were passed, for example, urging the governments to resuscitate the old German scientific laboratories at Amani and to undertake a thorough geological survey of East Africa. Another stressed the need for a north-and-south railway to open up southern Tanganyika. (Delamere pointed out that while the ridge of "white" land—country where settlement was climatically possible—ran north and south, all railways ran east and west.)

10

Delamere was frank enough about the political aims of his conference. It was intended to promote "the solidification of the white ideal", to unite the colonists of East Africa so that they were in a position, if it became necessary, to fight their common ruler, the Colonial Office. A resolution introduced by Northern Rhodesia and passed unanimously read that "Colonial Office control is too great, is increasing and ought to be diminished". Delamere explained in a telegram to the Secretary of State that nothing personal was meant: the resolution was "intended to deal with the principle that the combination in local councils of the wisdom and experience of colonists, officials and missionaries, guided as they are by experienced Governors, requires progressively less detailed direction from the Colonial Office in inverse ratio as the numbers and knowledge of the local community grow".

He believed that "the solidification of the white ideal" was a matter of urgency. For the ideal of white colonisation in Africa, of civilisation by interpenetration—his ideal—was being threatened by the extension of what he called the "West Coast policy". This he interpreted as a policy of developing African dependencies as purely native states where the white man had no place save that of temporary administrator and teacher, states from which the European would ultimately withdraw altogether, leaving no permanent mark on Africa save that which he had managed to impress upon the ways of life of the inhabitants—a crust of civilisation, perhaps, over the molten realities of barbarism.

For West Africa this system might well be the right one. Delamere did not pass judgment although he believed that it slowed down the economic development of countries in which it was applied. "It has lasted as long as it has as a living theory", he commented, "because of the great population, in Nigeria especially, and because of the high export value of certain tropical crops, of which such as palm kernels grow wild and need little more attention than periodic tapping."

But conditions in the west were totally different from those in the east. In West Africa the population was denser, the country richer, the natives harder-working, the climate unhealthy for Europeans. Delamere did oppose, with all the force at his command, the application to East Africa of policies evolved to meet quite another situation in a distant part of the continent.

He believed in the dual policy. This admitted the obligation to train, educate, protect and help forward the native inhabitants but allowed for a more permanent infiltration of European influence. It was prepared to encourage the white man to develop the country's resources because it considered that the country benefited from the industry and example of European settlers.

"The dual policy", he said, "sets out to keep the native in close and continuous touch with the work of the world; to break down those tribal customs which make for reversal to barbarism and to provide innumerable unpaid teachers of civilisation who themselves have to meet and overcome the problems of African life and economics." This policy was based, also, on a belief that a settler population supplied a core of stability to the sphere of European influence. Civilisation would prove to be less ephemeral in places where it was actually being practised and woven into the life and growth of the country than in lands where a band of independent Civil servants—spending only a part of their lives in Africa and with their roots, their homes and their futures still in England—were merely teaching its virtues.

Although the dual policy was not named until Coryndon's

time, its principles had been recognised, some seventy years before, by no less a man than David Livingstone. In his book *Missionary Travels* he said that emigration would ultimately benefit the natives more than missionaries; and he offered £2000 from the profits of his first book towards the expenses of sending out selected British families to colonise the shores of Lake Nyasa.[1]

Delamere was afraid that the political federation of East African territories would lead to the spread of the West Coast policy and the jettisoning of the dual policy. That was the doubt behind his reluctance to accept federation; that was one reason why he summoned the Tukuyu conference. "The first thing that we started to do", he said, "was to try and help to kill the spread of the West Coast policy in the East. . . ."

The first unofficial conference was a great success. No quarrels or bad feeling arose to destroy the good relations established at the outset, largely through the tact of the chairman, between representatives of all four territories. The conference lasted a week and then dispersed.

Three months later the first Governors' conference held in East Africa met in Nairobi. It was attended by the Governors of all five territories. Many of the subjects that had been discussed at Tukuyu were dealt with officially at Nairobi. The Tukuyu resolutions were considered by the Governors and many of them—including one urging the more active encouragement of settlement in Tanganyika, Nyasaland and Northern Rhodesia and another pressing for the extension of medical services to natives in all the territories—were formally endorsed.

11

Delamere's choice of the southern highlands of Tanganyika as a meeting-place had been dictated partly by a new interest which had started to occupy his attention.

The farmer, contrary to popular belief, is an indomitable optimist. When times are good he puts his profits to the expansion of his cultivation and the enlargement of his herds.

[1] R. J. Campbell, *The Life of Livingstone*.

He does not doubt that markets will continue to demand the output of his farm.

The colonial farmer is optimistic to the point of folly. His determination to increase production often amounts almost to a mania. So, in Kenya, the first good years since pre-war days—the "sunbeam period" which dawned in 1925—engendered a crop of new schemes of expansion. These concerned not only Kenya but also undeveloped parts of Tanganyika.

Delamere, once again, gave the lead. Early in 1925 he formed a small company called Colonists Ltd. to open up the southern highlands of Tanganyika by stimulating white settlement in the Iringa area.

His primary object was frankly political. Tanganyika was the weak link in the chain of white settlement that he, following Rhodes and Smuts, wanted to see securely fastened down Africa's highland backbone from Lake Victoria to Rhodesia. Its weakness, judged from his viewpoint, was the almost negligible number of settlers. The total unofficial community numbered less than 3000. Not more than a thousand were on the land. Only by increasing the white population could Tanganyika be headed along what Delamere considered to be the right road.

His second reason for launching his miniature settlement scheme was an imperialistic one. The fear that Tanganyika might at some future date be restored to Germany had been present, in spite of several reassurances by the British Government, ever since the mandate had been awarded to Britain. There was something essentially impermanent about a mandate. It was known that a group in Germany was working towards the recovery of their old colony, and it was suspected that German colonists already there were receiving financial aid from the fatherland.

Britain, on the other hand, had done little to stimulate development since the war and nothing at all to encourage settlement by British colonists, which alone could rivet the territory securely to the Empire. No railways had been built, no production schemes launched, and uncertainty as to the Government's intentions had undoubtedly kept capital away. Although the Imperial Government had been able and willing to spend at least £100 million—possibly as much as double that sum—on conquering the territory, a purely destructive operation, it had not seen fit to raise even a few millions as a loan for the more constructive and profitable purpose of developing the resources of its expensive prize.

Britain had been given a good start to establish her own colonists in the mandated territory. For the first seven years after the war no ex-enemies were allowed to return. She had not chosen to take advantage of this breathing-space, and in 1925 the seven years was up. After this Germans could immigrate in unlimited numbers, and there was a good deal of apprehension in East Africa that the country would become flooded with them. This was one factor which influenced Delamere in deciding to launch his scheme. He wanted to see British settlement well established before the Germans came back.

The southern highlands were the obvious setting for his attempt to increase the British population. Here was a big area of unoccupied land with an exceedingly sparse native population. There was room for settlement on a considerable scale without disturbing a single hut. (The population of the whole Iringa district was only 1·3 to the square mile.) The climate was good; adequate rainfall, cool temperature (the altitude ranged from 5000 to 6500 feet and there were sharp frosts at night), invigorating air. The land was well watered and the soil seemed fertile. Mixed farming, Delamere considered, could be carried on; coffee and tobacco were possibilities.

The greatest difficulty was transport. Iringa was severely handicapped by its distance from the railway. But a line to the south was projected and, at the time of Colonists Ltd.'s formation, it seemed almost certain that money would be allocated for it out of a £10 million transport loan that had been recommended by the Ormsby-Gore commission.

12

In May 1925 Colonists Ltd. was formed with a capital of only £6000, provided chiefly by Delamere, Lord Egerton of Tatton and Sir John Ramsden. The company was not to be run for profit. Its main activities were those of a land agency. A rough survey of the Tukuyu district was made and a transport unit of wagons and lorries was established at Iringa. The Iringa office became an information bureau for intending settlers and a central agency for existing ones. Later, a hotel was built at Iringa to provide the beginnings of a local market for perishable produce.

All went well at first. Word went round that the southern highlands were to become a second Kenya. The soil was almost as fertile, it was said, and the climate as good. Purchasers of land would double and treble their outlay in a few years when the railway came; survey parties were already in the field. Parts of the country were so well watered that the traveller came to permanent streams flowing between ridges every quarter of an hour as he marched. The country was well wooded, covered with protea trees whose young leaves were red and brown instead of green so that the hillsides were fired with a blaze of autumnal colour just before the rains. An exodus from Kenya to Tanganyika occurred. Settlers with some capital hurried down to apply for farms.

Difficulties started at once. The first related to title-deeds. Applications for farms selected by the newcomers and approved by the provincial Commissioner were sent in to Dar-es-Salaam but they often remained unacknowledged. Nothing further seemed to happen. The next step should have been the auctioning of the chosen farms. Months dragged by and no auctions were held. The Government did not seem at all anxious to attract new colonists, although the new Governor, Sir Donald Cameron, had announced as part of his policy the opening up of the Iringa province, and the land had been thrown open for settlement by the Government.

In 1926 the Germans started to arrive. They came in considerable numbers and soon there were more Germans than British. They, too, suffered from official delays. These settlers could not afford to wait—they had very little capital —and they built rough houses, ploughed up land and started development in anticipation of receiving titles. But still no titles came. Loans or mortgages could not be raised without them and the settlers had no security for their improvements. Government muddles added to the dissatisfaction and in one case at least the Government went back on its word. British and Germans united in their protests at their treatment and a petition to the Colonial Office was drawn up by the Iringa Farmers' Association.

Troubles did not end here. The soil and climate, for all their promise, proved disappointing. Coffee was planted, but it did not flourish. Tobacco grew well at first, but the danger of early frosts and the uneven distribution of rainfall—there was a dry spell lasting almost half the year—made the crop a risky one.

Delamere concluded that some enterprise which would give an immediate return and which was less uncertain than tobacco must be found. He was anxious to encourage mixed farming. To that end he decided to start a bacon factory, to buy pigs from the surrounding farmers, to transport the bacon to Dodoma and to sell it in Dar-es-Salaam. Towards the end of 1925 he took up a farm of 5000 acres, Uleti, imported the most up-to-date bacon-curing and pig product equipment available in London, and started to erect a factory.

13

Fortune seemed to be against Colonists Ltd. The new settlers round Iringa were, in effect, gambling on the coming of the railway; and the gamble failed.

Of the various routes which the projected southern line might take, two were finally selected, after preliminary surveys, as the best. One ran from Dodoma through the Iringa district to the north end of Lake Nyasa, and down to Fife in the north-eastern corner of Northern Rhodesia. It would tap first a native area, then the southern highlands. Produce from Nyasaland could be sent up the lake by boat and evacuated by way of Dar-es-Salaam. North-eastern Rhodesia, which was served by no railway at all, would be given an outlet to the sea.

The other route lay to the east and parallel to the projected Dodoma-Fife line. It took off from the central railway a hundred miles east of Dodoma and ran to Manda on the eastern shores of Lake Nyasa. This line would leave untapped the southern highland plateau, passing instead through a lower-lying area where the cultivation of ground-nuts and other native crops might be developed. At Manda it could tap Nyasaland's freight, but north-eastern Rhodesia would remain untouched. It had, however, certain technical advantages.

Rough surveys of both these lines were being made when the Iringa colonisation scheme was started. Delamere naturally urged the Government to decide in favour of the first route, which would open up the highland country suitable for white settlement. A resolution pressing for its adoption had been passed by the Tukuyu conference and this route was recommended by the Governors' conference early in 1926.

Before the matter had been settled the British Government, financially embarrassed by the general strike of 1926, decided that it could not afford, after all, to give East Africa a £10 million loan free of interest for the first five years, as had been proposed. A committee which was sitting under the chairmanship of Sir George Schuster to suggest how the £10 millions should be spent was forced to conclude that the Tanganyika Government would not be justified, in these circumstances, in building a new railway to the south at all. Whichever route was chosen the line could not pay for several years and the finances of the territory were not strong enough to make up the loss. For the time being, therefore, the question of the southern railway was shelved.

This decision did much to destroy the hopes of Colonists Ltd. Without exports there could be no real growth of settlement. Nor could land appreciate in value as a bait to attract new men. And, as an additional blow, overproduction of tobacco in Rhodesia and the consequent collapse of the market killed stone-dead the prospects of building up an export trade in the only crop sufficiently high-priced to stand transport charges of a penny a pound to the nearest railway.

Colonists Ltd. did not, however, close down for several years. "I look upon the settlement of the southern portion of Tanganyika and the northern part of Northern Rhodesia as vital in controlling the native policy of Eastern Africa," Delamere wrote, "and on this matter as being the key to the safety of this country, Kenya, as a colony of our own people; and I am going to keep this organisation for land business going whatever happens." The second-in-command of the 1820 Settlers' Association in South Africa was engaged to manage the organisation in Tanganyika and Delamere made frequent visits to Iringa to direct its policy. Often these trips were made with great difficulty, for sections of the road were sometimes washed away and bridges destroyed. It was a five days' motor journey from Nairobi to Iringa.

But in the end, after more money had been sunk and lost, Colonists Ltd. had to go. The little wave of Kenya settlers that had rippled down to the south receded, leaving Iringa to a few survivors and to German colonists assisted, to a limited extent, by a fund raised for their support in Germany. The prospects were not good enough to attract new colonists, the Government's attitude and transport difficulties discouraged existing ones, and the world depression gave the knock-out blow to Delamere's hopes.

The bacon factory at Uleti was kept alive until 1931. Delamere imported an expert bacon curer from England to run it and at first the products found a ready sale in Dar-es-Salaam. Transport costs, however, ate up the profits, and other difficulties developed. "Things that have to be squeezed at first are generally best in Africa," he wrote in reply to an appeal for more funds, "and the poor old milch cow has run dry for the moment anyway." He hung on obstinately to his project in spite of all discouragements until finance finally defeated him. He put, altogether, about £8000 into the plant, and ultimately lost it when the factory was forced to close.

CHAPTER XXII

THE FEDERATION ISSUE
1926–1929

I

IN 1926 Delamere paid a flying trip to England on personal affairs connected with the handing over of Vale Royal to his son. On the way he visited Nyasaland and the Rhodesias to prepare the ground for a second unofficial conference to be held in Livingstone. In Salisbury he secured a promise from the Premier that a representative of Southern Rhodesia would attend.

The Livingstone conference, held at the Falls hotel in September 1926, duplicated the success of its Tukuyu forerunner. All the unofficial members of the Northern Rhodesia Legislative Council attended. Five delegates from Kenya motored down the great north road, whose Broken Hill to Livingstone section was just completed. Delamere's caravan was, in fact, the first to come all the way down from the north along the new road. Tanganyika and Nyasaland were also represented and Colonel du Porte came on behalf of Southern Rhodesia.

Sir Herbert Stanley, Governor of Northern Rhodesia, opened the first meeting. "Though the conference is unofficial, we do not regard it in any sense as anti-official", he said. "Any resolutions which you pass will be examined by this Government at any rate in a spirit of much friendliness and with a keen desire to meet wherever possible the views which have been expressed."

Delamere's personal prestige reached, perhaps, its peak at the Livingstone conference. Newspaper reports in South African papers used the phrase "the Rhodes of East Africa". The following comments made subsequently by Mr. L. F.

Moore indicate the impression that he made on one of the leaders of unofficial East African opinion outside Kenya:

> Delamere of course presided and proved a most suave peacemaker. His powers were not strained at Tukuyu but at the Falls a savage split was averted more by his patient politeness than by the responses of the combatants.
>
> Whether the conferences could have produced any ultimate effect it is difficult to say. The slump has upset everything. We (Northern Rhodesia) were indisposed to involve ourselves in the Indian problem, and feared that responsible government was unlikely to be conceded from Tanganyika northwards, but anticipated a large influx of population in Northern Rhodesia.
>
> At that time we were opposed to amalgamation with Southern Rhodesia, but Delamere favoured it; he dreamt of a central African dominion including Southern Rhodesia. I thought this a most unlikely development. . . . Nevertheless, he considered that the combined and reunited representations—even pressure—of the peoples and their representatives on the Colonial Office would further his ideal.
>
> I sometimes wondered whether I really knew what D. was after. He expounded and argued and succeeded in obtaining acquiescence—but to what? He held these conferences at great expense, was the most genial and lavish host and entertainer I ever met, and went to extraordinary lengths to avoid abrading the sensibilities of his poorer coadjutors.
>
> D. was the dominant figure throughout, partly, no doubt, because he paid the piper, but more largely because he (I must presume) knew what he wanted. That he failed to achieve anything tangible discouraged further effort, for if he could do so little, what could lesser men do?

Federation was again discussed at Livingstone, but without enthusiasm. The Northern Rhodesian delegates were strongly opposed to linking themselves with the "black north" and feared "the uncertainty of the policy of the Colonial Office towards Asiatics in Kenya and Tanganyika".

After this conference Delamere concluded that closer union between all five East African territories was, for the time being, out of the question. The countries fell naturally into two groups: Kenya, Uganda and Tanganyika in the north, Nyasaland and Northern Rhodesia in the south. The first stage, he considered, must be to unite each of the two groups.

2

As soon as the conference was over Delamere and his colleagues hurried back to Kenya to prepare for the next general election. The occasion was an important one. For the first time a formal demand for an unofficial majority was put forward by the elected members.

To press by any constitutional means for a European elected majority over all parties in the Legislative Council.

To give favourable consideration to a scheme of co-ordination of the northern East African territories (Kenya, Tanganyika and Uganda) and possibly Nyasaland. . . . Provided that consideration of any such scheme is conditional on an elected majority having been granted and that the following essential safeguards are included. . . .

These were the opening and crucial words of the election manifesto drawn up by Delamere and signed by all the elected members in December 1926.

The eleven members returned to the Council were elected on this manifesto. Delamere was unopposed for the Rift Valley.

The European population of Kenya, then, had laid their cards on the table. "Federation, if——" The "if" was an elected majority. This, they believed, would safeguard their position as a British colony, "looking forward" in a former Secretary of State's words, "in the full fruition of time to responsible self-government".

For the next four years federation, or closer union as it was later called, was the central issue in East African politics. The story is one of delays, misunderstandings and a lost opportunity. Its outline, briefly told, is as follows:

Sir Edward Grigg spent the first eighteen months of his term of office exploring the two main questions on which Mr. Amery had instructed him to report: the safeguarding of native lands and the co-ordination of the East African territories. In January 1927, just before the Kenya elections, he was summoned to London to present his conclusions.

No doubt was left in his mind as to the right course to pursue. Closer co-ordination in East African affairs on the economic side was, in his opinion, essential. It was more than that; it was urgent. Several factors had brought it to a head.

Chief among these was the future of railway policy. The £10 million loan then projected was being parcelled out. Tanganyika had decided to spend most of her share on the construction of a branch line from Dodoma to Mwanza, a port on the southern extremity of Lake Victoria.

This line would, when completed, enter into direct competition with Kenya's line for the traffic of the basin of Lake Victoria. Both would tap the same area, leading the produce away to separate ports. A war of rates was inevitable. Even if agreement could be reached over rates, the completion of two lines and two ports could only mean that existing traffic would be spread more thinly over two systems. And both systems belonged to the same proprietor—Britain—and were wholly financed by the same shareholder—the British taxpayer.

Such competition was grossly uneconomic. In the long run, Sir Edward Grigg maintained—and he was supported by the Governor of Uganda, Sir William Gowers—both the British taxpayer and the African producer must suffer: the taxpayer because he was financing, at the same moment, two competing concerns; the producer because the money allocated to his transport needs was being dissipated on two rival channels instead of being concentrated on the efficiency of one. And one line was amply sufficient to deal with all the traffic. What, Sir Edward Grigg asked, was the object of conquering the ex-German colony at vast expense if it was then developed so as to compete with the next-door British state, as though the two were deadly rivals instead of fellow members of one Empire?

A resolution condemning the proposed branch line to Mwanza was passed at the Governors' conference of 1926. Four out of the five Governors supported it; but Sir Donald Cameron dissented, and the line was sanctioned by the Secretary of State.

3

This matter of wasteful competition between the Kenya and the Tanganyika railway systems raised the whole question of the central direction of policy. Railways had forced the issue of union in South Africa; history was repeating itself in the East.

There were many other arguments in favour of federation. Commercial interests were unanimous in their demand for a permanent customs union embracing Tanganyika. The reorganisation of defence was urgent. Kenya, the only one of the territories with a long, wild and unsettled foreign border to protect, was bearing a disproportionate and crippling share of what was in reality a common burden. Lack of a central authority was resulting in waste of energy and resources as regards research.

The creation of an East African dominion could not fail to stir the imagination of people in Britain and focus attention on the future of the three dependencies. Singly, they were of little account; small, remote places with tiresome governments, they seemed to many in England. But welded into a new unit, their resources would surely become better known; capital would embark on big developments; settlers would come to try their fortunes in the sixth and last dominion; bigger opportunities would attract men of ability and enterprise.

Not the least of the arguments for federation was that a man of wider outlook and a more constructive mind than was usually possessed by colonial governors would be found to fill the post of Governor-General. Imagination and statesmanship might be brought to bear in greater measure on East Africa's future. The dead hand of bureaucratic control might to some extent be lifted.

The difficulties of governing a slice of Africa from 6000 miles away were often mentioned. Federation would make them less acute. Although Downing Street would still retain the last word, the Governor-General would have wide powers to direct policy as he thought fit. And he would be on the spot—able to see things for himself, accessible to delegations, in touch with public opinion, and, above all, appointed to give all his time and intelligence to a study of East Africa's affairs. His presence would to some extent insulate the territories from the unsettling effects of political changes in England and make for that continuity of policy that had been so sadly lacking in East African affairs. Clearly the situation would be much more satisfactory than under the existing system whereby decisions were made by Civil servants who had never set foot in Africa, or by a Secretary of State immersed in party politics and with his mind on events happening in Honduras or Hong-Kong.

All these points were laid before the Secretary of State early in 1927. Sir Edward Grigg recommended the immediate establishment of a central authority to control the main transport services, the customs system, all communications by land and air, defence and research.

Federation in East Africa was an economic need. There was also a political side to the question; and this was more complicated, less straightforward than the economic aspect.

The difficulty was that the three dependencies varied too much politically for easy federation. One was a collection of native states governed by Britain as a Protectorate; another was a mandated territory under the supervision of the League of Nations; the third was a Crown colony directly under the Colonial Office but equipped with a system of electoral representation. There was a wide gulf between the constitutions and perhaps the destinies of the states; and, to make it more difficult, none of them wanted political federation and all three were suspicious of their neighbours.

No scheme of federation, Sir Edward Grigg considered, could be successful if the deep antagonism of any powerful section of the population was aroused against it. There was no question but that the strongest opposition would be offered by the colonists of Kenya to any change which deprived them of the political privileges they had won during the past twenty years, which abruptly silenced their voices on all major issues and which gave them nothing in return. It was only human nature to demand some compensation for the voluntary sacrifice of a cherished possession.

Kenya's Governor, therefore, supported—with important

modifications—the demand for an unofficial majority in the Legislative Council put forward in the elected members' manifesto of December 1926. He did not advocate a clear majority of elected members, but he suggested that there should be an unofficial majority composed partly of elected members and partly of members nominated by the Governor to represent native interests. The setting up of such a Council in Kenya was proposed, of course, only as part of a scheme of closer union which included a federal council for East Africa as a whole.

This, then, was the substance of Sir Edward Grigg's scheme for closer union presented to Mr. Amery early in 1927. The Secretary of State discussed it fully with its author and with Sir William Gowers and Sir Herbert Stanley, who were both in London. Sir Donald Cameron was summoned from Tanganyika to confer. Its main principles were agreed; but the question was a complex one and the Cabinet, to whom the matter was referred by Mr. Amery, appointed a sub-committee to consider it in detail. This sub-committee decided that an independent commission should be sent to East Africa to draw up a scheme for closer union. Their decision was announced in a white paper published in July 1927.[1]

4

This was the first pronouncement of policy made since the white paper of 1923. To the colonists it was an encouraging document. The acceptance of the "dual policy" by the Governors' conference was officially endorsed by the British Government and the colonists' claim to a greater share in the government of their country was pronounced justified.

Imperial trusteeship for the welfare of the native races was still, the white paper said, a primary obligation.

At the same time they [H.M. Government] wish to place on record their view that while these responsibilities of trusteeship must for some considerable time rest mainly on the agents of the Imperial Government, they desire to associate more closely in this high and

[1] Cmd. 2907 of 1927: "Future policy in Eastern Africa".

honourable task those who, as colonists or residents, have identified their interests with the prosperity of the country.

Mr. Amery, speaking on the appointment of the commission in the House of Commons, amplified the attitude of the Government in a statement which was frequently quoted in the years that followed.

All that is laid down in the white paper and all that constitutes any modification of the underlying principle of the white paper of 1923, is that we explicitly reject the idea of white and black dyarchy and affirm that progress towards self-government on the part of the white community does mean, and ought to mean, an association with the Government in the sense of trusteeship to the weaker and more numerous part of the population. . . .

One of the greatest mistakes made in the early history of South Africa was that the Imperial Government regarded itself as the one and only champion of the native races and alienated and thrust on one side the white community, which is often mistaken, perhaps, but sometimes right. The result was to breed in the white settlers not only hostility towards the government which denied them a share in the control of their own affairs, but hostility towards the idea with which that government was associated. . . .

The day will come when, with the growth of a large settled community, no government in this House can ultimately resist the demand for self-government. What we want to do is to make sure that the white settlers are conscious of the destiny of East Africa as a great country which they are called upon to lead and inspire; that they should be equally conscious of their responsibility towards other communities and should desire to bring these communities, in the fullness of time, into association with themselves on every matter affecting the development of the country.

Others shared with Mr. Amery his belief that to guard jealously the native trust as a private preserve of the British Government was to drive the settlers into an attitude of indifference or even hostility towards native interests which they would not otherwise have adopted.

Mr. Ormsby-Gore, now Under-Secretary for the Colonies and fresh from his first-hand study of East African affairs, supported the settlers' claim to increased responsibilities.

"It is not possible", he said, "in the twentieth century to govern people by the use of an official majority six thousand miles away as it was in the old days." To disregard the convictions of the colonists, he added, would be "one of the worst failures in British colonial history".

Delamere and his followers were reassured. Evidently, they felt, a more sympathetic and less rigidly bureaucratic spirit had at last possessed the Colonial Office and British politicians.

5

Shortly after the 1927 white paper appeared a third unofficial conference was held—in August 1927—in Nairobi. Delegates from Kenya, Tanganyika, Nyasaland and Northern Rhodesia went further than they had ventured at Tukuyu or at Livingstone towards welcoming federation. The new white paper had removed many of their doubts.

In his address from the chair Delamere came out into the open on the side of closer union. There were two alternatives before the country, and the moment had come to choose. One was "to face the issue and decide on the necessary safeguards and fix the lines along which the countries of Eastern Africa are to advance in the future". The other was a policy of drift: and "drift is always dangerous".

The question of safeguards, Delamere said—of an elected majority in Kenya—was vital. Federation could only be a success if the spirit of co-operation entered into all the communities concerned. So long as the colonists were afraid of obliteration they would fight shy of political fusion with their neighbours. He continued:

If we are to improve the position of the native races generally and permanently, our own people must be freed from fear for their own future as far as is humanly possible. Fear is the curse of so many policies and the father of so many narrow and selfish councils. If our civilisation is to be of any real use as an example during the years to come, it has to be firmly fixed in a position where it can keep its ideals. . . .

Any other policy is to my mind as absurd as trying to raise the standard of native maize throughout the country by planting your imported standard seed in the middle of native maize plantations, where it is at once made degenerate by cross-fertilisation from the lower grade it is expected to improve. Civilisation is nothing new in Africa, and it is quite ludicrous to suppose that the African native is likely to disappear before civilisation. On the contrary the real difficulty is to keep civilisation from being smothered, especially as it weakens, as all civilisations sooner or later do.

The instinct to revert to the easier way of living in the races of Africa is like the couch grass that was found to have smothered General Gordon's garden in Khartoum on the reoccupation after the Mahdi régime, and which would wipe out the whole of our cultivated areas in a year or two if we left this country to-day. . . . If your standards of civilisation are to remain fixed as an example, you have to be careful that the couch grass doesn't come into your own garden and smother the cultivated plants which civilisation has grown there.

Can we trust our people at home at all times to recognise this real danger to civilisation in Africa?

Can we altogether banish fear without safeguards?

Do our people at home really keep clearly in their minds that fear of competition by people living at a lower standard of living is a necessary instinct in a civilised man if he is to keep his civilised manners and ideals?

Get rid of fear for our own future and the whole outlook changes. Natives would then no longer loom as something alien—protected, right or wrong, by Downing Street, often owing to incorrect information or inaccurate data. They at once become part of our people whom it is our duty to protect and encourage. . . .

Our civilisation is here, and nothing can prevent its forward movement in the highlands of East Africa.

It will attain further control in the government by stages fast or slow as the case may be. I believe that is unalterable. The only question is whether our colonies will emerge into ultimate control of their destiny embittered by policies forced upon them and by the attacks of political enemies in England, or whether they will build up a sense of responsibility for the welfare of the native population living next to them in a calm atmosphere where their own future is secure.

Given the safeguards suggested in the elected members' manifesto, Delamere continued, federation would clear the cobwebs of controversy from the path and open the way for progress. "I believe that if we can get federation on our lines then we can sit down in safety to pursue our economic research and our work for ourselves and our native peoples without bothering our heads about politics. Politics have been the curse of Africa."

This address did much to convert the colonists to closer union. Where opinion had been doubtful at Livingstone it was favourable at Nairobi. "There is a strong opinion in Uganda in favour of federation", said one of the delegates from the Protectorate, which was represented at an unofficial conference for the first time. "Federation is vital to us in Tanganyika", echoed one of its representatives. "We have everything to gain and nothing to lose by it." Delamere even succeeded in convincing his hearers that Nairobi was the best initial site for a federal headquarters.

And so the commission to investigate closer union was born into an atmosphere of welcome and not of suspicion. Delamere's three conferences were largely responsible for this. Had no such meetings been held the commission would probably have been regarded with more hostility than cordiality by the East African colonists, particularly by those in Kenya. The Europeans in Kenya considered that, as they had advanced the furthest, they were risking most in allying themselves with countries both politically and economically less developed. These conferences taught them the essential unity of Africa's problems.

6

When Sir Edward Grigg sailed for Kenya in July 1927, the appointment of the closer union commission had been satisfactorily arranged.

Discussions between the Secretary of State and the Governors in the spring of 1927 had left no doubt that federation was to be brought about. The question was not one of its desirability; it was a practical one of designing the right machinery.

The commission's terms of reference were drawn up by the Cabinet sub-committee of which Mr. Amery was a member. They were submitted, when complete, to the Cabinet. Here a hitch occurred. The Cabinet felt that the question needed a more thorough study than had been given to it. They suggested that the commission should enquire whether federation was desirable as well as study the method of bringing it about.

The commission's instructions were therefore altered. It was told "to make recommendations as to *whether*, either by federation or some form of closer union, more effective co-operation between the different governments in Central and Eastern Africa may be secured, more particularly in regard to the development of transport and communications, customs tariffs and administration, scientific research and defence". But the original wording was left by an oversight in the body of the white paper. On a later page reference was made to the commission's enquiry "as to *how* closer union and co-operation between the territories may be most effectively secured".

This last-minute change in the wording of the white paper altered the whole basis from which the commission approached their problem. It resulted in their discussing for the greater part of 350 pages the theoretical pros and cons of closer union instead of devoting their time, as Mr. Amery had intended, to perfecting a practical scheme.

Seeds of the failure of the federation idea were sown, also, in the personnel of the commission sent to prepare for its realisation.

Mr. Amery chose Sir Hilton Young as chairman. Then he went off on a tour of the Empire and left the final selection of the other commissioners to the head of the team. Sir George Schuster was included as a financial expert and an Indian Civil servant; Sir Reginald Mant (with whom the chairman had served many years before on public bodies in India) was also appointed. It was decided to include a student of native questions and Mr. J. H. Oldham, secretary of the International Missionary Council, was selected.

The appointment of an Indian Civil servant to the commission seemed to carry with it the danger that the now buried Indian question might be resurrected. Sir Edward Grigg suggested that a South African should be added to balance the Indian member. The experience of this Dominion, who had herself faced similar problems only a short time before and whose leaders were therefore well familiar with the technical aspects of federation, would, he pointed out, be of value. He suggested that Mr. Patrick Duncan be asked to serve. Mr. Amery agreed, but Sir Hilton Young considered that the commission had already grown too big, and the idea was rejected.

When the commission came to the making of decisions it turned out to be badly balanced. Sir Reginald Mant was a strong supporter of the Indian case and found himself out of sympathy both with the point of view of the European population and with certain of the principles of East African policy already laid down by the Imperial Government. Sir George Schuster received the important appointment of financial adviser to the Government of India before the commission began to sit, and when the report came to be written demands upon his attention were inevitably made by preparation for his new position. Mr. Oldham's interests lay naturally more in the direction of native social and spiritual betterment than of practical economics. The chairman was the only one of the party who had a background of general political experience and who was more concerned with the practical requirements of the situation and the framing of a workable plan for closer union than with abstract theories.

The commission, as a result, tended to group itself into two camps, with the chairman in one and the rest of the commissioners in the other. This led to a majority report by the three members and a minority report by the chairman. And the orientation of the commissioners' interests resulted in their attention being directed towards theoretical aspects of native policy and away from the machinery of economic co-ordination.

7

The Hilton Young commission arrived in East Africa in January 1928. They spent ten days in Uganda, three weeks in Kenya and just over a fortnight in Tanganyika. In that brief time they probed into almost every political issue in East Africa. Their attention focussed itself mainly on the future political development of the native population.

Delamere gave evidence before the commission as the

principal spokesman for the colonists. He used this opportunity to outline his ideas as they had crystallised in his mind after a quarter of a century of experience. Since they comprise the last statement of his general conception of the future they may be summarised as follows in his own words. (The questions are interjected for the sake of clarity and are not taken from the evidence.)

(*Q.*) Do you believe that federation should embrace the southern territories?

(*A.*) "We all look on anything that is done between the three northern territories as the first step towards a possible federation of some kind with the Rhodesias and Nyasaland."

(*Q.*) What do you say to the separation of Barotseland as a native state and to the formation of a purely native province round the basin of Lake Victoria?

(*A.*) "I do not altogether believe in native states. I do not think they get on fast enough. In my opinion it is not a good policy for the future. I do not think it is wise to give native peoples the idea that they are going to work out their destiny entirely apart from us, or us from them. I believe that the only way we can civilise tropical Africa is through our own people—through this dual policy which we have accepted and adopted. I am one of those people who believe that there is no hope for Africa and the Africans except under the control and guidance of our own people."

(*Q.*) Do you approve of Lord Lugard's suggestion that the settled part of Kenya should be detached from the rest of the country and become a separate white state?

(*A.*) "I think it would be quite impossible to run a small highland country at the top of a hill cut off from the coast and from the Lake. I do not think it could be done economically, financially or in any other way. It is completely against the sort of ideal and policy which one hopes to see adopted in East Africa."

(*Q.*) Are you anxious to see federation brought about?

(*A.*) "In the past in Kenya there has been a very strong political feeling against federation. Therefore the matter has had to be approached by those who believe in federation from a rather tentative point of view. I myself and a great many others always believed that it was impossible for these states to go on drifting into agreements on different subjects without any peg on which to hang them, and without any idea of where they would lead us in the future. For that and other reasons many of us believed that a federation of some sort was necessary."

(*Q.*) Why do you suggest that the Kenya Legislative Council should be given an elected majority?

(*A.*) "We believe that the time has come. I feel that the longer the day is put off when our people get control, the more you excite questions between them and the other races of the country which will in the end give trouble. I feel that if you put the responsibility on your own people they will take it up, and that responsibility will be in the hands of people who, after all, belong to the country and are in a position to take part in the formation of its policy.

"Apart from that, I think a system of Crown colony government under an official majority is a terrific waste of time. You have a very large number of officials sitting on a Council who do not in the least want to sit there, and who take no part in the debates and are excluded from them by the official machine. If you had an unofficial majority the Government would allow its officers to give their own opinion as individuals.

"I have never found myself in the past two years in a position where we could not get a thing passed in Council, but the difficulty is to get it carried out. I believe myself that if the Civil service was to some extent under the control of the people of the country, things could be done in a very different way. Elected members can act as a spur on the Government—but the spur has got no rowels to it.

"The only reason why Kenya has pressed for this federation is that she believes that for certain imperial issues it would be best. We believe, on the other hand, that what we have lived for, our ideals, might run the risk of being lost if we had no last ditch into which we could get to cover up in case of difficulties. An elected majority would be our last ditch in the event of our allying ourselves with two countries at a lower state of development."

(*Q.*) Do you agree that there is a clash of economic interests between natives and Europeans which makes it undesirable to give the Europeans any control over native policy?

(*A.*) "I do not see any other outcome except to trust your own people. I cannot think of any other ultimate safeguard for natives.

"If the feeling that your own people are not to be trusted and that they do things to natives of which evidence would be hard to find, goes on sufficiently long, you will ultimately harden the feeling in the country that there is an economic or political split between the two.

"I do not personally believe that there is. I believe it is to our interests to develop the reserves for the benefit of the country as a whole and to push on with the development of the natives, remembering the effect that that development will have on the prosperity of the country as a whole. . . . The two interests are identical.

"We are not asking for complete control of natives. Under anything short of dominion status you would continue to keep the main control of natives in the hands of some impartial authority. The ultimate veto in all racial questions would rest with the Secretary of State."

(*Q.*) What do you think should be the future political destiny of the native?

(*A.*) "The policy we visualise for the time being is that the natives should to a very large extent govern their own affairs in their own reserves through the native councils. Ultimately some co-ordination of these native councils should take place. Finally there should be a central native council which should be brought into close liaison with the ordinary legislature, so that the whole thing would go forward together."

Little evidence could be obtained from the native community, for very few natives were sufficiently advanced to understand the issue. The overwhelming majority were inarticulate. The Kabaka of Uganda expressed nervousness lest a change of constitution should affect the agreement of 1900 under which his kingdom was recognised as a practically autonomous state. Three Warusha chiefs from Tanganyika opposed federation because they had been told that it would result in their having their finger-prints taken. But native opinion as a whole could not be gauged because it was non-existent.

8

The Hilton Young report was not published until January 1929, a year after the commission's visit to East Africa. It came as a disappointment both to people in Kenya and to the Secretary of State.

The keynote of the report was the need for co-ordination of the native policies in East Africa. In the main it was an essay on the future needs and aspirations of the natives. The commissioners had been asked to suggest ways and means of co-ordinating railways, customs, research and the like. They replied that the question of native policy was of such importance as to overshadow everything else, and they laid down the lines along which native development should, in their opinion, proceed.

In reply to the central question "Is closer union in East Africa desirable?" they answered "Yes". Federation was to start with two groups, a northern and a southern. For the northern group they suggested the setting up of a central authority, first a High Commissioner and then a Governor-General with far more dictatorial powers than had ever been contemplated. His main task was to frame native policy for the three territories. Nothing in the nature of a federal council composed of representatives of each territory was visualised to confirm his decisions, to act as a brake on his activities or to provide an outlet for local opinion.

The Governor-General was to be given authority to enact any legislation he thought necessary in the face of the united opposition of any or all of the three legislative bodies; and he was to be empowered to override any legislation passed in the local councils. He was, in fact, to be a virtual dictator. An advisory council comprised of the Governors of the three territories was to be the only body to assist him. The report defined his status as that of "a local projection of the personality of the Secretary of State".

From the colonists' point of view this scheme of closer union seemed to mark a retrograde step. If the entire direction of native policy, railways, customs and other services as well was to pass into the hands of a Governor-General, without even a council on which unofficial opinion was represented to advise him, the colonists would be surrendering rather than increasing their influence in public affairs. By no stretch of the imagination, they said, could such a scheme be said to associate them more closely (as the white paper had promised) in the Imperial Government's discharge of its trusteeship. On the contrary: trusteeship was to be more than ever a closely guarded prerogative of the Colonial Office.

The colonists' hopes of an increase in their power in the Kenya Legislative Council, which had been raised by the Cabinet's white paper, were dashed again by the commission. The idea of responsible government must, the majority report said, be abandoned for all time. It was out of the question. It could only come when the natives were advanced enough to share in the central government at least on equal terms with the Europeans. However long this might take, the Imperial Government must not contemplate handing over any part of its responsibilities to the colonists.

The chairman disagreed with Sir Reginald Mant, Sir George Schuster and Mr. Oldham on this fundamental issue. "I am unable to join in the opinion that responsible government and a majority of elected representatives in the legislature must be ruled out as a suitable form of government for Kenya", he wrote in his minority report. He maintained that the setting up of a strong central authority with full powers to settle any racial issue would do away with the objections to responsible government in Kenya. So long as the Imperial Government did not relax its hold on native affairs there could be no risk of a small group of whites imposing their will on a large mass of helpless natives. The Governor-General would be on the spot to hold the racial balance even.

9

Sir Hilton Young also parted company with his colleagues on another vital point. This was the matter of the common roll. The Indians, who had never reconciled themselves to the communal roll, won the sympathy of Sir Reginald Mant, and the question was reopened by the commission. The majority report suggested that the decision reached with so much difficulty by the Conservative Government in 1923 and categorically confirmed by the Labour Government in 1924[1] should be reversed and that a common roll should be

[1] Mr. J. H. Thomas, Secretary of State for the Colonies, endorsed the 1923 decision in these words, spoken on August 7th, 1924: "I have given careful consideration to representations in favour of a common roll, but I am not prepared to resist the conclusions arrived at in the command paper 1922 that in the special circum-

introduced for Europeans, Indians and detribalised natives, with an education and property qualification.

It was only to be expected that a report which bluntly declared the ideal of responsible government to be a hopeless one, which aroused Indian agitation by supporting the common roll and which proposed to amputate most of the powers of the Legislative Council, would have a cold reception from the colonists of East Africa.

An emergency meeting of elected members and the executive of the Convention of Associations was held in Nairobi and a strong telegram of protest was despatched to the Secretary of State. The conference felt, said the message, that the majority report was based on a bureaucratic conception and was a reversal of the spirit of the white paper. The tendency all through to minimise the interests of the Europeans and consider only those of the natives was "bound to encourage partisan and anti-native feeling among Europeans which hitherto has been absent".

"By banging the door to any prospect of ultimate responsible government," the message concluded, "the report is sure to bring about more vigorous action on the part of the colonists to assert their views." The theory that the more advanced and civilised section of the country's inhabitants "must stand still until the backward races (whom the report itself describes as twenty centuries behind the Europeans) have reached their standard is an impossible proposition, in which no white or governing race could be expected to acquiesce".

From Mr. Amery's point of view the report was little more satisfactory. The cleavage of opinion between the chairman and the rest of the members, for one thing, greatly weakened its force. And it had gone off at a political tangent. Mr. Amery had been thinking economically. He believed that the right way to approach closer union was to lead people up to it gradually by co-ordinating first one service and then another, showing them that their interests lay in co-operation and not in sectionalism. Political union should follow

stances of Kenya, with four diverse communities each of which will ultimately require electoral representation, the communal system is the best way to secure fair representation of each and all of these communities."

economic agreements by easy stages. But the Hilton Young commission had stirred up a hornet's nest. All the old suspicions that had been so carefully allayed by the white paper, by Delamere's unofficial conferences and by Sir Edward Grigg's propaganda, were revived.

10

Mr. Amery lost no time in trying to pull his federal baby out of the fire before it was too badly burned to survive. He despatched the head permanent official at the Colonial Office, Sir Samuel Wilson, to East Africa to discuss the recommendations of the Hilton Young report and to draw up a workable and acceptable scheme for closer union. His task, in fact, was to tone down the commission's findings to a pitch at which local agreement could be secured.

A few days' acquaintance with East Africa convinced Sir Samuel Wilson of the difficulties of his mission. Everyone with whom he talked seemed to reject any idea of closer union. The Europeans in Kenya had turned against it, he wrote in a report of his mission,[1] because they feared (after reading the Hilton Young report) that it would mean the abandonment of the dual policy and the sacrifice of their interests in order that Kenya policy might be brought into line with that of Uganda and Tanganyika. The Indians were "so imbued with the idea of obtaining the common roll that they were unlikely to consider any proposal for closer union until they had gained their main object." The natives of Uganda were "strongly opposed to any scheme because for some reason they feared that it would entail the control of their destinies being transferred to Kenya."

Everyone, in fact, was badly scared. To complicate matters still further the Rt. Hon. Srinivasa Sastri was sent officially from Delhi to present to Sir Samuel Wilson the case for greater political privileges for Indians. The Kenya Indians demanded that half the members whom the Hilton Young commission had suggested should be nominated to the Legislative Council to represent native interests should be Indians.

[1] Cmd. 3378 of 1929.

It was difficult to secure any agreement in this atmosphere of suspicion. Sir Samuel Wilson succeeded, however, in drawing up a concrete scheme of economic co-ordination to which the Governors and all sections of the population of the three territories, with the exception of the Kenya Indians, agreed. It provided for the appointment of a High Commissioner to be assisted by a federal council, with an official majority, on which all three territories would be represented. The Kenya Legislative Council was to be reconstituted with a complicated balance of four groups—officials, elected Europeans, nominated members to represent general (including native) interests, and Indians—none of which was to have a clear majority. The colonists abandoned their demand for a majority of elected members with considerable reluctance, but they agreed to the scheme.

The final plan was an intricate one, carrying all the germs of sectional strife. The Europeans suspected that the proposed council was too delicately balanced a piece of mechanism to stand the wear-and tear of ordinary political usage. But it did present a *modus vivendi* and reopened the door to an immediate measure of closer union. It was no small achievement on Sir Samuel Wilson's part to have persuaded the Kenya colonists to drop their claim for an elected majority in spite of their deep distrust of the federation idea engendered by the Hilton Young report.

But the Wilson scheme, which seemed at last to have rounded up the scattered points of view into a corral of consent, was never to be translated into practice. Once again action was strangled by delay.

Before Sir Samuel Wilson had completed his enquiries in East Africa a change of government occurred in Britain and Mr. Amery was forced to leave his scheme to the mercy of his successor. The Wilson report was presented in the summer of 1929 to Lord Passfield, the new Secretary of State for the Colonies. And closer union was not a child of the Labour Government. They were in no hurry to adopt it.

Even after the change of government, federation on the lines of the Wilson report nearly became a reality.

Sir Edward Grigg, who had been summoned to England for discussion once again early in 1929, left London in the summer under the impression that his new master intended to pursue the scheme. Lord Passfield had, at that time, indicated his intention of accepting the Wilson plan. But like other Secretaries of State before him, he changed his mind.

Sir Samuel Wilson's recommendations, in particular the granting of an unofficial majority in Kenya and the shelving of the question of the common roll, did not commend themselves to some of Lord Passfield's colleagues in the Labour Cabinet. The Secretary of State for India, Mr. Wedgwood Benn, was strongly opposed to them. The Wilson report was not accepted.

A year later the Government issued a further white paper embodying their own conclusions,[1] and, after another long and abortive enquiry, the idea of an East African federation was abandoned.

[1] See Chapter XXV, p. 277.

CHAPTER XXIII

THE SUNBEAM PERIOD
1927–1929

I

AFTER the elections of 1927 Delamere turned his attention for a time to his farm. His manager, Mr. Long, resigned in 1926, and in the interim before a successor could be found Delamere ran Soysambu and the Laikipia sheep farm himself.

No detail was too small for his attention. He kept the milk records, issued orders that the wheels of all cars passing from areas infected with sheep disease on to uncontaminated farms should be sprayed, ordered an eye-bath for a herd's children. His headquarters were at Soysambu but he spent much of his time on the Laikipia sheep-run, once more in a rough hut with sacking for a door, supervising the erection of more dips and wool sheds.

He was able to fit many activities into his day because he never wasted time. "As I have just had a burst tyre on the road I am taking the opportunity of writing to you", he scribbled to one of his assistant managers, sitting on the roadside while the driver changed the wheel. "You have about 1600 ewes with lambs for sale. They will be sold this year as soon after their lambs have been weaned as they can be got right. . . ." And again, "I happened to be coming through Nyeri and I found a lot of dissatisfaction about the difficulty of getting rid of their wheat. . . . Excuse this scrawl but I am on the road."

Records of correspondence at this period make curious reading. Accounts of dipping experiments on batches of wethers alternate with observations on the Nakuru drainage system. Instructions about the colour schemes of the flower-beds at Loresho follow a draft cable to the Premier of

Southern Rhodesia concerning an official conference. A telegram, "Send up as soon as possible six tubs of geraniums", indicates last-minute preparations for the arrival of week-end guests.

Delamere's character had undergone a remarkable change since the war. Before, he was inclined to be silent and abstemious. He disliked social events and only plunged occasionally into bouts of festivity. Now he spent frequent evenings at Muthaiga club, giving enormous dinner and supper parties. He had become extremely loquacious and the popping of champagne corks was as music in his ears. He would fritter as much on a week's parties as he spent, in his pioneer days, on a year's living.

His extraordinary vitality allowed him to live a treble life—as a farmer, as a politician and as a leader of local society. He seemed to need no sleep. Sometimes he would dance all night, breakfast at sunrise, drive home to bath and change, and then issue the day's orders for work on the coffee plantation. He would be back in Nairobi by ten o'clock for a meeting and continue all day. If Legislative Council was sitting he would make perhaps half a dozen speeches before the evening brought round another party.

No dance was complete without his bubbling flow of conversation, his antics designed to egg on the band to brighter efforts, his impish smile and, above all, his generous hospitality.

2

During the "sunbeam period" Kenya became fashionable. People had money to spend and some of them came to East Africa to do it. Rich sportsmen flocked there to shoot or photograph big game. Others came for less adventurous but, to their minds, no less entertaining forms of sport, for which the atmosphere of Kenya—African without being too uncomfortable and far enough off the beaten track to be original—provided a pleasant background. The country was acquiring a reputation, provided mainly by its visitors, which seemed almost to justify a wisecrack of the period: "Are you married, or do you live in Kenya?"

A branch of the bright young people (though few of them

were really young) established itself in the highlands and provided vivid local colour for the visitors. Under the stimulus of the altitude they found it easy to liquidate their inhibitions.

Many picturesque characters flitted across the Kenya stage during these few years of pre-depression prosperity. Few of them passed through without enjoying Delamere's hospitality. Muthaiga club achieved a reputation, or a notoriety, reaching beyond the borders of the colony. Only occasionally did it disappoint the hopeful guest. "I have heard of your Muthaiga in London, in Paris, in New York," a titled lady visitor, no longer young and amply proportioned, once complained, "but—where is the danger?"

This outburst of sophisticated gaiety was a passing phase. Then the depression came, the flow of visitors dwindled, and many of those who had settled in the highlands for reasons more frivolous than farming left the country. Only a few scattered outposts remained to keep up, as best they could, the traditions of a brief and vanished age.

In the prosperity period Delamere's farms at last started to make big profits. For twenty years he had kept his faith in sheep. Now they began to justify it. His flocks on Laikipia grew until 40,000 sheep were grazing over the downs. The wool clip went up steadily and prices were high. In the peak year—1926—he received £34,000 for his wool alone, and of this about £20,000 was working profit. But, of course, it belonged to the banks.

Delamere spent money so easily that he was often assumed to be a very wealthy man, even to have made a fortune. Had the sunbeam period lasted this might have been the case. As it was a huge overdraft had to be wiped off before any money that he made was his to spend. The sunbeam faded before it could melt his frozen debts.

3

Before the war Delamere had shown that the country could grow wheat. Then he had demonstrated that sheep could be profitably run. Now he turned to a third branch of farming—dairying. He resolved to prove that Kenya could be made into a first-class dairying country.

He had no doubt that this was so. Kenya had many of the advantages possessed by New Zealand: a mild climate with no severe winters, an evenly distributed rainfall, grazing all the year round and no winter feeding. Cattle diseases and high freights were to Kenya's disadvantage; cheaper land and labour were in her favour.

In about 1925 he started to develop his 1600-acre farm at Naivasha as a model dairying concern. He stocked it with high grade Friesian cows and continued to grade them up until they were practically pure-bred. He introduced milk-recording and balanced production rations, grew lucerne under irrigation for dry-weather feeding, practised scientific calf rearing. A fully equipped dairy was built and in a short time he secured a good contract for the sale of milk in Nairobi.

Satisfied with this experiment, he turned his attention to encouraging dairying in the country at large. He was anxious to do so for several reasons. One was idealistic: intensive dairying called for comparatively small farms and so encouraged closer settlement; like Rhodes, he wanted to see "homes, more homes" established in the highlands. Another was economic: dairying needed only a small labour force and Delamere believed it to be essential that settlers should become less reliant on large supplies of native labour. Besides, there was a good export market for butter and Kenya must, above all things, increase her exports. A third was scientific: the continuous production of a single crop such as maize exhausted the land. It would eventually become necessary to replace the nutriment extracted every year from the soil and the soundest way of effecting this was to shift on to a basis of mixed farming.

Two things were needed, he decided, before the industry could become a success. One was the establishment of more creameries; there was only one in Kenya. The other was a widespread and vigorous campaign against the greatest cattle scourge of the country, East Coast fever. He determined to tackle both.

His first step was to start a new co-operative creamery at Naivasha. He called a meeting of the surrounding farmers in 1925 and secured their support. As his contribution he gave a slice of his farm for the site of the factory and started the subscription list for the capital required with a sum of £2500. In order to ensure that the creamery should be started off on the most efficient and up-to-date lines he sent to Australia for an expert to plan and launch the new organisation.

Delamere recognised that co-operation often involved sacrifices in the early stages and he was quite prepared to make them. Under his contract for the sale of milk in Nairobi he received 1s. 2d. a gallon. As soon as the Naivasha co-operative creamery opened he cancelled this contract and sold all his butter-fat to the creamery at a rate which worked out at slightly under 6d. a gallon for milk. For the first six months of the creamery's life he waived payment for his cream altogether in order to give the factory a start.

The first butter sent out of Kenya was exported in 1926. The pioneer consignments fetched a price only slightly below that of the best New Zealand. Delamere and others who had urged the extension of dairying—Sir Edward Grigg was prominent among them—had not been mistaken.

4

After the Naivasha creamery proved itself a success a third was started. Then competition between the three began. It was clear to Delamere that if this was allowed to continue the creameries would eventually collapse, as so many co-operative enterprises had done before them all over the world for similar reasons. They must be persuaded to amalgamate.

Securing agreement among small bands of farmers to avoid internecine war reproduces in miniature the difficulties of securing agreement among nations to avoid international war. Everyone agrees with the principle; no one is willing to limit his right to manage his own affairs in his own way and to pursue his own immediate advantage.

Delamere worked incessantly at the task and eventually he succeeded. In 1930 Kenya Co-operative Creameries Ltd. was formed. Henceforward the creameries pooled their finances and competition ceased. The dairying industry expanded and in a few years two-thirds of the colony's output of butter was exported. Later, the creameries agreed to buy native as well as European-produced cream, provided it came up to the proper standards, and an example of black and white economic co-operation was set.

Delamere did everything in his power to encourage co-operative marketing. He handed over all his shares in the flour mill, Unga Ltd., for example, to the Wheatgrowers' Association. This later became incorporated in the Kenya Farmers' Association, an organisation for the co-operative disposal of Kenya's farm produce.

By 1926 Unga Ltd. had recovered from its financial difficulties. Delamere did not turn up for the annual general meeting and in his absence the other shareholders voted themselves a dividend of 10 per cent—the first ever declared.

At the end of the meeting, just as the shareholders were about to leave, Delamere arrived and was told of the decision. He refused to accept it. He was bound by his promise made to the Governor in 1922, when a protective duty on flour was imposed, never to make a profit out of Unga Ltd. He appealed to the shareholders to rescind the dividend and told them that he would dispose of his shares before the next meeting. The shareholders agreed, and the dividend was not declared.

A few months later he transferred his shares to the Wheatgrowers' Association. For technical reasons he was unable to make them over for nothing, as he wished to do. He was paid their face value—about half what he himself had given for them and about one-eighth of their market value at the time.

"It is the simple truth", wrote the manager of Unga Ltd., "that during the eighteen years in which Lord Delamere was financially interested in Unga Ltd. he was concerned with the sole object of fostering the wheat industry and with no thought of benefiting himself."

5

The biggest difficulty with which dairying in Kenya had to contend was the prevalence of animal diseases. Some, once fatal and widespread, had been virtually conquered by vaccines produced by scientific research. Such were rinderpest, anthrax and pleuro-pneumonia. (Delamere was largely to thank for checking a severe outbreak of pleuro-pneumonia after the war. The disease was rife throughout the Northern Frontier province and infection was threatening to spread southwards into reserves and settled areas alike. As a result of Delamere's insistence in Legislative Council a committee was appointed to go into the matter. It recommended the free distribution of pleuro-pneumonia vaccine. Again through Delamere's persistence, this policy was adopted and veterinary officers were enabled to immunise native stock and so to prevent the outbreak from spreading all over the country.) Other diseases had so far defied the patience and cunning of the research worker and could only be dealt with by guarding the susceptible animal from infection. Of these by far the worst was East Coast fever.

The only way in which East Coast fever could be tackled effectively was by regular dipping and by fencing into paddocks. In South Africa these measures had freed practically the whole of the Dominion from infection.

In East Africa the problem was much more difficult. Infection was not endemic in the greater part of the Union. All cattle were therefore susceptible when the disease was first introduced. Farmers had no alternative but to dip. But in East Africa infection had existed since time unknown, and native cattle in infected areas had gradually acquired a measure of immunity. Settlers were therefore able to obtain immune native cattle for draft purposes, so that the necessity to tackle the disease did not become acute.

An elaborate system of quarantine had been set up. The colony was networked with boundaries between clean and dirty areas and no cattle from a dirty district were allowed to pass over into a clean one. But in spite of these measures East Coast fever was spreading. Delamere saw clearly that until the question was tackled on a wholesale basis the disease would gradually encroach into clean areas until eventually the whole country would be in danger of infection.

The only way to deal with the matter, he believed, was to introduce compulsory fencing and dipping. For several years he campaigned energetically in favour of this measure.

"To dairy as a country", he said, "you must have cattle and plenty of them, and this is impossible until we tame our country. It is wild now. Fencing and dipping and destruction of vermin are necessities of the situation."

In 1927 a conference of stock-owners from all parts of Kenya was held in Nairobi and resolutions were passed urging the Government to take immediate steps to eradicate East Coast fever. In due course a compulsory dipping and fencing ordinance was prepared and introduced into Legislative Council by Delamere, who had been largely responsible for drawing it up. Any district could bring itself under the scope of the ordinance by a majority vote of two-thirds of the farmers. Then compulsion would be applied to the minority. The ordinance could also be enforced in the reserves at the wish of the local native councils.

This measure was purely an economic one. It had no political implications. Yet it became entangled in politics and held up, as a result, for an indefinite period. It provided a clear example of the interweaving of practical farming matters and political issues, and of the the way in which delays and arguments of politicians sometimes handicap agriculture just as severely as the inflictions of grubs, caterpillars, droughts and market fluctuations.

6

Dipping and fencing, both expensive improvements, could not, clearly, be made compulsory unless some provision was made to loan capital to the poorer settlers so as to enable them to carry out the provisions of the law. It was an essential part of the scheme that advances to farmers were to be made from the land bank.

But there was still no land bank. The settlers had asked for one persistently for the past ten years and more. Sir Edward Northey had put it high on his list of the country's needs in 1919, but he had failed to secure the money. Sir Edward Grigg had taken the matter up very shortly after his arrival. He was convinced that it was one of Kenya's most pressing necessities.

Kenya was probably the only purely agricultural country

in the world without any system of agricultural credits. Farmers had no way of borrowing money for permanent improvements except by securing an overdraft from their bank at 8 per cent or over. There was absolutely no machinery for short-term loans, an essential part of farm finance in any country, and the farmer who wanted to raise money for the planting of his next season's crop had often to borrow it at a very high rate from the brokers who handled his produce, on the security of the next harvest. As a result the brokers had in many cases secured a hold over their clients, and the banks had been forced to meet a necessity for which they were not designed to provide. Even England, most industrially minded of countries, had provided its farmers with some facilities for cheap credit.

Sir Edward Grigg endeavoured for five years to get a land bank scheme put through. He did not succeed within his term of office.

At first the difficulty of financing the bank delayed a settlement. The Colonial Office refused to agree to the floating of a loan and the Governor wanted to see at least a million pounds set aside as capital. By 1928, however, Kenya's finances were in such a sound position that she had managed to save up nearly £800,000 as surplus balances. The Colonial Office could hardly object to her using a part of this reserve to start a land bank on a small scale.

But the change of government in Britain in 1929 supervened just before an agreement was reached. Then the question took on a political tinge. Lord Passfield raised objections to the proposed land bank scheme because he felt that European settlers rather than natives would be getting the benefit of the surplus balances. And so the land bank was held up once more. It was finally established, on a very small scale, in 1931. By that time it was too late to save many farmers who had been forced to borrow money at a high rate of interest in the first stages of the world depression.

Until the land bank materialised the dipping and fencing ordinance—on whose necessity all were agreed—could not be enforced, the East Coast fever question could not be seriously tackled, the advance of the dairy industry was hampered and the colony's economic progress was delayed.

7

Running parallel with the development of dairying, mainly a European concern, was the task of putting the native stock industry on to an economic footing. In this Delamere was also interested and in 1926 he took part in the first experiment made to find an outlet for surplus native stock.

The problem of overstocking in the native reserves was a chronic one which neither the Imperial nor the local Government had made any serious attempt to solve. They had, in fact, refused to face it, in spite of repeated warnings from the Veterinary department and from experienced stockmen in all parts of the country that a day of reckoning would come.

The problem briefly, was this. Since science and British rule had preserved native herds from periodic decimation by disease, native-owned herds of cattle, sheep and goats had multiplied like mayflies. In 1924 there were estimated to be slightly more than three million cattle in the colony. By 1930 there were about five million head, and three years later the Kenya Land commission estimated the number at six million. In a decade, therefore, the cattle population had doubled itself. Sheep had been almost as prolific, and goats, the most useless of stock, had multiplied even more.

No corresponding improvement had been made in the pastures. The carrying capacity of the land had not been increased. Nor could the natives migrate, as they had once been accustomed to do, in search of new grazing from which, if necessary, they would drive the occupants with spear and sword.

In a few areas there was room for the increase. In others there was not.[1] Here overstocking became acute. The effect on the land was disastrous. Cattle, sheep and goats ate down

---

[1] It was calculated by the agricultural commission of 1929 that the Machakos section of the Akamba reserve was carrying 190,000 head of cattle, whereas the maximum number that could be adequately supported by the pastures was 60,000. A reduction of cattle by two-thirds of the total was therefore necessary to prevent destruction of the grazing.

An example of the amazingly rapid increase in stock is provided by the Samburu tribe. Before the Masai move they owned practically no cattle owing to fear of Masai raids. In 1928 there were 115,000 head of Samburu stock (largely cattle) owned by 6500 people on the Leroki plateau.

the grass so frequently that it had no chance to recuperate after the rains. Patches of it died, and in so doing bared the earth to the attacks of the elements. Rain beat upon it and swept the good soil away. The sun hammered on it and pulverised it into dust. Then the wind clawed it and whirled it away in clouds of broken particles. Erosion so robbed it of its virtue that no protective coat of grass would grow again to shelter it. The land was rendered useless, and the stock were concentrated more densely on surviving pastures until these, too, were eaten down to the point where erosion began.

So a vicious circle of overstocking and erosion was set up. Only certain areas were affected, but the process was one which was growing steadily and progressively worse in many parts of Africa. The longer it was left unchecked the more intractable it became. The policy of *laisser-faire* was one of robbing future generations. Nor could the question be solved by adding to the reserves, for more land merely stimulated an increase of stock, and it would only be a question of time —and a very short time at that—before the new pastures would be destroyed, like the old, by ever-growing herds.

8

The only effective solution, in the long run, was to persuade native owners to sell their surplus stock for cash.

There were many difficulties in the way. Chief among these was the African's immemorial regard for his animals as currency. A cow was not, in his eyes, a source of milk, or a sheep a satisfaction for hunger. It was a golden sovereign or a florin piece. With his stock he bought his wives and reckoned his wealth and standing in the tribe.

Education might change his attitude; but overstocking would not wait upon the erection of schools.

Few natives recognised the meaning of quality, and the conception of breeding from the best was foreign to the native stockman's mind. One cow was worth as much as another when it came to reckoning up the bride-price. Efforts to persuade the pastoral tribes to kill off their more useless animals met with blank opposition. As well ask a European to tear up a pound note because it was dirty and crumpled as to suggest to a Suk or M'Kamba that he should get rid of a bull because it was scraggy and malformed.

The resulting system was wasteful in the extreme. Flocks and herds multiplied rapidly in good years and perished like armies in modern warfare in a drought. Millions of animals were dammed up uselessly without an outlet to the markets of the world. Out of the 6 million native cattle in Kenya only 20,000 were annually sold. "The Masai have a country about the size of Denmark", Delamere remarked, "and the country draws nothing from it except for a few hides. This, after all, is rather a defeatist policy—that you only get the products of dead animals, animals that have died of starvation and disease."

What was to be done about it? The answer was not obscure. Factories should be erected in or near pastoral reserves to convert culls and surplus beasts into meat products—beef extract, dried meat, blood-and-bone meal, fertilisers and other by-products.

This scheme would benefit the natives in two ways. Their useless stock would be converted into wealth; and they would be enabled to buy cheap meat products. For it was a curious fact that some of the tribes richest in live-stock, such as the Akamba, rarely touched meat. They continued to live on a diet deficient in protein, to the great detriment of their health, while surrounded by vast herds of cattle. "In the midst of plenty", said the Kenya Land commission, "the natives in pastoral and semi-pastoral areas are living under conditions of extreme poverty."

The first effort to interest private concerns in the starting of a meat factory was made by the Government in 1923. An area of land at Kiu was offered to a British firm but the conditions were too severe to attract the necessary capital. In 1924 the veterinary adviser to the East African Governments, the late Mr. R. E. Montgomery, visited the Argentine to study methods there, but he was unsuccessful in persuading other British meat factory firms to take an interest in East Africa. One of them secured better terms from Southern Rhodesia and started a factory there.

9

On Mr. Montgomery's return to Kenya he determined to try an experiment for himself to prove the soundness of his beliefs. Early in 1926 he formed a small company to operate a trial factory at Mwanza in Tanganyika Territory. Delamere, who was an enthusiastic supporter of the meat factory idea, subscribed part of the capital and became a director. The other members of the board (besides Mr. Montgomery) were the director of a bank in Nairobi, a Kenya settler, the deputy director of Agriculture in Kenya and the Treasurer of Tanganyika. Meat Rations Ltd., as it was called, was given a free site for its factory, free grazing, and a guarantee of interest on the capital for ten years by the Tanganyika Government. The chief product of the factory was to be dried meat for local native consumption. The project was at first a success; but later, when the depression came, it had to call on the Tanganyika Government's guarantee.

The Kenya Government then appointed a committee to enquire whether a similar scheme would work in the colony. The members reported that a meat factory was unlikely to be a success unless the Government would guarantee a regular supply of stock. Failing this, the natives would probably refuse to sell their cattle to the factory at an economic price.

This question of bringing compulsion to bear on natives to sell their culls was the stumbling-block. All the big companies which had been approached by the Kenya Government had insisted on obtaining some assurance that the supply of stock would not be allowed to dry up without warning. Natives, unlike Europeans, did not have to sell their produce in order to live. They could take it off the market whenever they felt so inclined. Some sort of government compulsion as a substitute for economic pressure was needed if capital was to be sunk in an expensive plant which could not afford to stand idle at the natives' whim.

The Kenya Government had equipped itself with the power to exercise compulsion under an ordinance (passed in 1926) entitling it to compel natives to cull stock or grade crops in their own interests; but it was afraid to apply the ordinance—afraid partly of the reactions of difficult and temperamental tribes like the Masai, and even more afraid of invoking another storm of criticism from England on the grounds of ill-treating and exploiting the native. The principle of compulsion was therefore rejected.

Delamere believed that the Government, by refusing to contemplate compulsion, was shirking its duty. There was a great deal of talk about trusteeship for the natives, yet the Government on whom it rested seemed singularly unwilling to shoulder a concrete responsibility when one appeared.

Trusteeship, after all, was not just a matter of giving the ward anything he asked for and then accepting his grateful thanks. A good trustee must sometimes order his ward to do, for his own good, things that the ward dislikes. To shrink from this duty through fear of incurring unpopularity was a lamentable admission of weakness. If the Government was really as anxious as it claimed to be to encourage native development it could not find a better way to do so than to show the natives, if necessary with compulsion, how to turn their millions of useless cattle into a valuable asset.

Yet the only attempt to tackle the problem was left to a private company (and one with two settlers on the board); and an application from Kenya for imperial support was at once rejected.

A new meat factory scheme was submitted in 1930 to the committee administering the Colonial Development Fund in London. Under these proposals the meat works was to be an ambitious and costly affair owned and operated wholly by the Government. Sir Edward Grigg's original suggestion was that Meat Rations Ltd. should actually run the factory as agents for the Government. Delamere opposed and defeated this, because he felt that if the Kenya Government forced natives to sell their culls, it would lay itself open to criticism for using compulsion in the interests of a private company.

The scheme was rejected by the Colonial Development Advisory committee on the somewhat casuistical ground that its object was to check deterioration rather than to promote development. The Kenya Government was by that time nearing a financial crisis and could not itself find the money.

And so the project lapsed; and the overstocking problem remained as far from a solution as ever. With every season that it was allowed to go unattacked the reserves grew more denuded, and the sum that the Kenya Government would eventually have to pay out in famine relief to natives who were busily destroying their only source of sustenance mounted year by year.

10

In a colony such as Kenya the presiding Governor's personality is an important factor. A "live wire" will carry the current all through the country and energise every part of its mechanism. A man content to leave things as they are is apt to cause friction by his very inertia, for he is resisting the current of progress instead of creating it.

In Sir Edward Grigg Kenya had an imaginative and energetic ruler, and during his régime Kenya made rapid economic progress, in spite of the handicaps of a prolonged partial drought and a plague of locusts. He was a firm believer in "government by agreement"—"the only civilised method of government" as Delamere had described it—and during his five years of office co-operation between officials and elected members resulted in many important measures being discussed, agreed and put into effect with comparatively little friction. The principal advances, briefly summarised, were as follows:

DEVELOPMENT.—In 1926 exports exceeded imports for the first time, and in the following year they reached a record of nearly £3 millions. This was due mainly to white enterprise. Each European occupier exported, on the average, just under £1000 worth of produce in the year. More land was being taken up every year. By 1927 there were nearly 5 million acres under European occupation.

Sir Edward Grigg's development projects were financed out of a loan of £8,500,000 raised, on the colony's own security and without imperial guarantees, shortly after his appointment. The "cotton loan" presented to the colony in 1924 was repaid and a sum of £5 millions was left over for new development. With some of this, four new deep-water berths were built at Kilindini. When they were completed the port, with six such berths, was the finest on the east coast north of Durban.

RAILWAYS.—Most of the new loan was spent on railway expansion. The line to Uganda was completed, opening up a big area north-east of Lake Victoria for native cotton production. The extension of the Thika line to Nyeri was also finished. This passed through seventy miles of the richest part of the Kikuyu reserve and tapped a European coffee, wheat and timber area beyond. It was later continued through a stock and dairying district to Nanyuki. Two branch lines into closely settled maize-growing districts, and finally a branch through the north Kavirondo reserve where cotton growing and other native production was being encouraged, were added.

Under the combined stimuli of mounting exports, new development and good management the railway flourished. Earnings doubled between 1922 and 1927, while working expenses remained almost the same. The cost of carrying one ton of produce for one mile was brought down from twelve cents in 1922 to five cents in 1929, a figure slightly lower than the comparable cost on the South African railways. (In Nigeria and in Britain the figure worked out at nine cents a ton mile.)

There was one set-back to go on the debit side. This was the sudden death of Sir Christian Felling in 1928. The general manager had a physiological peculiarity: he could not take quinine. In 1927 he had a severe attack of malaria. He was strongly advised, while in England shortly afterwards, not to return to Africa, for another attack might prove fatal. He could have obtained an appointment elsewhere, but he was too devoted to his work in Kenya to abandon it. The warning was justified: he contracted malaria and died.

"I am so upset on hearing about Felling I do not know what to do", Delamere wrote. "Apart from the fact that it will be difficult to hold the finances of the country together as they depend to an extraordinary degree on the railway—apart from that, the country has lost its soundest man, and personally I have lost a great friend."

GOVERNMENT.—The introduction of a system of local self-government in the settled areas was the outstanding event. Up to 1927 the position in Kenya was a curious anomaly. The least-developed community, the Africans, had secured greater powers over their own affairs than the Europeans. Native councils could raise rates and spend the money in almost any way they thought fit, subject only to the Governor's formal approval. The Europeans were not entitled to levy rates to build roads, bridges or schools.

In 1926 a High Court judge from the Transvaal, Mr. Justice Feetham (who had been chairman of the Irish Boundaries commission), came up from South Africa to work out a scheme for giving Europeans in the settled areas as much scope to govern themselves as was already possessed by natives in the reserves. The plan was also to enable the Government to decentralise such functions as the upkeep of roads. Mr. Justice Feetham drew up a carefully designed framework of local government for settled areas and in the following year his plans were put into effect.

SURVEYS.—Technical experts followed one another to Kenya to advise on its development. An irrigation expert came from South Africa. Water-boring machines were imported and toured the country burrowing shafts to tap underground rivers, mostly in the native reserves. As a result of Delamere's inspiration an animal nutrition expert (Dr. John Orr) and a plant-breeding authority (Sir Rowland Biffen) came out from England to report on Kenya conditions. Dr. Orr was followed by a team of scientists sent out from his research institute at Aberdeen to study stock diseases and malnutrition caused by lack of certain minerals in the pastures, and also the effect of diet on the health of native tribes. Their findings were of great practical value. They demonstrated how, by the addition of mineral supplements to the diet of cows, the yield of milk could be largely increased and the health of the calves improved. Sir Rowland Biffen praised the wheat-breeding work already accomplished in Kenya and made suggestions for its future.

SETTLEMENT.—"The biggest need of the country is for more development and consequently more production to keep the railway fully employed", Felling pointed out. New lines needed new traffic. The Government sought to provide it by pushing ahead with the dual policy. Agricultural staff in the reserves was increased to stimulate native production. A closer settlement scheme for Europeans was drawn up by the Commissioner for Lands and passed by the Kenya Government. Its object was to help men with limited capital to establish themselves on small mixed farms on land already set aside for alienation. The shipping lines and the Overseas Settlement department in Britain agreed to assist the selected men, while the Government made plans to look after their training.

This scheme was first formulated in 1926. It was held up for several years waiting for the long-promised land bank. Then, in 1929, it was submitted to the Secretary of State in its final form. It was to apply, for a start, to two hundred settlers. Lord Passfield approved it, subject to its limitation to a maximum of twelve settlers. It was never carried into effect.

11

European education saw one of Sir Edward Grigg's principal reforms. The new generation of young Kenyans that was growing up had outstripped the facilities for its education. Schools were overcrowded, and in spite of the fact that the better-off settlers sent their children to England for education there were not enough places to go round. Many children were running wild on farms and receiving no training at all. The school buildings already in existence were not only inadequate but dangerous to health.

This was one of the matters on which Delamere gave the Governor whole-hearted support. He had strongly urged the expenditure of £80,000 from loan money on a secondary school for boys at Kabete in 1925, when the director of Education had opposed the idea on the ground that there would never be enough boarders to fill it. "There will be a waiting-list in two years", Delamere had prophesied; and he was right. Five years later there were over 1600 European children attending schools in Kenya. Delamere also urged the Government to erect proper sun-proof buildings instead of the existing wood and iron ovens in which children were taught. Experience had convinced him that much of the nerviness put down to altitude or to some mysterious effect of tropical latitudes on Europeans was due to bad housing and to disregard for the sun's rays. "People blame the country," he once remarked, "but after all if you go to Canada and go outside in the winter and do not protect your face you will probably get your nose nipped off from frostbite. I am quite prepared to believe that there is a specific action of the sun's rays on the nervous system, but this can be avoided by providing proper buildings, clothing and so forth."

Sir Edward Grigg took the matter up with vigour. All white men and women destined to spend their lives in Africa, he pointed out, were born into a special and inalienable responsibility. Throughout their lives they would have to set a standard of civilisation among people still far behind them (whatever the future might hold) in culture. They were assigned to an involuntary aristocracy, and they must be equipped as well as might be for the position that they would have to hold.

Europeans in Africa had, therefore, a right to the best education that the country could afford; in fact, the country could not afford to give them a poor one. The greatest danger of African colonisation was the growth of a class of "poor whites". Their poverty was primarily intellectual. Lack of education had aggravated, to some extent created, the poor white problem in South Africa. Kenya must avoid that tragic mistake.

"I am convinced that the future of this colony is secure—on one condition", Sir Edward Grigg said. "That condition is that all of you here that represent the British race should keep up the standards of your civilisation and see that your children maintain them too. In particular I say to you—look after your schools."

With the driving force of the Governor and the support of the elected members a school building programme, financed out of the new loan, was launched. The boys' secondary school at Kabete (afterwards named the Prince of Wales school) was a gesture of faith in the future of settlement. It was intended to provide an education as good as could be obtained, and to prepare Kenya boys for English universities. (In 1929 Sir Edward Grigg secured a Rhodes scholarship for East Africa, and a Prince of Wales schoolboy was selected to fill it.) It was to be not only a Kenya but a central East African school, attracting boys from the Sudan to the Zambesi.

Other schools sprang up at Nakuru, Eldoret and Kitale. The architecture of the buildings was an expression of the spirit that inspired their erection. They were designed by the best architect that Africa could provide, Sir Herbert Baker, and by his pupil, Mr. Hoogterp. Solid, enduring buildings, walls of whitewashed stone and roofs of red close-socketed tiles, cool open balconies and lofty rooms, they dominated the little up-country towns, still in the chrysalis stage of hotly shining corrugated iron, near which they were built. Just as in many English towns the gas-works is the first feature to strike the attention, and in French towns the barracks, so it is the gleaming white of the school buildings that catches and holds the eye of the visitor as he drives into the principal up-country towns in Kenya.

Until 1926 the money for the education of all races had come out of central revenues. It was now decided that each community should pay for its own education so that no arguments as to whether one race was receiving more than its fair share of revenue could be brought forward. After 1926 European and Indian education was supported by a special cess raised separately from the two races.

Native education continued to be financed out of central funds. It was not overlooked in the advance. Over twice as much government money was spent on it in 1930 as in 1925.

CHAPTER XXIV

LOCUSTS BRING TROUBLE
1928–1930

I

In May 1928 Delamere was married in Nairobi to Lady Markham, daughter of the Hon. Rupert Beckett. He left for England with his wife shortly afterwards for a holiday, and returned to Kenya in August.

On his arrival he found himself in trouble with his constituents and the colony in the throes of its first infestation of locusts since settlement began.

Dissatisfaction with their member had been brewing for some time among Rift Valley voters. Delamere was practically a stranger to them. He was too busy to give much attention to local affairs. He seldom answered letters. (He never kept a secretary for any length of time and his correspondence was always in confusion.) Nor was he particularly tactful with his constituents. He told an audience composed mainly of Nakuru traders that he was opposed to spending money on developing the township because he thought it wrong to encourage "cow-towns" in a small country.

The only local institution he supported was the War Memorial hospital. To this he contributed generously, and when someone hinted that he had secured the support of the *East African Standard* by virtue of being a shareholder in the company, he made a present of all his shares to the hospital.

On his return from England in 1928 Delamere was asked to attend a meeting which resolved itself into an attack on his behaviour and on the system of "government by agreement", which, the constituents protested, was nothing more than the Government's method of pulling wool over the elected members' eyes. A vote of censure was passed and he announced his intention of resigning. He did not do so, however, until ill-health forced him out of politics at the end of the year.

The temper of the Rift Valley settlers was not improved by the plague of locusts which swept over Eastern Africa in 1928, leaving a trail of ruined harvests, ravaged grazing and despondent feelings. The locusts followed a year of drought, when pastures were already weakened and the previous season's crops had been a partial failure.

Locusts had been unknown in Kenya since 1899. No one had anticipated an invasion. Early in 1928 dense swarms of the desert locust, the plague of ancient Egypt, darkened the skies and flattened themselves hungrily on the crops. They came from the north and north-west, from still undiscovered permanent breeding-grounds on each side of the Red Sea. Here, for reasons yet unknown, countless grasshoppers had gathered like armies before battle, had changed mysteriously in shape and colour and passed from the solitary into the gregarious form, and had started on their destructive flight to the fertile countries lying south in search of food.

Immense damage was done in Kenya. The native food supply was seriously diminished. Protection measures, sadly inadequate, were improvised. Tons of poison bait were scattered in an attempt to destroy immature locusts, or hoppers.

2

In 1929 the situation grew worse. Hoppers hatched out everywhere and advanced ruthlessly like vast steam rollers over crops, pastures, gardens. They ate everything—maize, wheat, barley, lucerne, native millet, beans, forage crops and grass. Swarms would settle on a field of wheat or maize just ripe for harvest, and in an hour's time nothing would be left but a waste of torn and broken stalks. Some farmers saw the whole of their crop wiped out before their eyes just as they were starting to harvest it, when in a week's time they would have been safe. There was nothing they could do. It was a heart-breaking devastation.

More flying swarms arrived from the north, some of them several miles long, solid clouds of winged grasshoppers blotting out the sun as they passed across it. Wherever they settled they swept the vegetation as bare as a bleached bone. When they alighted on trees the branches broke under their weight. In some districts coffee trees suffered in this way, although they were not eaten.

Kenya was not alone in her distress. These locusts swept down over the whole continent, through the Sudan to Uganda, Abyssinia, Somaliland and the Congo, across the Sahara to Senegal, Mauretania, Gambia, Nigeria and Sierra Leone. Huge invasions penetrated into Palestine, Transjordania and Iraq. Hundreds of thousands of pounds were spent in efforts to repulse them with flame-guns, trenches, poison bait and, later, even aeroplanes.

By 1929 an anti-locust service had been organised in Kenya. Two mobile units of flame-guns sprayed jets of fire on to heaving waves of hoppers driven by corps of volunteers into ditches and pits.

The depredations of 1929, coming on top of drought, led to widespread famine. A sum of £200,000 was voted early in 1929 for famine relief and a food control board set up to license exports. It was estimated that the colony, which in 1927 had exported over a million bags of maize, would have to import a quarter of a million bags. The Government was forced to draw upon surplus balances and so the process of building up reserves was reversed. Exports in 1929 fell off by nearly a quarter.

But this was not the end. While the desert locust was swarming over East Africa another species was preparing itself for flight. In 1928 the first hoppers of the migratory locust were reported from the swamps of the Niger, north of Timbuktu. Swarms multiplied and moved slowly east and west. By 1930 the vanguard had reached the Atlantic on the one side and the Nile on the other.

The next generation headed south from the Sudan. Early in 1931 they entered Uganda, Kenya and the southern Belgian Congo. Now there were two species of locust at large in East Africa, distinct but equally destructive. The desert variety was on the wane and 1930 had seen a locust lull. But migratory locusts were even harder to fight. They swarmed over larger areas to lay their eggs and the resulting hoppers were more scattered. The Northern Frontier area of Kenya became a favourite breeding ground.

In 1931 nearly half the maize and wheat in European areas and one-fifth of all native crops was destroyed by migratory locusts. The damage to crops was estimated at a quarter of a million pounds.

This was the worst year. The desert locusts passed on as mysteriously as they had come. Some of the migratory species remained, but in isolated bands. By 1932 the cultivated parts of Kenya were practically clear of locusts, and the infestation was over.

But it had been an expensive and for many a disastrous plague. Some men had lost their entire crop and had to borrow money in order to plant again. Grazing was severely damaged and cattle suffered accordingly. Science was left but little the wiser as to the reasons which lay behind these vast migrations of grasshoppers. The key to the puzzle might lie somewhere in the hidden breeding grounds of Eritrea and Arabia, the Niger swamps and the south-eastern Sudan. Here scientists suspected the existence of a permanent reservoir of locusts which periodically, for reasons still unguessed, overflowed into the fertile parts of Africa.

The locust outbreak of 1928 to 1931 cost the afflicted countries together over £7 million. A fraction of that sum spent on research might find a solution to the riddle.

3

Early in 1929 Delamere was forced by ill-health to retire from politics.

For many years he had been living at too fast a pace. Few men of nearly sixty could have stood the strain. Sir Edward Grigg's policy of associating the elected members as much as possible with the work of the Government, so as to educate them in the difficulties of ruling a country, made exacting demands on their energies. The practice of referring the budget estimates to a select committee on which the elected members were in a majority gave the unofficials a considerable say in public affairs, but it proved correspondingly hard work. And Delamere was never skilled in the art of getting work out of others. He kept things very much in his own hands, trusting to his personal ascendancy over his colleagues to prevent revolt.

In 1928 the Prince of Wales came out to Kenya and Delamere took a lead, as he always did on such occasions, in the parties held to celebrate the royal visit. The year was in every way a crowded one. Delamere's heart had never been the same after his severe illness in 1915. He had been warned then that to live a strenuous life at a high altitude was to court disaster.

The collapse came suddenly. For some weeks Delamere was critically ill and at one time he was not expected to recover. When the crisis was over he was ordered away for a complete rest. He resigned from the Legislative and Executive Councils and left for South Africa with his wife.

Delamere's political career might have ended here. His heart could never wholly recover. He was warned by doctors that any prolonged strain or worry would probably be fatal and that he must slow down the tempo of his life. But activity was in his spirit and idleness was to him anathema. He had nothing in him of the philosopher who is content to welcome age as an opportunity for retrospection. His whole nature demanded action. All his life he had been a rebel—against nature, against governments, against the inertia of bureaucracy. Now he rebelled against the inevitable breakdown of an engine which had been consistently run at too high a speed.

After a few weeks in Cape Town he felt better, and began to grow restive. Sir Samuel Wilson was on his way to Kenya to concoct his scheme for closer union. Mr. Sastri had left Delhi for Nairobi to present the Indian case. Delamere felt uneasy. One morning he decided to return home immediately, mainly to see Sir Samuel Wilson. He and his wife caught the first train to Lourenço Marques, found that there was no regular boat for a week, and came up to Mombasa on an old tramp plying between India and the east coast.

They reached home in time to entertain at Loresho Sir Samuel Wilson, and, later, Mr. Sastri, who had never before visited the country in whose politics he had so often intervened.

4

Delamere could not keep away from politics for long. Shortly after his return from convalescence he became chairman of the Elected Members' organisation, in spite of the fact that he had not yet returned to the Legislative Council. He seemed as alert as ever, although he was more easily tired than before his breakdown and gave up his supper parties and riotous evenings at Muthaiga. In any case, he could no longer afford them. Two years' drought and the locusts put a sudden check on the prosperity of his farms, his overdraft began to mount again and he was forced to reduce his personal expenses to the minimum.

Experience had never taught him to be a good public speaker, but his wits were still keen and quick in debate. Often he would leap to his feet and launch into a rambling, inconsequential speech which barely made sense in print. All the time his mind would be searching for the winning point while his flow of words formed a sort of smoke-screen to confuse his listeners. Then, suddenly, the point would come to him. He would break off his speech in the middle of a sentence and bring out the argument forcibly, emphasising each point with fluent gestures. While he was speaking his hands were never still. He would twirl a pencil or fiddle nervously with his notes.

He was at his best in committees. Often he would pass tense and barbed little remarks as if he was talking to himself and then, before he could be called to order, turn to the chairman and say, with the greatest apparent distress, "I beg your pardon, sir! I shouldn't have said that." But the thrust had gone home, and there was a twinkle in his eye as he apologised.

He seldom let his opponents in debate score a point unchallenged. On one occasion a difference of opinion had arisen between Delamere and the director of Agriculture on the question of locust control. Delamere was pressing for a big campaign against locusts designed to exterminate the hoppers throughout the hatching areas. The department's policy was to concentrate on crop protection.

The director was asked if he could give an estimate of the

extent of locust infestation expected in the following season. He replied that it was impossible. "You might as well ask me how many bald-headed men eat oysters on Thursdays", he added. "That's easy", Delamere replied. "I can tell you that. Kill off all the bald-headed men and you have your answer —none."

Delamere was skilled in the use of sarcasm in debates. People who were not accustomed to his methods found them confusing. He once, for example, disconcerted the Uganda representatives on the Railway Advisory Council, of which he was appointed a Kenya unofficial member in 1930, at a meeting at Entebbe. The subject of rates was a frequent bone of contention between Uganda and Kenya. Uganda suffered from a chronic hang-over from past grievances and was always suspicious that rating policy might favour Kenya at the expense of the Protectorate. On this occasion Uganda was objecting strongly to the "country produce rates" which enabled Kenya to rail her fresh produce to Uganda at a comparatively low cost. Uganda demanded as a *quid pro quo* low "in transit" rates on imported necessities coming straight through Kenya to the Protectorate.

The principle was agreed, and Uganda was asked to prepare a list of necessities which she regarded as eligible for the special rate. A long list of provisions was produced. Biscuits were passed, and preserved fruit. Delamere said nothing when the council considered caviar, and that was passed too.

Finally they came to perrier water. There was a brand of Kenya-made mineral water sold in competition with the imported article. Delamere pursed his lips and spoke in a quiet, silky tone.

"Of course", he said, "we all agree that perrier water is a poor man's drink. The water is bottled 6000 miles away, carried 6000 miles by sea and then over 1000 miles of railway and then perhaps another 100 miles by lorry. Undoubtedly it is a poor man's drink. And as for caviar, of course that is unquestionably a poor man's food. Certainly Uganda should have the low rates on these items on the poor man's list."

The Uganda delegates were uncertain how to deal with these methods. They looked a little uneasy. The items had been duly passed; but later they were quietly removed from the schedule.

Delamere had changed in public as well as in private life since the war. Most of the old fieriness had gone. He had adopted different methods, the soft answer in place of the impetuous outburst. He possessed—when he chose to use it—the old-fashioned quality of courtesy. "The last of his race", a friend once described him. He kept open house at Loresho, and nothing was too much trouble to secure his guests' comfort. For his own part he cared little for luxury and the habit of living in huts was so deep-rooted that he used as his bedroom an out-building designed as a garage, and left the comfortable stone house to visitors. He always slept between blankets, having grown accustomed to do without sheets.

5

Delamere went frequently to Tanganyika in an effort to keep his bacon factory and Colonists Ltd. alive. In 1929 Lady Delamere took over the management of the hotel at Iringa, and made it pay its way. At the same time her husband was appointed by Sir Donald Cameron to a commission formed to draw up a scheme of land settlement in Tanganyika. This involved several visits to Dar-es-Salaam and took up more time.

Frequent motor trips to Iringa over bad roads—during the heavy rains of 1930 they became impassable—did not improve his health. On one occasion he became paralysed by lumbago and had to be carried into his car to return to Kenya. The car broke down and he spent a night in a trench in the sand scooped out for him at the side of the road by his companion. He made one more trip by road to Livingstone and on the way he gave evidence by telegram before a commission sitting in Nairobi. He always sent long wires in place of letters when it was possible to do so. This was the record telegram of his career.

The commission in question had been appointed largely at his own instigation. Dissatisfaction with the Agricultural department had been growing for some time among the colonists. Large sums were spent on the department and the settlers questioned whether the country was getting value for money. An idea also had arisen that one of the unofficial members of Legislative Council should be appointed as a minister of Agriculture. A man with actual experience of farming in Kenya would be better qualified, it was felt, to direct agricultural policy than a Civil servant with little practical knowledge, or even a bachelor of science who came direct from some tropical colony where agriculture was of a totally different type. Kenya was peculiar among British colonies in that conditions in the highlands were temperate and not tropical; and an understanding of palm kernel production in Sierra Leone or of the copra industry in Fiji was of little help to an official faced with problems of creamery organisation or rusts of wheat.

This idea of an unofficial minister of Agriculture had been supported by Sir Edward Grigg, and the Hilton Young commission had advocated its adoption as an experiment; but nothing further had been done. At the end of 1928 Delamere moved a motion for the appointment of a commission of enquiry into the progress of agriculture and this was accepted. Sir Daniel Hall, the distinguished agricultural scientist, agreed to come out from England to preside over the commission.

Delamere happened to be passing through Abercorn, in Northern Rhodesia, when the commission started its sittings. He scribbled his views at some length on a sheaf of telegraph forms and asked his wife to hand them in at the local post office. Somewhat taken aback at the length, she suggested that he should cut it down. He agreed, and returned in triumph a little later to say that her advice had been followed. On investigation it was found that six words had been eliminated. The telegram was despatched, to the amazement of the native clerk, and the cost was nearly £40.

This telegram outlined Delamere's ideas for a complete agricultural policy for Kenya. The first essential, he said, was that agriculture should be recognised as the one and only foundation of the colony's existence. "If it succeeds everyone, whites and natives alike, benefits; if it fails or falters, everyone suffers." Kenya was responsible for three large loans and she could pay interest only out of the proceeds of the land. "The plant of prosperity must be watered at the root: concentration of all resources on agriculture is vital to the future."

Because Kenya had only a small area of good agricultural land this area must be developed intensively and to the full. Good farming land must not be bottled up by the Government in forest reserves and elsewhere and left unoccupied. Afforestation on a big scale was needed to safeguard the water supplies. A land bank should be started immediately, financed if necessary out of savings.

The reorganisation of the stock industry was vital. "Today the industry is moribund because an ordinary, perfectly understood step for controlling disease, universal in South Africa, is not taken. . . . All that is needed is to pass and enforce ordinary dipping and fencing laws." A market for native stock was essential and Delamere suggested that loan money should be lent to the native trust fund to establish two meat factories. These factories would then be the property of the natives themselves and so no objection could be taken to the enforcement of compulsory culling.

In due course the agricultural commission under Sir Daniel Hall reported and many technical recommendations were made. A board of agriculture with an unofficial chairman was advocated as a first step towards giving the settlers more say in the running of the department that most closely affected them. This suggestion was put into effect. The creation of the board was clearly visualised as a preparation for the appointment of an unofficial minister of Agriculture. Strong recommendations were also made that meat factories for dealing with surplus stock should be immediately established.

6

Delamere managed to keep away from active politics for nearly a year. His first public reappearance was in the rôle of chairman of the fourth unofficial conference held in Nairobi in January 1930.

The future of the tariff agreement between Kenya, Uganda and Tanganyika was the main subject at issue. For some time past a feeling had been growing in Uganda and Tanganyika that their interests were being sacrificed to those of Kenya settlers. This unofficial conference was called to thrash the matter out.

Kenya was anxious to develop the local East African market for her produce. It seemed, on the face of it, absurd that Uganda should import canned butter (as she did) and wheat flour from Europe, or even America, six or ten thousand miles away, when excellent fresh butter and local flour were produced next door.

Of late years Kenya had been pushing, successfully, the sale of her fresh farm produce in the two neighbouring dependencies. The railway gave specially low "country produce rates" to locally produced articles for sale in East African territories. This was a recognised form of protection, quite common in young agricultural countries of Kenya's type.

Uganda objected to these rates on the grounds that she was not interested in whether her imports came from Kenya or from overseas, but only in securing the lowest possible rates on her purchases. In 1929 she pushed her objections vigorously and a Governors' conference was summoned at the beginning of 1930 to decide this question, together with the further one of the amount of protection to be given to locally produced articles through the common customs tariff.

Uganda, whose customs system had been amalgamated with Kenya's in 1917, complained that prices in the Protectorate were kept up by customs duties imposed in the interests of Kenya producers. Tanganyika, who had come wholly into the customs union in 1927, to a large extent supported her.

Kenya, on the other hand, was determined to stick to her protectionist guns. A tariff committee appointed in 1929 to review the subject reported that protection had achieved its object of allowing local industries to put down their roots, without raising prices to the consumer. In the case of each protected article prices had actually been lowered since the duties were imposed.[1] To meet Uganda's wishes, however,

[1] Kenya flour, for example, had supplied less than half the market in 1922 (before protection); by 1928 it was feeding the whole East African market with a

the committee decided that the duties should be reduced and they recommended the scaling down of the tariffs on each item to about half the previous level.

There were not a large number of protected articles. The argument was concerned only with wheat, sugar, hams and bacon, butter and cheese, ghee and timber. Uganda pressed for the complete removal of these duties, threatening to withdraw altogether from the customs agreement if she did not get her way. The tangle was a hard one to straighten out: how to maintain a customs agreement between three countries with totally different policies and without a central authority to settle disputes.

7

Delamere was nervous about the outcome of the Governors' conference summoned to settle the matter. Protection in the local market for such of Kenya's young agricultural industries as could prove themselves economically sound was the keystone of his economic policy. He decided to make a bid for the conversion of unofficial opinion in Uganda and Tanganyika. In the long run, he considered, it was to the advantage of both these countries to encourage the growth in Kenya of products which they could not raise in sufficient quantities themselves, even if it meant a small sacrifice for the first few years. Once the industries were established they would benefit by securing cheaper and better goods.

Besides, it was a question of the parochial versus the broader point of view. If East Africa was to be regarded as a unit, soon to be federally linked, then products of the Kenya highlands would count as home-grown in Uganda just as Scottish potatoes are home-grown in England.

Uganda did not send representatives to the fourth unofficial conference and the Tanganyika delegates arrived in Nairobi in a frame of mind unfavourable to conversion. Delamere took the chair. All the Tanganyika representatives voiced

small surplus over for export. The acreage under wheat had increased more than sixfold and the flour industry was worth £200,000 a year to the colony. At the same time Kenya flour was selling in Uganda at a price which would have undercut by a comfortable margin imported flour brought in duty-free.

discontent with the working of the customs union, and fear of "exploitation" by Kenya.

Delamere heard them out in silence. Then he spoke for over an hour, answering each of their objections in turn and appealing to them to sink sectional jealousies and to look at the matter from the point of view of East African development as a whole. He reminded the Tanganyikans that they themselves would soon develop their agriculture to the point of needing some security in the early stages in their own local market.

He succeeded in his object. His speech was admitted to be one of the most convincing he had ever delivered. The Tanganyika delegates abandoned their previous standpoint and unanimous resolutions were passed by the conference asking that every effort should be made to "retain and retrench the customs union of East Africa, provided that the principle of adequate protection is retained".

These resolutions were laid before the Governors' conference, which was then in session, by a deputation from the unofficial conference. A way out was found in the form of "suspended duties". A low basic tariff on the protected articles was adopted by the customs union and additional, or "suspended", duties were agreed. The basic duties were for revenue, the suspended duties for protection. Each country could enforce the suspended part of the rate whenever it wanted to after consultation with its neighbours. This compromise resolved the deadlock.

8

In the New Year's honours list of 1930 Delamere was created a K.C.M.G. in recognition of his thirty-years devotion to the country he had helped to build. This was the first civil honour awarded to a Kenya settler for services within the colony.

Early in the same year Lady Delamere returned to England for a visit. While she was away Delamere wrote to her every morning as soon as he was called, before the day's work began. His letters reflected a strenuous life. Meetings to deal with creameries, Congo Basin treaties, agricultural credits, meat extract factories; plans for manuring coffee, pooling butter sales, lowering costs of cattle feed; trips to Uganda to serve on Railway Council; narrow escapes on churned-up roads (in 1930 the rains were exceptionally heavy) and hours spent stuck in mud-holes—such activities as these made up his daily routine. The following extracts give some idea of the matters with which he was concerned at this time:—

Loresho, Kabete
March 31*st*, 1930

... I got a piteous wire from Marsden in Tanganyika yesterday saying that the escarpment road had been covered by earth slides and that the bridge over the Ruaha couldn't be got to, so that the Dodoma-Iringa road is closed completely. Also that the Tossamaganga bridge on the other side had been washed away. Iringa is isolated and presumably the bacon factory is cut off from Iringa. Bad luck, just when our factory was within an ace of paying its way.

I suppose the hotel has now run out of all supplies. Our little hotel showed a profit for the nine months up to the end of January, including interest and depreciation, and it is unlucky that the railway and the roads should again be washed away, when the rains are supposed to finish in the middle of February down there. . . . The only methods of communication with Iringa now are by air or telegraph. It really does seem as if Providence was against us for the moment.

April 1*st*, 1930

... We had an excellent dinner last night cooked by the nursery cook. Everyone pleased. Only Francis, Dutton and Martin. The purpose of the meeting was to get from Martin his impressions of the position as he saw it in England with regard to the new constitution, federation, etc.

He says (*a*) that Sir S. Wilson has for the moment no influence, nor indeed have any of the permanent people; (*b*) that since Drummond Shiels took over from Lunn, Passfield has passed into the background. Drummond Shiels' idea of Kenya was, apparently (according to Martin) that there are a large number of very respectable settlers who would like to come into line (with what?) but that they are led by a few aristocratic politicians headed by myself—in the wrong direction.

Martin came to the conclusion, after a long interview with Drummond Shiels just before he left, that they had no idea how they were going to settle Kenya affairs. D.S. wandered from one idea to another, but we thought, and Martin agreed, that these might be different *ballons d'essai* to find out what Martin thought. The chief impression left on Martin's mind was that D.S. leant again towards what Thomas called the "islands" (the highlands) being isolated and given over to us to govern—an impracticable scheme but one which makes one laugh because it has of course terrified our friends like Oldham & Co. who, Martin says, are now leaning towards the Wilson scheme for safety.

I said just now an impracticable scheme, and it is from every point of view, politically and economically, but it might possibly have to be our last ditch.... I want to come home badly and find out facts for myself, as I am completely in the dark....

April 6th, 1930

...We spent yesterday morning on the Native Lands Trust bill. It is rather an awkward fix as, apart from the fact that Passfield's amendments seem impracticable in fact, our members have already voted against them and H.E. withdrew the bill in sympathy with their opinions and wrote a despatch arguing against the amendments.

As the old man (P.) has been quite civil in his replies and shows a desire to be pleasant and reasonable about it, we have decided to vote against the amendments, but to be pleasant about it too, and it will be passed by Government. If we are going to have a real fight in Council we cannot have it on this ground. The question of native land rights is one we are sure to lose on.

I think we shall really stick our toes in over Drummond Shiels' amendments to our budget. Although he has a constitutional right to interfere, it is never done except on quite definite racial questions. We have paid our own way for years, we have made our own loans, we have collected an accumulated surplus of over half a million, notwithstanding locusts, drought etc. Now this busy creature has sent our budget back with amendments. We shall have to stop that sort of thing somehow. It has not happened for years....

I played golf with Francis and then went across to the Ritchies. They were on the point of going to dinner with the Martin Johnstons, where they were looking forward to being fed on chop suey, noodles and waffles, drink without alcohol and tobacco without nicotine, which were apparently the things on the menu.

April 13th, 1930

... Francis has got a case he is fighting for the White Sisters near Thika. The *Government* made a mistake a few years ago about the boundary between them and the Kikuyu reserve, and altered the White Sisters' original survey line and put a piece of their land, which they bought on the open market, into the native reserve. Whereupon the Kikuyu pulled up the original survey pegs.

When it was properly surveyed, again by Government, the other day to demarcate the boundary of the reserve, it was found that a mistake had been made, which the Sisters had always contended. Between the two surveyings the natives had put some *shambas* on the land in dispute. Now Government coolly admits the Sisters are right, but says they must bring an action to get the natives off their land. Francis of course contends that it is the business of D.C. to remove them, and if necessary for Government to compensate them. . . .

In the meantime there is a lot of friction. Charles Taylor knew a case where the exact opposite occurred on his property on the opposite side of the river from the White Sisters. A mistake of boundary was made there, and he ploughed up about 80 acres of land thinking it was his. The D.C. found he had made a mistake and he had to withdraw over his own side of the boundary, leaving the ploughed land to the natives. The D.C. there, of course, insisted on his withdrawal from the reserve, quite rightly. In this case, because it is natives, the White Sisters are expected to go to the expense of an action.

April 22nd, 1930

... Lunched at the Avenue with the Cobbs and the Harpers. I am so sorry for the Cobbs. They have been hoping against hope that the rain would stop and let them harvest their crop, but now with the heavy rain of the last week or two the last 700 acres of beautiful barley has simply rotted on the ground. They harvested the rest, a good many thousand bags, and it is hardly worth taking to the station at the price. Mrs. Cobb finally deserted her post the day before yesterday and came down to Nairobi to join him. I have never before seen her disheartened, but she says this has really been the last straw after working herself on the harvesters ever since you and I and the Neville Chamberlains went there together.

I'm afraid it means their selling the developed part of their farm and starting again on another bit. Rather hard at Cobb's age to start all over again, and for her after making their house so nice. But it has happened to all the pioneers in all the countries they have made. Their joy is in the creation of something out of nothing. Cobb has already left one beautiful place, Keringet, into which he put years of his life, and now he is probably going to do it again, leaving a home made out of the bare veld for someone else. And he will probably do it again.

New capital comes in and takes over in a different spirit, investing in proved things.

Cobb has made large profits out of farming, but it has always gone back into increased acreages or something he is trying. The result is the first two or three bad years on end leave him stranded and he starts again. The pioneer mind only sees forward. If it didn't it would never do what it does. But it seldom consolidates for the same reason.

April [Undated]

... An extraordinary letter turned up last night from Hayward. He says: "Legalishu (the chief of the biggest Masai clan, the Purko) has sent his son Sitabo here to report that he has found what I take to be a thunderbolt. It was found after very heavy rain—on the surface, the grass being burned—and it throws a light at night for about 200 feet. A number of Masai lifted this thing and took it to the village and put it in a box, and even then it throws a light through the wood. It is cold and very heavy. The police know nothing about it as yet (I rather like that touch!). He is anxious to get enough money to bring the thing here by lorry to you. Sitabo says he will await your reply here till Sunday. . . ."

Boy Long and I agree that it is too interesting to be let slip, so I have sent a wire to Hayward to tell him to send Sitabo here by first available method, and that if I am satisfied I will send a car or lorry. I suppose he wants to sell it to me, or knows that I shall look after his father's rights in the matter if it has any value.

I must make a real effort to straighten things out, and the only possible way to do so is to try and sell land at a low price. Things *might* improve and probably will in a year or two, but in the meanwhile one is in danger of being caught completely owing to my carelessness of my own business, and changes of management, in the year or two before I married you. The average sales from the farms for the last four years have been about £30,000 a year gross. Of this an average of £24,000 a year has been from Laikipia and Soysambu and about £6000 a year from Manera. About half this must be subtracted for expenditure to-day.

But now the sales have dropped enormously and everything is swallowed up (and more) by interest, etc., on mortgages and on overdraft. Even at present prices of land one could clear things up by selling a proportion of land, but the difficulty nowadays is to find buyers. There are a certain number of sales, but they are flukes.

IN THE TRAIN
May 1st, 1930

Just off the *Clement Hill* and in the train running through the Kavirondo reserve. It shows how much rain we have had that the Victoria Nyanza has risen three feet already. If one thinks of the area (isn't it 640,000 square miles?), it shows what the floods must have been. The rain has done in about half of the cotton crop in Uganda, bringing it down from 200,000 bales to 100,000. This has all happened since the railway estimates were made up for presentation to Railway Council at the end of last year. That means that the railway loses about £140,000 on actual transport, and an estimated amount of about £100,000 in decreased importations, because the people will buy much less. Nearly a quarter of a million. Luckily Kenya estimates are up about £50,000 from a railway point of view.

The administration of the railway and the Council have during the last six years reduced rates to the extent of an annual loss of revenue of about £322,000 a year. This has been mostly on high-rated imported articles. The result is a loss of a revenue on imports which makes it difficult to go on with the low export rates on low priced commodities. But these low rates are going to be continued if I have anything to say. The railway will have to go slow in reducing rates for a year or two.

In the meantime, we cut down the betterment for the year by £100,000 and made savings. The thing is sound enough. The earnings have gone up by half a million a year in four years. But the lowering of rates too rapidly and the taking over of branch lines from the Government too easily means that during that same four years the increase of earnings over ordinary working expenditure has only been £100,000.

We have, however, £1,600,000 in various reserve funds, so we have a margin to get straight in.

NDERIT, ELMENTEITA
May 3rd, 1930

Such a curious mixture, this house. An enormous house (for a farmhouse) costing thousands to build and yet only about six rooms altogether. Good furniture mixed with things made by the local *fundi*. Chairs and carpets covered with enormous half-starved Borzois or wolf-hounds. High grass all round the house. But such delightful hospitality.

I went over to Soysambu for lunch. Everything seems better at the moment. The Laikipia death-rate is almost down to normal. We seem to be turning out about 6000 lbs. of butter fat per month.

Got back for tea and found Commander K. there. I'm so sorry he has had to give up his farm. The two dry years and then the world slump in maize did him. He does not grouse a bit, poor man, and says that he doesn't regret a bit having come to Kenya and taken part in its development. So good to meet that spirit.

LORESHO, KABETE
May 14th, 1930

... We spent yesterday going into the question of saving the maize hung up on the Trans Nzoia and elsewhere. Owing to the wet year, instead of drying on the cob in the cribs the maize is getting damper. The ordinary moisture content for shipment is fixed at 12½ per cent. The drying plant at the coast is entirely insufficient. There are about 400,000 bags on the Trans Nzoia and probably another 300,000 elsewhere, to get out in the next three or four months. All that the department of Agriculture has done is, quite rightly, to refuse to increase the moisture content allowed for export, but there it has stuck.

It is very undesirable that individual farmers should dry maize, because for starch-makers and others one has to be very careful that it should either be dried naturally or that it should be artificially dried at a regulated temperature which must not go too high. You cannot tell by look if it has been dried too fast but it alters the value for certain trades. ... Now we shall have to rush up one or two driers at Kitale and possibly one at Hoey's Bridge to save the crop. ... The Trans Nzoia maize alone is worth between £100,000 and £150,000 even at these bad prices, and that would make all the difference to a single district.

Even if we got a couple of driers up, to do about 3000 bags a day between them, we are still confronted with weevil trouble. Generally, maize on the cob in a crib is pretty safe for some time, but the wet this year has started weevils in the maize actually in the field. An attempt has got to be made to tackle that while the maize is waiting for drying. That means gas, and to gas maize in cribs with tarpaulins and rolls of stuff round the cribs to keep the air in. is not going to be easy, and may be too expensive. Luckily we have a supply of the stuff for the gas and it must be tried. We are going on with this to-day. Anyway the Governor has agreed to the expenditure pending meeting of Legislative Council. The Trans Nzoia people have come down with two sets of local plans for dealing with the job.

May 17th, 1930

... This morning had meeting of debenture holders of Naivasha creamery. Got all we wanted passed unanimously so we now have a free hand to get on with negotiations for amalgamation with Lumbwa. The surprise of the meeting was produced by a one-armed man who started farming at Naivasha, having retired from being a railway guard, a good many years ago.

I was talking about the difficulty of raising debentures at the present time at a low rate of interest and pointing out that our own were at 8 per cent and Nanyuki's at 10 per cent, when suddenly he said: "Well, I'll give you £3000 at 5½ per cent". This was afterwards modified to 6 per cent, but it is a marvellous thing that he should be able to produce £3000 out of his pocket at a moment's notice. ...

The future of the dairy industry depends on getting things right at first; but it is extraordinarily difficult with small farmers, living under rather isolated conditions, who all think their own way is the best.

One of the troubles lately has been that one can't get anywhere by road without running the risk of being permanently stuck or not getting back. Thomson's Falls were wavering between coming in with us and sending their milk to Naivasha, and building a creamery of their own. Of course just at that moment their branch railway collapsed in the floods and they have been cut off for weeks except for a motor lorry that gets through twice a day and can only carry two cans besides the passengers. So they have decided to build their own. That doesn't make things easier and is bound to be against their own interests. They have calculated on 21,000 lbs. monthly of butter fat, I expect on an optimistic basis. We last month put through 40,000 lbs. The trouble at the moment is the very low price of butter on the London market.

CHAPTER XXV

IN DEFENCE OF SETTLEMENT
1930

I

"The main object of our policy and legislation should be to found a white colony."—SIR CHARLES ELIOT, 1902.

"Primarily, Kenya is an African territory, and H.M.'s Government think it necessary definitely to record their considered opinion that the interests of the African natives must be paramount, and that if and when those interests and the interests of the immigrant races should conflict, the former should prevail."—White paper, "Indians in Kenya", 1923.

"With the statement in the white paper of 1923 in all its aspects and with all its implications H.M.'s Government express their complete concurrence."—White paper, "Memorandum on Native Policy", 1930.[1]

So the needle of British policy swung round the compass from north to south—from "white" to "black". It was this change of course that was responsible for colonists' discontent, for the sense of uncertainty which led them to ask for safeguards, for the outcry which greeted the publication of the Labour Government's East African policy in the white papers of June 1930.

The colonists had booked their passages for a harbour made by many vessels before them, that of colonial self-government. The master of the ship had repeatedly confirmed its destination. Familiar ports of call on the route had been reached and passed. Then, without warning, the sailing directions had been reversed. The ship had swung off her settled course and was heading for strange, dangerous seas lying in another direction. The passengers were first bewildered, then alarmed, now dismayed.

Obviously, the interests of the other communities, European, Indian or Arab, must severally be safeguarded. Whatever the circumstances in which members of these communities have entered Kenya there

[1] Cmd. 3573 of 1930.

will be no drastic action or reversal of measures already introduced . . . the result of which might be to destroy or impair the existing interests of those who have already settled in Kenya.

So had the 1923 white paper qualified its assertion of African paramountcy. But how long would this pledge be kept? the colonists asked. Other pledges, expressed or implied, had been dissolved. This, too, might go. The policy of the Imperial Government, culminating in the white papers of 1930, seemed to them—wrongly or rightly—to be moving inexorably in the direction of hostility towards white settlement.

Fear lay behind the colonists' agitation against the Labour Government's pronouncements in 1930. Fear led them to exaggerate the meaning of the memorandum on native policy, to detect innuendoes in every sentence. It was fear that had prompted them in the first place to ask for political powers which reason should have told them were still beyond their reach.

I am always afraid of fear as an ingredient of policy [Delamere said]. It is the most unreasonable and the most cruel of all human qualities.

The progress and development of Eastern Africa has been held back by fear of three things in the last few years. Fear that Tanganyika would be handed back to the Germans—fear of an all-black policy which would submerge the Europeans—fear of swamping from Asia.

Delamere could not escape the influence of the very fear he dreaded. Anxiety for the future of white settlement drove him to extremes in his demands. The Imperial Government did little towards creating a more reasonable attitude by allaying these disquieting fears. Instead, they told the colonists bluntly that their co-operation was not wanted. They did not conceal the fact that they distrusted settlers.

2

The Labour Government's anxiously awaited conclusions on closer union were issued in June 1930 at the same time as an outline of their native policy.

It was the tone of these documents—the "black papers", they were called—rather than any of the statements contained in them that was resented, not only in Kenya but in other parts of East Africa, notably in Northern Rhodesia.

The memorandum on native policy managed to create the impression that now, for the first time, native welfare was being considered by a high-minded Imperial Government intent on seeing justice done in a colony hitherto wilfully insensible to native rights. Nothing was said about all the work for native betterment that the East African Governments had been carrying out steadily and consistently ever since their funds had permitted.

Most of the principles laid down had, in actual fact, been in general acceptance for many years. "These opinions do not constitute any novel doctrine", the white paper itself admitted. "They have long been implicit in the policy with regard to native races in different parts of the Empire." Then why, the colonists felt, did the home Government go out of its way to force these opinions in so patronising and self-righteous a manner down East Africa's throat?

No mention was made in either of the documents of the part white settlement had played, and would play in future, in the development of East Africa. On the contrary, European interests were to be overridden and native paramountcy was to be complete. "All proposals designed to promote the well-being and interests of any non-native race", the paper on policy remarked, "must be carefully examined at the outset from the standpoint of their effect on the native races."

The colonists felt that their efforts in the past and their fate in the future were being callously ignored. They had lived in the belief that they were the builders of a new British colony; now it was implied that they were "immigrant communities" encumbering a native state.

They were the victims of another reversal of imperial policy. After the Indian settlement the colonists' right to share in the trusteeship for the native's future had been definitely conceded. "The trusteeship lies upon the shoulders of every man and woman of European race in Africa", Mr. Ormsby-Gore had said. In 1927 the Imperial Government had accepted this principle in a public declaration of its policy. But the 1930 white paper repudiated the association of the colonists in the task of trusteeship.

> They [the Imperial Government] fully accept the principle that the relation of H.M.'s Government to the native population of East Africa is one of trusteeship which cannot be devolved, and from which they cannot be relieved. The ultimate responsibility for the exercise of this trusteeship must accordingly rest with them alone.

In three years the British Government had changed its mind on this fundamental point as to whether or not the colonists were to be invited to share the burden of trusteeship. The reaction was correspondingly abrupt. "I am convinced", said Sir Edward Grigg, "that there is no large body of English opinion conscious of these fluctuations or of the unfairness, the grievance and the material injury which they produce."

The memorandum on native policy was, in effect, a red herring drawn across the path of closer union. It did much to frighten unofficial European opinion off the federation idea without contributing anything new to the structure of native policy.

3

The unpopularity of the "black papers" was increased by suspicions held as to their origin. Sir Samuel Wilson's framework for closer union, to which all principal parties in East Africa had agreed, had (it was said) been accepted by Lord Passfield, but the scheme had been rejected by the Cabinet, owing mainly to the opposition of the Secretary of State for India, Mr. Wedgwood Benn. Thereafter East African policy, it was believed, was dictated largely by the India Office. The white paper on native policy was thought to have been written by Mr. Wedgwood Benn, assisted by Sir Reginald Mant.

Nothing was more calculated to inflame Europeans in Kenya than the suspicion, justified or not, of India Office intervention in African affairs. Indian influence was traced in the passage in the white paper dealing with that old bugbear, the common roll.

"H.M. Government are of the opinion", it read, "that

the establishment of a common roll is the object to be aimed at and attained"; and an enquiry was to be undertaken at once as to how the common roll might be introduced "in the immediate future".

This was going even further than the Hilton Young commission, which had at least qualified its recommendation for a common roll by the provision that local agreement to its introduction must first be secured. Nothing was said about consulting East African opinion in the 1930 document. And it was a direct reversal of the Labour Government's policy as publicly announced by Mr. Thomas in 1924.[1] Only strong pressure from the India Office, it was felt, could have brought about so complete a *volte face*.

The rest of the conclusions reached by the Imperial Government about closer union[2] were little more satisfactory from Kenya's point of view. A High Commissioner, equipped with all the dictatorial powers suggested in the Hilton Young report, was to be appointed to "supervise" Kenya, Tanganyika and Uganda. He was to be assisted by a council with a strong official majority; and the Kenya constitution was to be left unchanged.

These decisions, together with the Hilton Young and the Wilson reports, were to be considered by a joint committee of both Houses of Parliament which was to produce a final settlement.

On the publication of the two papers a joint meeting of the Convention of Associations and the elected members was hastily convened. Delegates from Tanganyika, including members of its recently established Legislative Council, attended. The conclusions on closer union were unanimously pronounced "unacceptable". An angry cable was sent over Delamere's signature to the Secretary of State:

> Attitude of Imperial Government as now expressed involves breach of previous pledges. East African colonists stand on principle that the white race is the only people which has proved its capacity to govern mixed races.

We must challenge the doctrine of political and economic para-

[1] See Chapter XXII. (footnote on page 230).
[2] Cmd. 3574 of 1930: "Statement of Conclusions of H.M. Government as regards Closer Union in East Africa".

mountcy of natives as interpreted in these documents, and claim the closer association in trusteeship foreshadowed in the 1927 white paper.

White settlers permanently domiciled in East Africa cannot accept designation "immigrant community" as applied to themselves, or the right of Indian immigrants to participate on same basis as Europeans in the government of East Africa. They regard Indian representation on local legislatures desirable only as a convenient method of enabling Indian sectional views to be voiced. They also consider it imperative that closer union should be accompanied by an unofficial majority in at least one territory.

The principles of a common electoral roll and a racially mixed federal council cannot be accepted. Although closer union involving constitutional changes is still considered desirable the conference regrets that the retrogressive spirit of the new proposals has definitely antagonised European opinion.

Delamere himself regarded the white papers with intense resentment. In a speech at Nakuru he inveighed against the "insufferable patronage of the wording". Feeling was widespread throughout the country. The East African Women's League, a non-political welfare organisation, held a special general meeting of protest against what it regarded as a threat to the future of white settlement, and sent a cable to the Secretary of State.

It was Delamere's idea that South Africa should be approached for support. He cabled to General Hertzog and to Mr. Moffat, the premier of Southern Rhodesia, and received encouraging replies. The conference at Nairobi passed a resolution instructing its leaders to "investigate the lines on which the sympathy of the Union of South Africa and Rhodesia could be enlisted to maintain white settlement in Kenya and Tanganyika which is jeopardised by the proposals contained in the white papers".

4

The Nairobi conference decided to send a mission to London to present the colonists' case to the joint Parliamentary committee foreshadowed in the white papers. Delamere was appointed leader. Mr. T. J. O'Shea, elected member for the Uasin Gishu plateau (one of the most active of Kenya's politicians with an Irish gift of oratory), and Mr. W. McClellan Wilson, an ex-missionary turned settler, were chosen to support him. The Tanganyika settlers were represented by Mr. A. A. Menkin, a former editor of the *Tanganyika Times*, and the East African Women's League sent Lady Eleanor Cole as their delegate.

Delamere drew up his own mandate in the following words: "It will be the duty of the deputation to put forward every argument against the subordination of European interests in East Africa; to press either for a complete withdrawal of the present proposals and the substitution of proposals acceptable in this country, or to secure for us a period of lull—with the door quite definitely left open for us to consider any fresh proposals—during which this country can consolidate its economic position and have a rest from the politics which have disturbed business and exacerbated local opinion for so long."

The leader of the team was anxious to lose no time and the delegation sailed in August 1930 before the joint Parliamentary committee had been appointed.

Within twelve hours of his arrival Delamere and his colleagues had interviewed General Hertzog and Mr. Havenga, who had reached London shortly before to attend the Imperial Conference being held that autumn. The South African premier agreed, as General Smuts had done, that East African affairs had a special interest for the Union—itself, as well as Britain, a mandatory power. General Hertzog promised to raise the matter at the Imperial Conference if circumstances seemed to demand such action.

For the next two months the delegation devoted itself to interviews with the press, public dinners, addresses to members of Parliament, luncheons with politicians and publicists, and other familiar methods for the propagation of a point of view.

Delamere himself was not at his best and the deputation did not work well together as a team. The leader kept the initiative in his own hands but often failed to make good use of it. He was to deliver all the important speeches, for example, but on several occasions he never appeared at the function and one of his colleagues had to deputise without warning. He seemed to have lost his old grip. At meetings of the deputation he was inclined to ramble over general ground without coming to definite decisions on specific points. The other delegates were unaccustomed to teamwork and Delamere was irritated by their independence.

Delamere always felt himself to be at a disadvantage in London. He had been out of touch with trends of thought in England for too long to be able to adjust himself immediately to the new atmosphere. This feeling—the germ, perhaps, of the colonial inferiority complex—made him diffuse and unconvincing. In Kenya, in his own surroundings, he was much more effective.

Everything had changed so much since he had left England to make his home in Africa. The whole basis from which people argued things had shifted.

In Delamere's mind there were certain fixed triangulation points on which he based his policy. One was that the extension of European civilisation in Africa was in itself a desirable thing. A second was that the British race, with a history of culture and civilisation behind it, was superior to heterogeneous African races only now emerging from centuries of relative barbarism. ("I believe that the essential art of ruling is bred in the inherent characteristics of a people", he said; "in fair dealing, in honesty of purpose, in strength of character. It has been granted to few nations in the world's history. It is a gift which cannot be handed on by teaching or by example.") A third was that the opening up of new areas by means of genuine colonisation was to the advantage of the world.

These were axioms. You either rejected or endorsed them. If you rejected them, then it was no more use entering into a discussion on the conclusions arising out of them than it would be to attempt to prove Euclid's theorems without accepting the definitions of a straight line, a circle or a point.

The trouble was that opinion in England, or at any rate a considerable body of it, no longer accepted—and even despised—these axioms. Reason could show them to be fallacious, or at the least not proven. Instinct, too, seemed to have changed. The spirit which led to British colonial expansion was almost dead—withered, perhaps, by the disappearance of the biological factors that had nourished it, the rapid rise of population resulting in the swarming of the British people in its new imperial hives.

To affirm as the British Government's policy that the interests of the ruling race were on all occasions to be subjugated to those of the more backward race seemed to Delamere both a heresy and an impossibility. It was a negation of colonisation. He could not understand the new mood —was it of disillusionment or of altruism?—that dictated this attitude.

Those in the opposite camp found it equally hard to sympathise with Delamere's point of view. It was one which they abhorred. To them he was a die-hard imperialist, an exploiter of backward races, a capitalist avid for profit and unscrupulous in getting it, a jingo imbued with Rhodes' nationalistic hysteria. The philosophy to which he subscribed was too recent to be regarded with tolerance.

5

So both sides faced each other over a barrier of misunderstanding. Delamere was a man of sixty and he could not, in a few weeks, tune himself in to the new wave-length of English—and, in particular, Labour—sentiment.

The other side, for their part, could not see that colonisation no longer followed along the old and often evil nineteenth-century lines. It, too, had changed; but the anti-imperialists were reluctant to admit it. They still clung to worn-out notions left over from slave-trade days.

The modern colonist did not, as was sometimes assumed, regard the native as a lump of brawn created for the sole purpose of labouring for the white man, for a starvation wage, until he dropped. He recognised the African as a fellow human being entitled to fair treatment and to consideration in the way of health, welfare, education and the rest. He was as anxious as anyone to see the native's standard of living raised and was quite prepared to assist by paying higher wages to men who could earn them by maintaining a higher standard of workmanship and diligence.

Nor was the object of colonisation merely the ruthless exploitation of the resources and people of the country for the benefit of the ruling race. Its aim went deeper: to the founding of permanent homes and the making of a new country where the two races would progress together without enmity, and where an offshoot of European culture would take root firmly and enduringly in the soil. It was an experiment, but at least a constructive one.

No one could say how it would develop; but it had gone too far to be reversed. Mere opposition to white settlement was as sterile an attitude as the out-dated one of jingoism. The settlers were there, and it was impossible to ignore them or to attempt to shut them out from the country's future. The insignificance of their numbers was apt to blind English politicians, saturated with a democratic faith in quantity, to the strength of their position. For the colonists were making the future while others talked about it.

They had, also, a love for their country which engendered a conviction that they had a right to take a part in the direction of its future. It was this factor that lay behind their resentment to the words "immigrant communities" used of them in the white papers. Their children, born in the country, were not immigrants. They belonged to it as much, the settlers felt, as natives who had themselves been immigrants a few generations before.

The highlands of Kenya have a peculiar property of inspiring emotional affection among those who have made their homes there. This power has never been analysed, but it has its own importance in East African affairs as a political factor. It is compounded, perhaps, of the beauty of the country, of the grandeur of distant views, of space and freedom without the sting of hostility and harshness often felt in untamed continents. The variety of the landscape, ranging from silent mountain forests resting always in cold green shadow to the brilliance of open plain and broken horizon where rocks burn to the touch, is an element of Kenya's charm. The friendliness of the people, the hospitality of comfortable, irregular homesteads with their bright and carefully tended gardens—spacious cottages with a castle's outlook—and the good humour of natives, who seldom pass a traveller by without a greeting, play their part.

There is a natural cheerfulness in the atmosphere, perhaps because gloom, even in the face of disaster, is not indigenous to countries with perpetual sunshine where clouds are a changing decoration against a back-cloth of blue skies rather than dense blankets between earth and sun. There is an exhilaration in the clearness of the air, a sharpness in the outline of the distant escarpments, a width of skyline on the downs swept clean by wind, a depth of tone in the blues and purples of far-off hills not found in sunless northern countries where the air is denser than it is among mountains.

It is a country that always holds the unexpected in store, that rouses high hopes and seldom satisfies them, and yet charms the bitterness out of disappointment. Its scenes live in the memory of those who have left it, flashing back on to the mind so vividly that the nostrils seem to sense the sweet smell of a *vlei* after the rains or the tingling of red dust from untarred roads, the ear to catch the melancholy hoot of a rain-bird or the strangely moving rhythmic chant from the throats of distant Africans.

It is a land where the individual counts for more than in Europe because he is not elbowed out by his fellows; a place of opportunity and of disappointments, where years of work may be wrecked by sudden calamities and where fortunes are easier to lose than to make. Perhaps its attraction lies partly in the challenge that it throws down—the challenge of all new countries—to master its resources: or perhaps it lies in the pleasantness of life in constant sunshine and on a fertile soil. Whatever the secret of this charm, it draws back to the country men and women who have left and inspires many of those who have adopted Kenya as their home with an almost passionate concern for its future. "I believe that you and the future of Kenya", Delamere once wrote to his wife, "are the only two things I care for." Neither Delamere nor his colleagues were prepared to leave that future wholly to others—to people who neither knew nor cared for Kenya —to shape.

6

The Kenya delegation came to England with a mandate to persuade the Labour Government to withdraw and rewrite their white papers. This mission was doomed to failure from the start. Governments are seldom ready to admit themselves mistaken; and the Labour Cabinet was not open to conviction that its policy was wrong.

The main discussion centred round native policy. Delamere maintained that it was contrary to British principles of impartial government to declare the interests of one section of the community paramount above those of all other sections, and to lay down as a matter of policy that whenever the interests of two groups of the governed clashed, then one of the parties to the dispute, by virtue of race and regardless of the rights of the case, must always prevail. The business of government, he said, was to hold the scales even and not to play advocate to one section of the population. The present policy could only lead to one result: to divide the country on racial lines and to implant in the minds of the Europeans a sense of injustice which would force them further and further into opposition to native interests, instead of bringing them more clearly to see that native and European interests were interdependent.

In Kampala the rickshaw-boys had a song which they chanted as they ran to the effect that iron is useless without wood: the axe must have a handle: so the European needs the African. The converse of this, the colonists believed, held true. Wood wants iron, the handle an axe-head, the African needs the European. The Government's policy took no account of this mutual community of interest.

"Short of getting rid of the colonists in Kenya and indeed also in Tanganyika", Delamere said, "you have got to adapt your native policy to their position as future governors of the country."

This was the main burden of the delegation's attack on the white papers. They raised other points. One was that the 1930 white paper broke the pledge given by the Imperial Government in 1927 to associate the colonists more closely in trusteeship for the natives.

We ourselves did and do consider ourselves trustees for the future of the indigenous races [Delamere said]. Our trusteeship (cannot we go back to the real meaning of the word which is responsibility?) is that of all governing peoples for the uncivilised races under their rule. It means that during the long period of time likely to elapse before they can take their place on a civilised plane, we will see that they have every chance in the state of life and the standard of civilisation to which, as a whole, they rise. . . . Certainly not that their interests should be paramount over those of all other inhabitants of East Africa.

Another point was that a highly developed, politically conscious group of people such as British colonists could not be expected to arrest their progress indefinitely until a community still lagging many centuries behind in the march of civilisation caught up sufficiently to join on equal terms in the political advance.

I think the difference between Lord Passfield's policy and ours is a definite one [Delamere said]. His policy is that until these backward peoples are capable of taking part in the government of these countries, the whole political future of Eastern Africa is to stand still. Until that time bureaucratic rule is to hold the field and no further political advance is to be made.

Our policy visualises the future as a period of native advancement in their own reserves, on their own councils, before they are capable of taking part in the central direction and government of these countries.

We visualise native councils going forward gradually from the present small units to a point where over those small units is a central native council, dealing with native affairs under the central government, but with wide powers. That is as far as we can see at present. During that long period it is impossible to stifle the rights and aspirations of the civilised community which has to develop the whole of the rest of these countries.

7

In attacking the white papers the delegates found themselves involved in a justification of Kenya's native policy. "No one can deny", Delamere said, "that the general impression of the native memorandum was that all sensible native policies could only be proposed and carried out by the

Imperial Government and that the future of the native races must therefore rest in their hands for all time. It was our duty to undermine the foundations of this theory."

So the colonists took up the challenge. They undertook to argue that settlement was entitled to support not only for its own sake but because it benefited the native peoples. The tactics adopted were to show that Kenya had already done far more than she had received credit for to advance her native population; and that natives in Kenya were no worse treated, and in some ways better cared for, than those in other African dependencies under more direct Colonial Office control and possessing fewer settlers.

The delegation attempted to answer a long list of accusations that had been made against Kenya's policy by an assiduous band of critics during the past ten years.

The first was the old question of land: that the settlers had stolen all the best parts of it and left only rejected land, and not enough of that, for the natives.

Thirty-one million acres, an area roughly equal to that of England and Wales, had been set aside, the delegation pointed out, for the perpetual use of a native population equal to about one-third that of London. That fact ought to dispose, they suggested, of the accusation that the Kenya natives were starved for land. Even in the most crowded of the reserves, that of the Kikuyu, there was an allowance of about thirteen acres to every family. Taking the colony as a whole there were over fifty-five acres of gazetted reserve to a native family.

Only 10,200 square miles out of the colony's total area of 220,000 square miles—about 4½ per cent—had been alienated to Europeans. But an area over four and a half times as large—48,000 square miles, or 22 per cent of the colony's area—had been set aside as native reserve. Even if the semi-desert Northern Frontier and Turkana provinces, occupied solely by indigenous natives, were subtracted, less than 10 per cent of the remaining land had been given to settlers.

The reserves embraced, contrary to frequent statements made by ill-informed critics, a large proportion of the best land in the country. The two biggest tribes (the Kikuyu and the Kavirondo) had between them more land than the whole of the white highlands put together. And it was better land. Practically the whole of the Kikuyu reserve consisted of rich, red, fertile forest soil, excellently watered and all over 5000 feet, of the type which, in European hands, grew the finest coffee; and the Kikuyu tribe had over 3¼ million acres of it

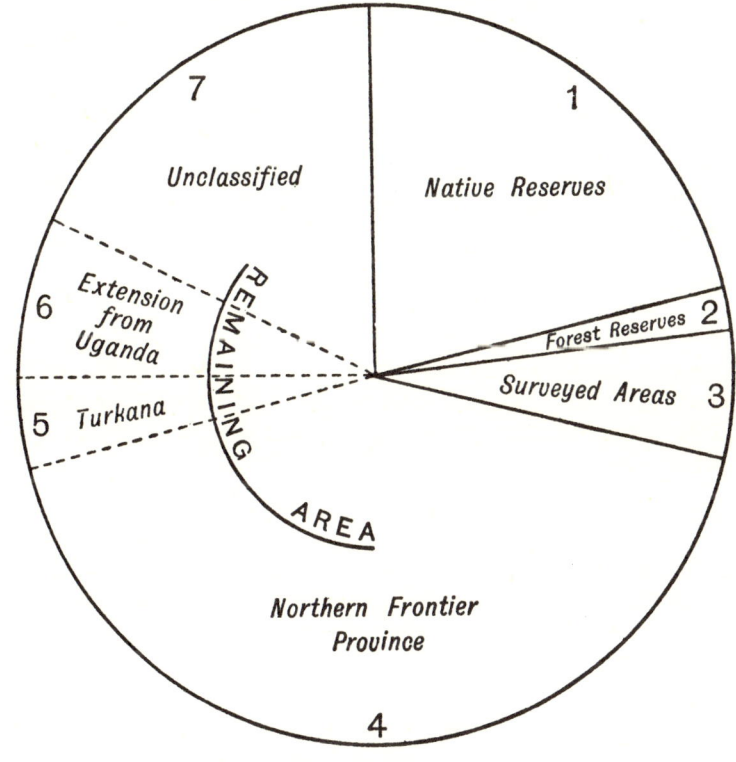

Pie chart with sections:
- 1 Native Reserves
- 2 Forest Reserves
- 3 Surveyed Areas
- 4 Northern Frontier Province
- 5 Turkana
- 6 Extension from Uganda
- 7 Unclassified
- Remaining Area

LAND IN KENYA, 1933

Diagram showing the proportion of the total area—224,960 square miles—occupied by different categories of land. "Surveyed areas" includes all land alienated to settlers, together with townships and other unalienated Crown land.

—an area half the size of the entire European highlands. The Kavirondo reserve was still larger. It included the richest agricultural land in the country, and enjoyed a better rainfall than any other part of Kenya.

Much of the grazing in the Masai and Nandi country was as good or better than any that the Europeans had secured.

These contentions were later borne out by the Kenya Land commission. "The greater part of the Masai reserve", its report remarked, "includes some of the finest agricultural and pastoral land in Kenya."

The fact was that the natives, not the Europeans, had got the best land. This was confirmed by the man probably in the position to know best, the director of Agriculture. Speaking in Legislative Council in 1928 he said:

> I should like to voice the opinion, with all the authority that I am able to exercise, and with all the knowledge I may possess, that the best land and the most fertile land in this colony has not been occupied by the non-native peoples. The natives have been left in possession of the most fertile land of the colony.

A few years before the deputy director had said:

> The European is wrongly accused of having become possessed of the best land in Kenya. He knows how to use land in comparison with the native, who possesses as good land and even better in many parts . . . it is this difference in the use of land which has blinded observers.

This same officer added:

> For proper cultivation the native reserves need a population about three times as great as is living there at present. Enormously valuable agricultural areas in native reserves are hardly populated, and if populated are treated pastorally.

Nor was it correct to state that the Europeans had taken all the highlands, leaving the lower-lying parts to natives. Only about one quarter of the area of Kenya over 4500 feet had been alienated for settlement.

Not only did the natives own enough land and good land, but they were secure in their possession of it. (In the past this had not been so.) In 1926 the reserves had been finally gazetted and now the Native Lands Trust bill, which had been supported by all the elected members, had passed on to the statute book. Under this law the reserves were "set aside for the use and benefit of the native tribes of the colony for ever", and a Native Lands Trust board, with the Governor as chairman, was established to guard their security. Never again could the fringes be clipped as had happened in a few instances in the past.

So much, the delegation said, for the libel that the settlers had stolen all the natives' best land.

8

Then there was the question of labour. The bogey of "forced labour" had been laid but accusations had been made that natives were compelled by high taxation to work for Europeans against their will.

In regard to labour two definite tenets of policy had been laid down in Kenya. One was that the Government, in the words of Sir Edward Grigg, "neither can nor will produce labour from the reserves by compulsion of any sort". The other was that every able-bodied male was expected to pull his weight in society by doing a certain amount of work, either within his own reserve or, if he preferred it, for wages under a European employer. He was to have an absolutely free choice as to which type of labour he undertook.

It was sometimes maintained that his choice was not in fact free, because he could only earn money to pay his tax by going out of his reserve to work. It was stated, however, by the chief Native Commissioner in Legislative Council that the amount received by the natives as a whole for the crops they exported from the reserves, after providing for their own needs, almost exactly balanced the total amount of native direct taxation. "The native can and does provide for his tax by the sale of his surplus produce", said the Commissioner. In addition to this they earned (*circa* 1930) about £2,000,000 a year in wages. All this was extra to their direct taxes and their own sustenance, and was available for luxuries and for the improvement of their standard of living.

Another argument advanced against white settlement was that the demand for labour would soon increase to a point where the male population of the reserves was not large enough to satisfy it. Figures showed, however, that the labour demand, even in the year it reached its maximum, could be met by one-third of the men in the reserves. Taking the native population as a whole, that is, two men out of three could always remain at home without thereby creating any shortage of labour. After 1929 the proportion of men needed outside the reserves steadily declined, and by 1931 there were more men seeking employment than could be absorbed by the labour market.

The delegation also did its best to dispel the impression (deliberately created, in part, by men with a grudge against the colony) that the Kenya settler was a harsh, exacting and unduly self-seeking employer.

Relations between settlers and natives, the delegates affirmed, rested on a solid basis of goodwill. Labourers were housed and fed on rations laid down by the Government. Every farm maintained a dispensary to deal with minor ailments, and there were few settlers' wives who did not, as a matter of course, treat the sores and burns of innumerable babies brought to them by native women. Some farms provided schools for their employees' children. In times of famine the labourer was freed from all anxiety while his relations in the reserve went hungry. Government inspectors toured the country to see that labour conditions were enforced. A native who was dissatisfied with his treatment could, by complaining to a district officer, set the whole motion of the law in progress against his employer.

Much of the labour was provided by squatters who lived, rent-free, with their wives, children, goats and cattle on European farms. The fact that squatters were rapidly on the increase—there were calculated to be about 200,000 natives living outside the reserves—proved that this relationship between master and man was not an irksome one.

There were, of course, occasional abuses, for in every country in the world there were bad employers and good; but over the country as a whole African labourers were well treated and contented. Most settlers took a personal interest in the welfare of their employees, and were fair and lenient masters. Employment under Europeans created opportunity. Intelligent natives could rise to positions of considerable trust and authority and so find an outlet for their abilities. Successful skilled workers could earn wages that would make them rich men among their fellows. Work outside the reserves provided something of adventure for the young men. It brought them into contact with men of other tribes, taught them new things, enabled them to see a little of the world—the strange world of the white man—beyond the narrow boundaries of their tribal life.

Probably nowhere in the world [the chief Native Commissioner wrote in a report] are relations between employers and employed better than in Kenya. But quite apart from that, the concern of the unofficial population for the development of native communities has manifested itself in many and diverse ways and is a particularly noteworthy factor in the life of the colony.

9

One of the most persistent accusations made against the local Government by its English critics was that natives were being taxed to pay for European services. It was suggested that they did not get a fair return for their hut tax, and that money which should have been spent on hospitals and schools in the reserves went to European education and agriculture.

Sir Edward Grigg had emphatically refuted this allegation in the Legislative Council in 1928:

Every penny of direct taxation raised in native reserves is spent on direct native services in those reserves.

I mention this fact because this Council is continually being accused by those who will not look at facts of taking revenue from the native and spending it on European and other services. I desire to say here, with all the zest at my command, that that reiterated charge against the colony is entirely false and untrue. The contribution made to the general system and machinery of government throughout the colony by the native tribes comes entirely from their contribution to indirect revenue.

This was definite enough. The Kenya delegation proceeded to drive home the statement with a battery of figures.

Kenya's accounts were not kept on a racial basis. Many

of the services could not be divided into the proportions which benefited Africans, Europeans, Indians or Arabs. Who was to say, for example, how much advantage, in terms of cash, each race derived from the cost of defence? The only immediate benefactors were, in actual fact, nomadic Turkana and Rendile tribes who contributed nothing at all to the revenue. They paid no hut tax but their wives were protected, at the expense of the rest of the colony's population, from being raped by Abyssinians. Since the war, over a million pounds of Kenya's revenue had thus been sunk in the useless deserts of her northern provinces. It was obvious that the principle of returning to each community the amount it paid in direct taxation broke down at once.

In spite of difficulties, however, the cost of such services as education, health and agriculture could be divided up amongst the races. This was done, and a despatch was written by the Governor separating the expenditure for 1929 into native and non-native components. Only one-third of military expenditure was put down as a native service. The resulting figures showed that, in 1929, a sum (in round figures) of £681,000 was spent on direct native services, whereas the revenue from native hut and poll tax amounted to £540,000. The natives, therefore, had received in direct services £141,000 more than they had contributed in direct taxation.

Another line of attack against the colonists was that the Europeans did not pay their fair share of taxes. They had succeeded in getting income tax removed, it was said, and since then they had rejoiced in negligible taxation while the natives groaned under the weight of heavy imposts.

In reply to this the Kenya delegation quoted the figures worked out by the statistician to the Governors' conference. These showed that the Europeans in Kenya paid an average of over £36 a head in taxation, while the average for the native population was 6s. 6d. a head. This sum, the Europeans claimed, could not be considered excessive considering that the native population had free land and an enormous wealth of stock (on an average for the whole country there were nearly 20 head of stock to a family; the Masai had about 180 head to a family—probably more than any other tribe in Africa), and that the average native cash wage throughout the colony worked out at 20s. a month.[1]

No exact figure of the proportion of total revenue contributed by each community could be worked out. Various estimates indicated, however, that the European population, which numbered about 17,000, or less than 2 per cent of the population, provided at least two-fifths of the revenue.

10

The last point in regard to taxation to be refuted was the suggestion that the natives of Kenya would be better off if there were no white settlement, for the Government would then be able to spend more on the African and less on the European. The colonists held that this was a fallacy. The stimulus of settlement, they said, had so increased the country's trade that a bigger pool of wealth had been created on which the native, with the rest of the community, could draw. Had it not been for settlement Kenya would have been economically far poorer, revenues smaller and African social services less developed.

They supported their case by comparing the amount allocated to native social services in Kenya with that spent in Uganda and Tanganyika.

Kenya, with a population of less than 3 million natives, had spent more on education every year up to 1928 than had Tanganyika, with a population of 4 million. Tanganyika had now forged ahead, but only by very little, and the amount spent per head on native schooling was still much larger in Kenya.

Kenya was spending considerably more per head on native medical services than either Tanganyika or Uganda. She possessed, by 1930, the best native hospitals in East Africa, and a larger number of patients received treatment in Kenya than in Tanganyika, in spite of the mandated territory's bigger population. Since the war the medical service had

---

[1] This figure included the wages of the higher-paid classes such as personal servants and artisans. The average for farm labourers was, of course, lower—about 12 to 14 shillings. This did not include costs of rations and housing.

succeeded in almost abolishing what had been the most prevalent disease in Kenya, yaws.[1]

It was clear, therefore, that the native was better rather than worse off, at least in these respects, in a country where white settlers had established themselves than in almost wholly native states. Even a hostile critic of Kenya, Professor Buell, admitted in his book, *The Native Problem in Africa*:

> The attitude of respective governments toward mission education is best shown by the amount of financial assistance they give to mission schools. In this respect, Kenya is making larger grants than in native territories. . . .
>
> It seems clear that so far the Kenya Government has done more for native education than the Uganda Government, and that the Kenya Government has, in comparison with Tanganyika, done a great deal more for its natives in the way of medical work. In agricultural and veterinary services for natives Kenya lags considerably behind Uganda and somewhat behind Tanganyika. (Vol. i. p. 387.)

These facts proved the injustice, the deputation said, of accusing the colonists of standing in the way of native progress. They claimed to have consistently supported it and, to a large extent, to have made it possible.

They could not avoid the feeling that the home Government's attitude was sometimes tinged with hypocrisy. A great deal was made of the supposition that the Imperial Government alone was impartial and fitted to watch over native interests. Yet when it came to the point its behaviour hardly fitted with its declarations. There was, for example, the matter of the arrears of pay owing by the Imperial Government to relatives of porters in the Carrier Corps who had died or been reported missing during the war. This sum, totalling about £50,000, had been described by

---

[1] The following comparative figures are given by Professor Buell (*The Native Problem in Africa*, vol. i.), of expenditure per hundred natives:

	Kenya	Uganda
Agriculture	£1·75	£2·36
Medical	5·74	4·37
Education	2·43	1·47

"There are more European doctors and government educators in Kenya in relation to the native population than in Tanganyika and Uganda", Professor Buell stated. (1928.)

Mr. Amery as a debt of honour. The Kenya Government had repeatedly reminded Secretaries of State that its payment was long overdue. Yet the British Treasury had refused to sanction it and the debt still remained — twelve years after the war — unhonoured. This behaviour was later described by a commission as "a much more callous violation of the principle of trusteeship to the natives than any of the injuries which the natives have suffered by alienation of their land".[1]

II

The final point made by the delegation was a defence of the dual policy on the ground that its European arm had developed and opened up Kenya for British commerce. The trade of Kenya had doubled in the last seven years. It could double again in the next seven if the dual policy was vigorously pursued. It was European enterprise that had provided the stimulus. In spite of efforts to increase native production, Europeans were still responsible for nearly nine-tenths of the total exports. Kenya, Delamere further pointed out, had a greater trade per head of her population than any other Crown possession in Africa of similar age. Nigeria, for all its natural wealth of tropical produce, had a trade of 35s. a head. Kenya and Uganda together had a *per capita* trade of 57s. The railway traffic was greater by over £100 a mile in Kenya than in Nigeria. Delamere remarked:

An area of over a million square miles is awaiting development and British trade. The only part of it which has been developed with railways and ports since Rhodes died and the railways of Rhodesia were carried into the Congo and the Katanga is Kenya — because it has a vigorous white resident population to push forward its development.

Kenya started last in the race. The greater part of the country consists of Masai steppes. There was no question of growing valuable native crops and starting an industry of that sort. And yet now it heads the list of the African countries under the Colonial Office of anything like its own age.

[1] In 1935 — some eighteen years after it was contracted — the debt was honoured by the National Government by paying over £50,000 towards the cost of carrying out readjustments recommended by the Kenya Land commission.

Surely Britain, he asked, was not indifferent to the possibilities of trade in Africa at a time when other continents and countries were rolling themselves up like hedgehogs, exposing an armour of tariff and quota prickles to the rest of the world? The dual policy had justified itself, he maintained, as the soundest basis for increasing trade and at the same time enriching (as increase of trade must do) the indigenous population of East Africa; and so it had earned its right to imperial support.

This was, in essence, the case prepared by Delamere and his colleagues to answer the charges so repeatedly brought against the good faith of colonists and government alike.

As for the future, Delamere said, it was futile to plan too far ahead. No one could foresee the ultimate political development of the native. No one could tell whether, in the long run, education would change the fundamental outlook of the mass of the African people or whether they would reach a certain point and then—apart from a few exceptional individuals—progress no further. As the geneticist Bateson had put it: "The stick will not make the dwarf pea climb, but without it the tall can never rise. Education, sanitation and the rest are but the giving or withholding of opportunity."

The use that the African would make of that opportunity was still an unknown factor. To rush him off his balance would be a fatal mistake. He still had a long road to travel. Before he could take part in the central government some method would have to be found of getting round the difficulty of the tribal divisions which had provided the framework of African society since time unknown. It was an easy but a dangerous mistake to think of "natives" as comprising a homogeneous population. Hamitic, Nilotic and Bantu were possibly as different in stock and origin as Nordic Germans, Latin Frenchmen and Slavonic Russians. Their languages were of a different structure. Thirty years before they had been constantly at war with each other, and in a few years they would be at war again if British rule were to be withdrawn. Tribalism died hard; as hard, perhaps, as nationalism in Europe. If western races had not yet learnt to forget their traditions of enmity and join in a united states of Europe, surely it was premature to make plans for the day when Africans would drop their no less deep-rooted tribal and racial differences.

12

The Europeans, in the meantime, must be left free to follow the natural evolution of political responsibility as they showed themselves fit for it. They were not aiming at responsible government in the lifetime of the present generation. "For many years to come", Delamere admitted, "final responsibility, not only in active affairs but on all major issues, must rest with the Imperial Government". They wanted "a policy of gradual devolution of responsibility".

The evolution of Europeans, no less than that of natives, could be determined only by time. White settlement was still an experiment. Fundamentally its future depended not upon government but on biology. If the white races could establish themselves permanently in tropical highlands and breed and thrive there without loss of virility, then their ultimate right to control their own destiny could not for ever be denied. Two thousand children, many of them Kenya born, were now in Kenya schools. They were experimental material in the human laboratory. Science was only beginning to formulate the questions that would have to be answered before any conclusions could be reached as to the future of white races in the tropics.

Did the ultra-violet rays of the sun affect the nervous system in some unknown way? The power of the sunlight in Kenya was equal, all the year round, to that of a mid-summer day in the Alps. Could the northern races maintain their vigour indefinitely in this intensity of light? At the altitude of the highlands the body was obliged to make an extra effort to obtain the oxygen needed for its upkeep. Did this strain result in a loss of efficiency, or would children born in the country adapt themselves naturally to these increased demands, as they seemed to have done in South Africa and throughout the immense sections of South America and the United States where people lived and bred, without any ill effects, at altitudes of over 5000 feet?[1]

[1] The belief held by some people that the altitude of the Kenya highlands must be deleterious to Europeans does not appear to be supported by comparisons

Did the more violent fluctuations of temperature—often a fall which in northern Europe would be spread over a season took place in the tropics between noon and night-time—place a strain on the body of the European? Humidity, also, was much more changeable. Did the quick adjustments that the body was called upon to make in some way exhaust the nervous system of men and women, and particularly children, adapted through centuries to a slower, steadier climate?

Until research had analysed these factors and time had provided the data, no conclusions could be reached as to the future of white settlement in Kenya. It might well be that the body, with its tremendous powers of adaptability, would find little trouble in adjusting itself to these conditions. It had met and conquered harder difficulties, from the winters of northern Canada with fifty-below-zero temperatures to the tropics of Queensland where white men worked on sugar plantations in the sun and showed no loss of vigour or fertility or health. Kenya might perhaps evolve a new human type best suited to her conditions, as other countries had done.

Delamere believed that the strains of adjustment could largely be avoided by taking simple precautions.

It is often wondered how far the European can permanently inhabit central Africa [he remarked]. My own belief is that the difficulties at present inherent in life in the cool climate of the tropics above certain altitudes are those arising from lack of knowledge and lack of organisation for carrying out the results of research.

As each trouble is investigated it is found to be specific and capable of being dealt with. It is only a few years ago that malaria was supposed to be caused by some mysterious exhalation from swamps or newly turned over land. Now that we have discovered its cause, surely we can deal with it in time.

The ultra-violet rays or the actinic ray is our greatest difficulty, and yet this ray is necessary to healthy life and in the smoky towns of England it may have to be artificially applied. Its effect seems to be to stimulate the nervous system and to improve the capacity of

with conditions in other countries. Johannesburg, for example—the second largest city in Africa—is 5700 feet above sea-level, and Denver, Colorado, is at about the same altitude as Nairobi, 5200 feet. In neither of these cities are people more prone to insanity than elsewhere.

the body for extracting nutrition from certain food substances. It is probable that an excess of the ray causes nerve exhaustion, and it seems to me one of the matters that requires careful research.

How many hours' exposure to the ray is good? How much is that affected by thickness or colour of clothing and hats? We all know that the Latin races in sunny countries spend a proportion of the day in darkened rooms. I think the Dutch in South Africa do the same thing.

Generally speaking, there is probably no reason whatever why Europeans living under civilised conditions should not live on the high veld of tropical Africa. I can well remember when it was said that English people could not live in Johannesburg without going home frequently.

13

All these points were raised in speeches, interviews and memoranda during the delegation's stay in England.

The settlers had an interview with the Secretary of State at which they failed to obtain a promise that, following the pledges of his predecessor, closer union would not be imposed upon East Africa in the face of opposition from the Europeans. He was adamant on the subject of an unofficial majority in the Kenya Legislative Council. His replies to questions about the common roll were, from the delegation's point of view, unsatisfactory. It was evident that no toning down of the white papers could be anticipated.

On one point only was reassurance obtained. A suggestion in the white paper that land outside the reserves might be provided for natives who wished to lease plots on individual tenure had aroused fears among the colonists that alienated land would be bought for the purpose. Would this, they wondered, be the beginning of an attempt to squeeze the settlers out of Kenya? Lord Passfield, however, promised them that the "white highlands" were not to be threatened. Whatever happened, he said, the Government would not go back on that reiterated pledge.

It was after this meeting that Delamere and his colleagues decided definitely to oppose any form of closer union. They felt that it could only be brought about on terms which would deprive the Kenya Legislative Council of the power it had already secured without giving anything in return. Further examination of the proposals had shown that, far from saving money, the setting up of a High Commissioner would cost more. The beginning of the world depression had already affected East Africa and the financial aspect assumed a new importance. There seemed to be few advantages to be gained. It was best, Delamere said, to "put closer union into cold storage" for the time being.

Delamere was accused of inconsistency at this change of front. He was, however, consistent to the extent that he had always qualified his support for closer union with the provisos that it was to be brought about on lines which would safeguard the future of white settlement, and that it must bring with it some constitutional advance for the Europeans. These provisos had not been fulfilled. Closer union had taken a very different shape from that which he had first visualised and he believed that no alternative was left but to oppose it.

Before returning to Kenya Delamere made his second and last speech before the House of Lords. It was not a success. He was always at his worst in formal surroundings and before a strange audience. The solemn, dignified atmosphere, the tiers of benches sparsely filled with dormant peers and bishops oppressed him.

The occasion was the moving of a motion by Lord Passfield for the setting up of the joint select committee. Delamere made a halting and ineffectual speech. His health was not good and a strenuous two months of apparently fruitless discussion had worn him out. His mind had lost its snap. After a few disconnected sentences he sat down, conscious of his failure. He had missed an opportunity, and disappointed many who had hoped to hear a colonial statesman with a reputation as the *enfant terrible* of the Colonial Office and the breaker of Governors expounding the Kenya settler's case.

In November 1930 he returned to Kenya. Shortly after his arrival he was reappointed to the Executive Council. During his absence in London the settler who had taken his place as elected member for the Rift Valley—Mr. Powys Cobb—had given up his seat and Delamere had been re-elected. He was deeply gratified by this gesture of confidence in his leadership.

CHAPTER XXVI

WORLD DEPRESSION
1931

I

DELAMERE arrived in Kenya to find the colony staggering under the first blows of the world depression. Causes far outside her control once again checked her advance just as she seemed to have settled into a steady stride towards prosperity. Only a country of exceptional resilience could have survived.

In the autumn of 1929 the New York stock market collapsed with spectacular abruptness. All over the world newspapers carried stories of distracted brokers, tickers two hours late and panic which swept America like a veld fire. Few readers saw in the Wall Street crash the first ominous crack in the precarious structure of post-war economics.

Then commodity prices began to drop with alarming speed. In industrial countries unemployment figures started to soar. Demand for agricultural products shrank and prices fell again.

The Canadian wheat pool failed in its attempt to hold up grain prices and North American farmers found themselves plunged into insolvency as dollar wheat fell to fifty cents.

Gold accumulated unhealthily in Paris and New York. Deflation, already acute, squeezed debtor countries to breaking point. The stability of currencies was threatened. Germany announced her inability to pay further reparations. The Austrian banking system gave way under the strain. The credit of the world was shaken.

Tariff walls were raised and frightened nations took shelter behind them, erecting a barbed wire entanglement of quotas on the top to make doubly sure that other countries' goods could not pass the barriers. Only the minimum of foreign trade was allowed to enter. Every nation tried to sell more to others and to buy less from them. Goods accumulated unsold in factories. Grain piled high in elevators. Stacks of cotton rose to the roofs of warehouses. Coffee was burned as fuel for locomotives. Shiploads of molasses were poured into the sea. In thousands of homes men and women went hungry for bread and ragged of shirt and dress, while unemployment figures rose month by month as mills and factories closed their doors. Commodity prices continued to fall.

So widely spread was the web of world depression, so fine its meshes, that no one could escape. Even primitive Africans living lives little different from those of their ancestors felt its effects. A chain of economics bound them to a world of which they lived in ignorance.

The chain started somewhere, perhaps, in an industrial city, where the creeping paralysis of unemployment was gaining ground. A big store cancelled its order for boots. A factory reduced its purchases of leather. A tannery cut down its demand for hides. The price on the London market sagged.

A shipper decreased his next consignment from abroad. A Mombasa produce merchant offered a lower price to Indian and Somali middlemen. The word went out into the scattered *dukas*. Somewhere a native herdsman, to whom Europe was not even a name, found that suddenly, for some reason totally inexplicable to him, the price that he received for his ox hide at a trading outpost had dropped by half.

Nor did the chain end there. His hides fetched half their previous price but his tax did not vary. When the time came he could not pay in full. Thousands like him reduced their contribution to the revenue. The estimates were not realised, retrenchments followed and purchasing power fell further; and the budget could not be balanced.

2

Agricultural countries felt the depression most acutely and with the greatest violence. Between 1925 and 1930 the average value of every ton of produce exported from Australia fell by 60 per cent. As a result of the depression the cash income of American farmers dropped from nine and a half to four billion dollars. Kenya, dependent wholly on farm produce, was desperately hard hit. She had no second string of industry on which to rely.

Prices of her major crops fell disastrously. Coffee dropped, in 1930, from about £120 to £70 a ton. It cost the Kenya producer, experts calculated, £71 to £75 to get each ton of coffee to the London market, not counting interest charges.

In 1929 maize had sold for 12s. a bag. In the middle of 1930 it fell to little over 5s. By the end of the same year it was fetching less than 2s. 9d.

Sisal slumped from £40 a ton in 1929 to £20 in the following year and, later still, to £12 a ton. Wheat fell almost as steeply. The depression reduced the price of butter in London from 180s. to 84s. a cwt. The prices of all Kenya's principal exports reached a level, in 1930, well below the cost of production. "The growth of one essential arm of the dual policy", said Sir Edward Grigg in July, "has been paralysed." The slump was cataclysmic in its abruptness.

Native produce was no better off. The price of *wimbi* and beans dropped by half, that of ghee by nearly two-thirds. Hides fell from 30s. a *frasila* (at Narok) down to 6s.

It was not surprising that revenue fell far short of the estimates and that the year 1930 yielded a deficit of nearly £200,000.

Kenya suffered more severely than most countries because her position was already weakened by the locust invasion. The 1929 budget should have shown a comfortable surplus, as the previous five budgets had done. But unforeseen calls upon the colony's resources to fight locusts and to relieve famine, combined with a fall in revenue following the destruction of crops, had resulted in a large deficit. Kenya had been obliged to weaken her defences by drawing upon her savings before the depression set in.

The railway suffered with the countries that it served. A bad cotton crop in Uganda coincided with the fall in the price of the raw material. Uganda's 1930 exports dropped, as a result, by over £2,000,000, or 50 per cent. This catastrophic falling off of traffic reduced the takings of the railway by some £400,000.

While Uganda's exports fell by half, Kenya managed to increase her output to a higher total than she had ever reached before. In spite of the fall in values her exports rose from less than £3,000,000 in 1929 to slightly under £3,500,000 in 1930. Only this spurt in production saved the situation for the colony and the railway.

Delamere used this fact to point a moral that he often stressed—that the "single crop policy" followed by Uganda was a dangerous one. All Uganda's eggs, he said, were in one basket. In times of crisis such as this the single crop policy displayed its weakness, and the basis of mixed farming —his ideal for Kenya—showed its strength. A country that spread its production over a variety of crops was less subject to violent fluctuations of trade and he believed that its progress, in the long run, would be greater. In support of this he pointed out that Kenya's exports had risen steadily year by year, until in 1930 they were 50 per cent higher than in 1924. Uganda's exports, during the same period, had remained stationary.

3

An increase of exports such as Kenya had managed to achieve was, for an agricultural debtor country, the only alternative to default on her loans.

For while prices dropped, debts and fixed charges such as freights remained the same. Interest on debts, both private and public, could only be paid with the proceeds of the sale of produce. So it became necessary to sell two or three times as much produce as before in order to obtain the same amount of money with which to pay interest.

The burden of debt, in other words, was suddenly doubled or trebled—or, in some cases, even more drastically multiplied. It was calculated that the East African sisal grower had to send ten times as much fibre to London in 1931 as was required two years before to repay a given amount of debt.

All over the world agricultural countries were faced with the same problems. In one important respect Kenya was worse off than most of her fellow-sufferers. The Dominions could, and some did, devaluate their currency in terms of sterling.

The Australian and the British pound parted company, so that for every pound paid in London for her produce the Commonwealth received over 28s. in her own currency. Kenya, as a Crown colony, was tied to sterling and could take no steps of this sort to alleviate her position. She sold her butter in London for the same price as that obtained by Australia, but the Kenya farmer received considerably less for it than did the Australian.

Against these handicaps she had one great advantage on her side—low costs of production. Few countries could produce more cheaply. In this lay the ultimate soundness of her economic position.

Delamere saw, as soon as he returned from England, that the only policy for the elected members to adopt was to drop politics altogether in favour of economics. "The one thing that stands out", he told a meeting of settlers, "is that Kenya *cannot afford* to give so large a proportion of her time to politics. . . . Let us all concentrate on getting on with our work and consolidating our economic position, and leave political argument for the present."

Delamere followed his own advice without delay. Although doctors had warned him that his heart was in no condition to stand worry and overwork, he allowed himself no rest. He studied with thoroughness the effect of the crisis on Kenya and decided that the first necessity of the situation was the appointment of an economic and finance committee, composed jointly of officials, elected members and business men, to consider the whole question of Kenya's financial situation and the measures needed to strengthen her agricultural position. He pressed for a committee on these lines in January 1931. The Government replied that it was already engaged in making such economies as were necessary, and that it saw no need for a committee to advise it.

It was unfortunate that a change of Governors was taking place at a time when financial difficulties were gathering so rapidly. Sir Edward Grigg departed in August 1930; Sir Joseph Byrne, promoted from Sierra Leone, did not arrive until February 1931. Kenya was, therefore, left for half a year without a Governor.

The departure of a Governor whose policy is known and

the arrival of a successor new to the country and its problems must always have an unsettling effect, especially if the shuffle coincides with a crisis. Continuity of policy, more than ever a necessity, becomes impossible. The matter is complicated by the colonial system of transferring heads of departments from one country to another at frequent intervals. Sir Joseph Byrne arrived to find that almost all the senior officials on whom he had to rely for advice were newcomers to Kenya.

At one period during Sir Edward Grigg's régime ten heads of departments had been on leave at once. Government in Britain would be unduly complicated if ten members of the Cabinet were holiday-making in South Africa at the same time.

4

During Delamere's absence in England the Government had taken action to give the agricultural industry breathing space in which to make readjustments to the new conditions.

The maize industry was the hardest hit—the price fell by two-thirds in a single season—and the danger of wholesale collapse had to be averted. Maize provided a livelihood for more settlers than any other crop, and one-third of the area of European cultivation was under it. A maize conference was held in 1930 and the Government agreed to subsidise exports by means of a loan of £108,000 from surplus balances. A sum of £100,000 was also set aside to provide short-term credits to farmers at the ordinary rate of interest.

The object of this was to enable settlers, already partially crippled by drought and locusts, to plant their next season's crops. The banks, scared by the world financial crisis, had withdrawn abruptly into their shells and refused to make further advances. The Government was obliged to take over the responsibilities that the banks had hitherto not only accepted but actively sought. Had the land bank been in existence such an emergency measure would not have been necessary. For three years it had been momentarily expected, but it was still held up on matters of detail by the Secretary of State and action of some sort could no longer be delayed.

These were the only measures of assistance granted to agriculture by the Government.

A thorough investigation into the means of reducing costs of production had, in the meantime, been undertaken by the board of agriculture, which had been set up in May 1930 on the lines recommended in Sir Daniel Hall's report. It had an unofficial majority and was under the chairmanship of a settler, Mr. J. F. H. Harper. Delamere was one of the members. It was intended to be a step towards associating the colonists in the machinery of government and a method of making use of their experience in the framing of policy.

The board analysed costs of production of each principal industry and showed where reductions could best be made. Good use was made of its advice. Costs were drastically reduced by all Kenya's leading industries and in many cases they were pared down to half their boom-time level. The Government, however, at first did little to assist this effort. When the world depression grew worse and prices fell still further, railway rates on some exported products were raised and taxation was further increased.

5

At the fourth general election, held in March 1931, Delamere outlined to the Rift Valley electors his programme for meeting the depression. Political issues were left altogether out of the picture.

The country's greatest need, he said, was the reorganisation of agricultural credit. A planned system of long-term credit was essential to replace the present haphazard method of financing permanent improvements out of bank overdrafts which were liable to be called in at any moment. "In every country in the world where agriculture has been a success", Delamere said, "this method of a low rate of interest on long-term loans has been adopted to put agriculture on its feet."

Another necessary step was an enquiry into the best methods of encouraging the shift over from single crop to mixed farming which was taking place in Kenya. "The highlands of Kenya have not got enormous acreages of land suitable for ranching and partial development of the soil", Delamere said. "Like New Zealand and other small countries with a rich soil, Kenya must ultimately depend on a more intensive system."

A further suggestion was that a closer settlement scheme based on the subdivision of existing farms should be launched. This was the only way, Delamere said, that the basis of production on which the railway rested could be broadened.

The final plank in his election platform was the need for economy in the Civil service. Since the Bowring committee's feat of pruning, government expenditure had doubled. If times were hard and the country and all its inhabitants were suffering, Delamere held, it was only just that officials should make their share of the sacrifice.

Civil servants were apt to complain of unfairness in that they suffered in bad times but had no chance to profit by prosperity. Delamere pointed out that this complaint could not in justice be made in Kenya. Officials had received an all-round increase of one-third in salaries and pensions after the war, and another windfall at the time of the currency change. Then when trade improved after the post-war slump, they had benefited again. One of Sir Edward Grigg's first actions was to raise the salaries of all Civil servants by 20 per cent. Pensions were generous—an officer might retire on an annual income equal to two-thirds of his maximum salary—and however much the cost of living might fall and the colony's revenue shrink they could not be reduced.

Delamere therefore supported a graduated cut in Civil service pay. He believed that the drastic economies essential to the country's solvency could not be made without it. Decentralisation was another method of economy. In a farmers' country like Kenya, he said, government machinery should be simple and "the enormous superstructure which overshadows us all, officials and non-officials, at the Secretariat, should be reduced to something more in keeping with the colony's true position".

He was anxious, also, to see the nucleus of a local Civil service formed. Every year larger numbers of Kenya youths were leaving school. One of the recognised openings for the able in all countries was the administration. In Kenya it was closed to those whose homes lay in the country. The settlers were beginning to resent this, and Delamere pressed for an enquiry into how far the best among the new generation of Kenya boys could be offered chances in the Civil service.

This was the outline of his programme early in 1931. He was returned unopposed, for the last time, for the Rift Valley. All members were elected on a manifesto binding them to drop politics until the depression was over.

6

The Legislative Council reassembled in June 1931 under the new Governor. World conditions had worsened between the dissolution of the old council in January, and the gathering of the new.

The 1931 budget had been rashly framed in the belief that it was "only reasonable to assume that there will be some revival in market prices." This reasoning had been at fault; prices had further to fall. Locusts were still rampant and while the Council assembled in Nairobi they were engaged in destroying the equivalent of a million bags of maize. The yield of hut tax and customs duties was dropping ominously.

The need for action had, however, been realised by the Government. The new Governor announced in his first address to Council that the 1931 estimates of expenditure had been cut by nearly a quarter of a million and the budget balanced on the new level. The unofficials congratulated the Government and moved that the revised budget should be referred, as usual, to the select committee on which the elected members sat. The Government refused to accept this motion. Their official spokesman indicated that the cuts had been made and were unalterable.

The practice of referring the estimates for criticism to a select committee had become firmly established during the past ten years. It had grown into a recognised custom. It was an essential part of the system of "government by agreement" now accepted on all sides as a local tradition.

The Governor's refusal to refer the revised budget back to the select committee could only mean one thing, in the opinion of the elected members. It could only mean that "government by agreement" was to be scrapped, and the unofficials treated as opponents instead of as partners in the country's business. Rumours had already been circulated that Sir Joseph Byrne had come out with instructions "to break the unofficial influence". At a time when all the brains and energies of the country were needed to co-operate in straightening out the financial tangle and consolidating the economic position, this attitude on the Government's part seemed to the elected members to be a disaster.

Delamere exploded once: "In all the years I have been in this Council", he said, "I have never before heard of a case where Government refused the request of the united body of the unofficial members on such flimsy arguments."

The departmental cuts in the 1931 budget were later criticised in England on the grounds that they pared down too severely the native social services. The colonists were accused of influencing the Government to deal more leniently with European than with native benefits. This charge was somewhat ironical in view of the bitterness felt by the unofficial members at the Government's refusal to allow them any say in the recasting of the estimates. As the cuts were made in the interval between two Legislative Councils, the settlers' representatives could hardly be held responsible.

Delamere took the Government's change of attitude—another of those reversals of policy from which Kenya had suffered so often—very much to heart. The Government's refusal to accept the elected members' offer of co-operation embittered the last few months of his life. He saw the system which he had worked so hard to build up destroyed, the colonists antagonised at a time when their goodwill was most needed, while the finances of the country grew worse and the savings which it had carefully put aside dwindled steadily.

He accused the Government of dragging politics back into the arena after the colonists had offered to bury them. The development of a colony was basically an economic business. The Government, Delamere said, had continually allowed political red herrings to distract it from the line of economic advance. Because of political considerations it had put obstacles in the way of the taking up of land, wavered for years over a labour policy, built up no system of agricultural credit, failed to alienate available land, negatived every closer settlement scheme, done nothing to attract new settlers. Now, when it was most essential that all classes should pull together if the colony was to be extricated from the economic morass, the Government had cold-shouldered the colonists because of a purely political desire to see their privileges curtailed.

7

Throughout Delamere's last session he urged the Government again and again to work out a constructive policy for increasing production, European and native alike. The limit of economies, he said, must eventually be reached and the problem of carrying on a trade big enough to support the superstructure of Kenya's loans would remain. "I believe that unless we continue to accelerate a forward policy of reconstruction", he said, "we must fall by the weight of the interest on our loans, which are too large for this country unless we keep up its forward development."

Kenya's loan commitments had reached a total of £17,000,000. Less than a quarter of this debt had been incurred by the colony. The remainder had gone to the construction of railways and ports, and the railway had to find the interest.

The depression had placed the colony in the same position as the individual farmer: between two and three times as much produce had to be sold as in 1929 to pay the interest on debts. The loans had been floated by the Crown Agents at a high rate of interest—the first was paying over 6½ per cent—and there was no provision for converting them to a lower level. Every year more interest was falling due. In 1931 colony and railway combined had to find the formidable sum of £1,000,000 to meet their obligations.

If prosperity had continued they would have experienced no difficulty. Under Sir Christian Felling's management the railway had earned a profit of over £6,000,000 between 1923 and 1929, had built up a large betterment fund and had made substantial rate reductions. It was in a sound enough position. But it had been built wholly on the assumption that settlement would increase, that production would expand and that more traffic would flow along it every year. Now Felling had gone, the depression had descended and development was at a standstill. Only increased production could avert default. "A greater density per mile of traffic", Delamere said, "is the key to the railway position."

He continued to urge until his death that a committee should be set up to consider this question of reconstruction, and that Government and colonists together should hammer out a planned policy for agriculture.

The rapidly growing tree of this colony [he said] has got to be watered at its roots—agriculture. This period of economic drought has brought about the psychological moment when that must be done.

It is said sometimes, by people who don't always consider these things very carefully—why should not the branches and flowers be watered too? The answer is that if you water the root it makes every part of the tree grow through the sap that the water has allowed the roots to release. If you water other parts of the tree and leave the root dry, the watered branches and flowers are soon killed by the death of the tree. In my opinion you must water agriculture with money or credit if the colony is to flourish and its difficulties to be overcome.

Finance for agriculture on a proper scale will produce more traffic and also better-paying traffic for the railway. It will start new production by new people, which means imports. It will enable men who are here already gradually to change over to mixed farming, which means a gradual increase in higher-priced products. It will enable the ordinary man, the original man who is on the land, in many cases to get out and to start afresh with new capital.

The Government refused to listen to his plea and no economic committee was set up. The land bank was at last established in 1931—thanks, as Delamere acknowledged, to Sir Joseph Byrne—but the original scheme had been so whittled down by the Secretary of State that it was little more than a twig to prop a tower. A capital of less than a quarter of a million, which was all it was allowed, would not go far in a country where 9 or 10 millions were out on loan and mortgage.

No constructive policy for helping production was produced. Heavy departmental cuts were made but, in spite of this, expenditure could not be brought down sufficiently to meet a drop in revenue of £450,000, and 1931 closed with another deficit. It was Delamere's tragedy that he was to die while the crisis was at its worst and before he could see the finances of the country straightened out and the dangers of insolvency passed.

8

While Delamere was appealing vainly for reconstruction in Kenya, the joint select committee of both Houses of Parliament, presided over by Lord Stanley of Alderley, was sitting in London to reach a final decision on the closer union issue.

Delamere was originally to have led the colonists' deputation, but he felt that his presence was more necessary in Kenya than in London. Interest in the colony's affairs was focussed now upon economic questions to be settled on the spot; closer union had faded into the background. The findings of the joint select committee were to a large extent a foregone conclusion.

Lord Francis Scott, the elected member who had been marked down as Delamere's successor, was chosen to give evidence on behalf of the colonists, assisted by Messrs. H. E. Schwartze and J. F. H. Harper. Their mandate was to ask that the issue should be postponed until the "economic blizzard" had spent itself, and until some new and practical form of federation had crystallised out of the immense mass of opinion and data advanced from all sides. At the same time all immediate claims to increased political power were abandoned by the colonists. These demands had arisen out of the movement towards closer union; they died with it.

Closer union found few champions before Lord Stanley's committee. The settlers were at one in their opposition with many sections of East African opinion. Three natives from Tanganyika expressed a deep-rooted objection to being associated with Kenya or with Uganda on the ground that the native policies pursued in both countries were different from that followed in the mandated territory. The delegate representing the Kabaka of Uganda claimed that the natives of that Protectorate had reached a much higher stage of development than any neighbouring African races and that they would only lose by closer association with Tanganyika or Kenya. Both Tanganyika and Uganda native spokesmen feared the influence of Kenya settlers in any form of federation.

The three Kenya natives (a Kikuyu, a M'kamba and a north Kavirondo) were equally opposed to closer union. They felt that a High Commissioner would stand between the native peoples and the Secretary of State, whom they regarded as the mouthpiece of the King, and that the submergence of Kenya in a larger state would postpone the day when they would be able to take a part in the central government.

The Indians of Tanganyika and Uganda also opposed closer union and the Arabs of Kenya were against it.

The joint select committee came to the only conclusion possible after hearing evidence of the almost universal distrust with which closer union was regarded. "This is not the time", they said, "for taking any far-reaching step in the direction of formal union."[1] For a considerable time to come the progress of East Africa could best be assured by each country continuing to develop along its own lines, subject to the closest possible economic co-operation.

The committee also settled another controversial point: the interpretation of the phrase "paramountcy of native interests".

> The doctrine of paramountcy means no more than that the interests of the overwhelming majority of the indigenous population should not be subordinated to those of a minority belonging to another race, however important in itself.

The settlers expressed themselves as perfectly satisfied with this definition. Their delegation created a good impression and the policy of white settlement was given a qualified blessing. "It would be difficult to find any other instance of a white population settling in a native country with so little disturbance of the original population", the report of the committee said; "nor", it added, "can it be denied that the natives as a whole have benefited from the presence of a settler community."

The visit to England of the colonists' deputation had one

---

[1] Report of the Joint Select Committee on Closer Union (H.M.S.O., 1931).

indirect result which caused a good deal of resentment. This was the death, after a brief year of existence, of the board of agriculture.

This board had been regarded with satisfaction in Kenya as a token of the Government's genuine intention to associate the colonists more closely in the direction of policy. Its constitution was framed on a non-racial basis cutting across the lines of white and black. Each major industry was represented and the board was intended to deal with native no less than with European agriculture. It had in it the beginnings, perhaps, of a pattern of government based on economic rather than on political divisions, on representation by industries and not by races or parties.

The colonists had reason to believe, however, that it was not popular with the administration. There was jealousy, they suspected, lest it should usurp the functions of the Agricultural department.

Then the chairman, Mr. Harper, was appointed to give evidence before the joint select committee. He left Kenya on the understanding that he would return to his position and the board was suspended temporarily during his absence.

At a meeting of the joint select committee the Secretary of State quoted the establishment of the board as an example of the Government's intention to associate the colonists in the execution of its trusteeship towards the natives. "I look upon the board of agriculture", he told Sir Edward Grigg and the committee, "as part of the constitution of the colony."

Lord Passfield's example of the Government's wish to co-operate with the colonists was not a well-chosen one. A few months after this public reassurance, the board was abolished. This incident was regarded in Kenya as another and particularly blunt indication that the new Governor's policy was one of depriving the colonists of such privileges as they had already won.

9

The last months of Delamere's life saw no slackening in his activity. He had the good fortune to die in harness.

His own farming affairs claimed much of his time. In common with all farmers he was losing money. The price of wool fell by 65 per cent. The creameries were obliged to lower their price for butter-fat to a figure below normal costs of production. One of Delamere's last activities was to help draft a bill imposing a cess on local sales of butter to adjust the difference between internal and export prices.

There was no doubt that, in his own interests, Delamere should have dropped politics altogether when the world depression started and devoted his whole attention to his farms. Had he done so he might have held down his soaring overdraft and consolidated his own position. Whenever he spent a hurried week-end on one of his properties he astonished his managers by his gift for being able to pick out the essential thread from a tangle of figures, and by the soundness of his technical knowledge of stock.

But he could not find time enough to set his own affairs in order. Delamere's critics often hinted that he used his position in politics to feather his own nest. In reality, the opposite was the case. He neglected his personal interests for what he believed to be the greater interests of the country and postponed for too long the reorganisation of his farms. He died when the depression was at its worst, before readjustments to the new price level had been made. At his death his assets, shrunken to half the value at which they stood two years before, only just balanced his liabilities. Yet there were still some who claimed that he had made a fortune out of exploiting the country.

Every day he spent many hours sifting figures and examining details in committee rooms. "Curse all this work", he wrote, in a bitter moment, to his wife. "It is only because they put rabbits to govern who bolt into their burrows directly there is a chance of having to take responsibility if the hole is left unstopped for a second."

He chafed at the waste of time which many of these meetings entailed. On Executive Council, for example, hours were spent considering such matters as a bill to prevent a Christian widow being inherited under tribal law by a pagan brother-in-law, or the terms of sixteen draft labour conventions which the Secretary of State wished to see applied to Kenya. (One of them was named "convention concerning the employment of women during the night"; and the

Governor had to write a despatch pointing out that its application to Kenya would serve no useful purpose since women were not employed in industry, either by day or by night. Another convention fixed "the minimum age for the admission of young persons to employment as trimmers or stokers at sea", an employment hardly common in Kenya; but the convention had to be incorporated in a draft amendment to the Employment of Natives' ordinance.)

At the end of his career Delamere adapted himself with remarkable completeness, for a man of his age, to a new way of living. Mud huts and rough surroundings were replaced by a comfortable house with good English furniture, a civilised environment and a daily game of golf. He became a well-known figure on the golf course. Sometimes he would start out for a round at the head of a little procession of retainers, the first native carrying his clubs, the second a pair of field glasses and a dozen balls, and the third a large box of cigars.

After fourteen years of widowerhood he was still able to readjust himself immediately to married life, and though he had always been essentially a solitary campaigner he came to rely more upon his wife's judgment than upon that of anyone he had previously consulted. He still entertained generously, but at home and no longer at clubs. He became devoted to his three small step-children and was constantly buying them presents. Once, while he was in England with the delegation, he spent a whole day searching shops all over London for a miniature red wagon for which one of his step-daughters had asked.

In a sense Delamere was a victim to the world depression. Worry, both over his own affairs and over the country's difficulties, hastened his end. He never doubted that things could be righted; but the process of readjustment needed every ounce of his energy and the strain was too severe. The position was too critical for him to take a holiday. He was attending meetings until a few days before his death. Up to the end he did not lose his adroitness in debate. In his last speech in Legislative Council he caught the Government out over an error of drafting in a bill to regulate the traffic in arms which meant, he said, that the only way in which an aeroplane was entitled to enter Kenya was by "folding its wings and alighting in a warehouse at Mombasa".

10

The end came quickly. Early in November he had five attacks of angina in quick succession. So strong was his constitution that he managed to survive them, and for ten days he lay, his consciousness regained, nursed at Loresho by his wife.

His intense desire to find out the facts about everything that was going on around him—a vital curiosity which had characterised him all his life—persisted even when he was lying on his death-bed half drugged against the pain. Practically the last thing he wrote was a list of questions that he wanted the doctor to answer about the scientific action of drugs on the human body.

Inevitably, a further attack of angina followed and on November 13th, at the age of sixty-one, he died.

His death had been expected, and yet when it came people could not realise that Delamere was gone. He had always been there; hardly anyone could remember Kenya before his time, and it seemed inconceivable that the colony should be without him. He had been the mainspring of so many activities. Whether it was in Legislative Council or Convention, at a race meeting, a dance, or an agricultural show, his short, restless figure, his Puck-like smile and his quick wit were as familiar as some feature of the landscape. Such events, without his presence, would seem empty and flat. It was hard to believe that his irresistible vitality had at last been stilled.

Delamere's leadership, unquestioned for thirty years, had become a habit. There was hardly an industry in which he had not experimented, a society to which he had not belonged, a political issue in which he had not joined. Every European knew him by sight, nearly all Africans were familiar with his name. Whenever a new enterprise was started it was always Delamere who was first approached for support. Whenever a problem arose people waited for Delamere to give his opinion before they took action. Whenever a man had a grievance it was Delamere to whom he wrote for support. The thread of his existence had become inextricably woven into the web of Kenya's development. Now that thread had snapped; and the pattern of the web could never again be quite the same.

The sense of loss which the colonists felt at the death of their leader was more than personal. Delamere was a symbol. He stood for a philosophy that had been great in its day; now it was passing and no one knew what would replace it. In East Africa he was the spear-head of a generation's ideals.

Although, like all leaders, he had many enemies, none who knew him questioned his sincerity or his integrity. He loved Kenya more than he cared for his own interests, or his health, or even, ultimately, for his life. Because of this his own people trusted him and his opponents respected him. Whether the ideals that he worked for were considered great or misguided, with his passing Africa lost one of the men who had helped to shape the beginnings of history in the most enigmatic and fascinating of the continents.

Delamere's death was felt as an African and not merely as a Kenya loss. His name was more than a word throughout the eastern territories. Tributes to his memory were sent from many parts of Africa, by opponents as well as by friends. "It would be idle to pretend that in Uganda all sections of the community have been in agreement and sympathy with Lord Delamere", said the acting Chief Secretary in the Legislative Council at Entebbe. "Those of us who have been associated with him on councils when questions of difficulty are discussed almost to a point of physical exhaustion cannot fail to have been filled with whole-hearted admiration for the energy, the enthusiasm, the alert ability and the unerring consistency with which he championed causes and principles which had enlisted his support."

"He was the most satisfactory public man to do business with that I have ever met", Sir Donald Cameron wrote from Tanganyika. He revealed that he had offered Delamere a seat on the Tanganyika Legislative Council when it had first been formed, because he felt that the country wanted a man of Delamere's calibre and experience to advise and criticise.

Other messages came from such different sympathisers

as the Secretary of State in London and the local native council at Embu, where the leading chief moved a resolution, unanimously carried, expressing the sorrow of his tribe. General Hertzog and General Smuts sent messages of sympathy from South Africa. The Governor and the premier of Southern Rhodesia telegraphed their condolences. In the Northern Rhodesian, the Uganda and the Tanganyika Legislative Councils, and in the Nyasaland Convention of Associations, resolutions of regret were passed.

11

Delamere was buried at Soysambu on a rocky knoll above the lake, looking over the view he had loved so well in his lifetime.

The knoll stands out from the plain lying below and around it, but the grave is sheltered by a natural screen of bush. There is no tombstone, only an outcrop of grey boulders baking in the hot sun; no flowers but the harsh flaming red of the wild aloes which blossom in tall clumps among the rocks. Veld grass, pale and fibrous except when the rains seem to drench it overnight with a fresh bright green, grows up to the heap of stones which covers the grave. Game graze near it, and the distant chatter of flamingoes standing in the blue waters of the lake comes faintly on the air through the dusty curtain of bush. Beyond rise the rounded peaks of Eburru with their dark crest of forest and deep changing shadows of clouds passing always across the massive flanks.

In his life Delamere loved the plains and never cared for shaded and enclosed places, and there are no trees to thrust their branches between his tomb and the sky. Only the shadow of a flying bird flickering quickly over the boulders or a bank of heavy thunder-cloud rolling down from the Mau comes between his burial place and the sun or the stars. Delamere's grave is as he wished it to be, a part of Africa and out of the sight of men.

It was a strange assortment of mourners that followed the bier across the veld. People drove to Soysambu from several hundred miles away to attend the funeral. The manager,

Mr. Dempster, had heard the news of Delamere's death when he reached the sheep-farm on Laikipia at ten o'clock at night after a long motor drive from Loresho. He turned the car round and drove back to Soysambu and from daybreak the next day he worked to hollow a grave out of the rocky hillock that Delamere had chosen. Old-timers who had known Delamere twenty-five years ago came to the funeral in torn and stained farm clothes, shorts and a khaki bush shirt. There were bearded Dutchmen, officials in white uniforms and decorations, clergymen in surplices and sun-helmets. Copper-skinned Masai stalked after the procession in their short hide cloaks and oily pigtails, carrying their long spears. Some of the older herds had worked for Delamere for twenty years and more. They knew and respected him as well, perhaps, as any of his settler friends, and after his death they remained to serve his interests as faithfully as they had done during his lifetime. One, who was on leave, heard the news in his village in the reserve and came by train from Voi clasping a bunch of withered veld flowers to place upon his employer's grave.

There were few mourners who did not feel, as they turned their backs on Soysambu, that with Delamere's death the country had lost a part of itself. One chapter of its history was forever closed.

APPENDIX

CHRONOLOGY OF SECRETARIES OF STATE AND GOVERNORS, 1895–1931

I. *Secretaries of State*

On June 15th, 1895, the East Africa Protectorate was transferred from the Imperial British East Africa Company and placed under the Foreign Office.

1. The Marquess of Salisbury. Secretary of State for Foreign Affairs. Appointed June 1895.
2. Lord Lansdowne. Secretary of State for Foreign Affairs. Appointed November 1900.

In 1905 the East Africa Protectorate was transferred from the Foreign Office to the Colonial Office.

3. Earl of Elgin and Kincardine. Secretary of State for the Colonies. Appointed December 1905.
4. Earl of Crewe. Appointed April 1908.
5. Rt. Hon. Lewis Harcourt. Appointed November 1910.
6. Rt. Hon. A. Bonar Law. Appointed May 1915.
7. Rt. Hon. Walter Long. Appointed December 1916.
8. Viscount Milner. Appointed January 1919.
9. Rt. Hon. Winston Churchill. Appointed February 1921.
10. The Duke of Devonshire. Appointed October 1922.
11. Rt. Hon. J. H. Thomas. Appointed January 1924.
12. Rt. Hon. L. S. Amery. Appointed November 1924.
13. Lord Passfield. Appointed June 1929.
14. Rt. Hon. J. H. Thomas. Appointed August 1931.
15. Sir Philip Cunliffe-Lister. Appointed November 1931.

II. *Commissioners and Governors*

1. Sir Arthur Hardinge, H.M. Consul-General in Zanzibar, 1895–1900. In 1896 Sir A. Hardinge was appointed H.M. Commissioner and Consul-General for the East Africa Protectorate.
2. Sir Charles Eliot. 1901–1904. In August 1902 the office of Commissioner for the East Africa Protectorate was created.
3. Sir Donald Stewart. 1904–1905.
4. Sir James Hayes-Sadler. 1905–1909.

In November 1906 the East Africa Protectorate was placed under a Governor and Commander-in-chief, and Executive and Legislative Councils were created.

5. Sir Percy Girouard. 1909–1912.
6. Sir Henry Belfield. 1912–1917.
   Sir Charles Bowring: Acting Governor. 1917–1919.
7. Sir Edward Northey. 1919–1922.

In June, 1920, the Protectorate became a Crown Colony.

8. Sir Robert Coryndon. 1922–1925.
9. Sir Edward Grigg. 1925–1930.
10. Sir Joseph Byrne. 1931–

INDEX

Aberdares, i. 53, 68, 96, 99, 135, 267, 292; ii. 90
Aborigines Protection Society, i. 236; ii. 63, 141
Abyssinia, i. 12, 29, 30, 36-40, 42, 49, 51, 57, 72, 220, 241, 242, 244, 245; ii. 102, 142, 257, 294
Aden, i. 9, 11, 12, 13, 16, 17, 26, 59, 60; ii. 30
Aggrey, Dr., ii. 181, 182
Agricultural Commission (1929), ii. 244, 262-4
Agriculture, Department of, i. 142; ii. 196, 262-3, 273, 317
Ainsworth, John, i. 51, 112, 113, 115, 155, 194, 252; ii. 60
Ainsworth Circular, ii. 60-61, 63, 69
Amani Institute, ii. 19, 204
Amery, L. S., ii. 72, 73, 74, 77, 83, 178, 188, 193, 198, 215, 219, 220, 223, 224, 225, 231, 232, 233, 297
Andrews, C. F., ii. 140, 145, 146
Anglo-Abyssinian Boundary Commission, i. 39
Archbishop of Canterbury, ii. 63
Archer, C. K., ii. 140
Archer, Geoffrey, i. 244
Arnoldi's Scouts, ii. 4, 14
Arthur, Dr. J. W., ii. 63, 140
Astraea, H.M.S., ii. 3
Atkinson, Dr. A. E., i. 24-6, 28, 31, 35, 87, 93, 135, 139, 150, 161
Australia, i. 8, 80, 93, 95, 96, 97, 106, 108, 124, 141, 158, 163, 173, 175, 247, 253, 288; ii. 28, 32, 121, 125, 238, 304, 307

Badminton Magazine, i. 18.
Bagge, Stephen, i. 51, 129, 130
Baillie, Arthur, i. 227, 229, 233, 236
Baker, Sir Herbert, ii. 200, 254
Baringo, Lake, i. 18, 19, 50-51, 53, 66, 85; ii. 90
Barth, Sir Jacob, i. 274
Bateson, Professor, ii. 298
Belfield, Sir Henry, i. 196, 197, 276, 279; ii. 10, 22, 33, 35, 51, 53, 54, 62
Belgians, the, ii. 25, 37

Biffen, Sir Rowland, i. 171, 280; ii. 251
Board of Agriculture, ii. 264, 309, 317
Boma Trading Co., i. 242-5
Bonar Law, ii. 35
Boran (tribe), i. 31, 36-43, 48; ii. 28
Bowker, Russell, i. 227
Bowker's Horse, ii. 4, 10, 12
Bowring, Sir Charles, i. 246; ii. 41, 97, 104, 140, 162, 164
Bowring Committee (1922), ii. 104-9, 310
British India Line, i. 9
Brussels Convention, i. 34; ii. 35
Buell, Professor Raymond, ii. 66, 296
Burghash, Sultan, i. 9
Burton, G. L., i. 174
Burton, Sir Richard, i. 220
Byatt, Sir Horace, ii. 168, 169, 170
Byrne, Sir Joseph, ii. 307, 312, 314

Cameron, Sir Donald, i. 273; ii. 209, 216, 219, 262, 321
Canada, i. 88, 93, 170, 171, 173, 176; ii. 34, 121, 125, 253
Canadian Land Laws, i. 84, 85, 88
Carrier Corps, ii. 39, 296
Ceylon, i. 97; ii. 103
Chamberlain, Joseph, i. 85, 117, 118, 193
Chamberlain, Neville, ii. 270
Chamberlain, Robert, i. 177-8; ii. 129, 130, 261, 262
Chatham, H.M.S., ii. 20
Church, A. G., ii. 190, 191
Church Missionary Society, i. 11; ii. 64
Church of Scotland Mission, ii. 140
Churchill, Winston, i. 207, 212, 213, 234, 241; ii. 70, 104, 121, 124, 126, 127, 128, 130, 131, 133, 135, 150
Closer Union, *see* Federation
Closer Union Commission (1928-29), ii. 223-232, 233, 279
Cobb, Powys, ii. 270-1, 303
Coffee Industry, i. 109, 214, 215, 227, 247, 248; ii. 26, 27, 50, 72, 172, 236, 250, 289, 305
Coghlan, Sir James, ii. 185
Cole, Berkeley, ii. 5
Cole, Galbraith, i. 134; ii. 90

327

Cole, Lady Eleanor, ii. 281
Collective Punishments Ordinance, i. 202
Colonial Development Fund, ii. 248
Colonial Economic Development Committee, ii. 96, 98
Colonial Office, i. 85, 193, 195, 196, 235, 246, 247, 269, 276, 277, 278, 279, 282; ii. 23, 36, 51, 55, 71, 73, 75, 76, 79, 85, 89, 92, 93, 96, 97, 98, 99, 100, 101, 102, 119, 121, 124, 126, 132, 133, 134, 139, 142, 151, 153, 154, 155, 157, 160, 161-4, 168, 177, 186, 195, 204, 210, 214, 218, 221, 230, 232, 243, 288, 297, 302
Colonists' Association, i. 189, 190, 191, 195, 209, 225, 230, 234, 241, 261, 262
Colonists Ltd., ii. 207-12, 262
Coney, J. E., ii. 104
Congo Basin Treaties, ii. 267
Congo, Belgian, i. 3, 23, 27, 32, 256; ii. 97, 195, 257, 297
Connaught, Duke of, i. 153
"Connecting links", ii. 135, 165
Conscription, ii. 21, 23, 24, 40, 42
Constantine, A. K., ii. 106, 107
Convention of Associations, i. 262, 277; ii. 51, 52, 58, 59, 60, 81, 104, 112, 114, 119, 122, 126, 128, 140, 141, 163, 165, 169, 231, 279, 320
Cooper, Brigadier-General, A. S., i. 252
Co-operative Creameries, ii. 91-2, 238-240, 267, 274
Corbett, G. L., ii. 120, 150-51
Coryndon, Sir Robert, ii. 53, 72, 132, 139, 140, 156-7, 162-3, 166, 169, 170, 173, 176, 180, 195-7, 205
"Country Produce Rates", ii. 261, 265
Crewe, Lord, i. 195, 196, 246
Crowdy, W. M., ii. 140
Crown Lands Ordinance, 1902, i. 85, 89; ii. 117, 175, 177
Crown Lands Ordinance, 1915, ii. 175, 177
Cyprus, i. 85

Dar-es-Salaam, ii. 3, 5, 9, 11, 37, 202, 209, 210, 262
Delamere, Lady (Florence), i. 60, 63, 66, 92, 147, 164, 167, 240, 251, 280, 282, 313
Delamere, Lady (Gladys), ii. 255, 259, 262, 263, 267, 285, 319, 320
Dempster, Mr., ii. 323
Desai, M. A., ii. 140
Deventer, Van, ii. 24, 25, 37

Devonshire, Duke of, ii. 133, 147, 151, 154, 163, 164, 169, 170
Dipping and Fencing Ordinance, ii. 242-3, 264
Dodoma, ii. 25, 201, 210, 216
Donaldson-Smith, Dr., i. 5, 23, 30, 39, 47
Dorobo (tribe), i. 74, 112, 113, 114, 152
Drummond Shiels, Dr., ii. 268-9
Dual Policy, the, ii. 53, 192-3, 205-6, 219, 226, 232, 251, 297, 298, 305
"Dummying", ii. 176-9
Duncan, Patrick, ii. 225
Du Porte, Colonel, ii. 213

East Africa, ii. 15
East Africa Commission (1924), ii. 19, 187, 189-94, 201, 208
East African Chamber of Commerce, ii. 169
East African Mounted Rifles, ii. 4, 7-12, 13-14, 24
East African Standard, i. 246, 261; ii. 18, 65, 125, 169, 177, 255
East African Syndicate, i. 100, 127, 129
East African Women's League, ii. 280, 281
East Coast Fever, i. 94, 142, 145-6, 178, 243, 289, 297; ii. 238, 241-3
Economic Commission (1919), ii. 33-5, 113
Economic and Finance Committee, see Bowring Committee
Education, native, see Native Education
Egerton of Tatton, Lord, ii. 208
Egypt, i. 34, 106, 219, 220, 285; ii. 72, 189, 256
Elected Members' Organisation, ii. 99, 128, 260
Elgin, Lord, i. 193-5, 196, 209, 287
"Elgin Pledge", i. 209; ii. 117, 120, 127
Eliot, Sir Charles, i. 55, 71, 77-9, 81, 82, 87, 89, 91, 93, 96, 97, 98, 104, 110, 121, 122-8, 129-32, 143, 151, 156, 185, 191, 192, 199, 204, 208, 210, 264, 272, 280; ii. 49, 275
Elkington, J., i. 153, 257
Elmenteita, i. 74, 146, 178, 212, 287, 288, 289, 290, 293, 301, 303, 304, 306, 311, 314; ii. 5, 17, 43, 44
Erosion, ii. 244-5
Equator Ranch, i. 135-52, 154, 158-73, 176, 178, 179; ii. 106
European and African Trades Organisation, ii. 179-80
Evans, G. W., i. 171, 172, 173, 174; ii. 20
Exchange Settlement, ii. 71-81, 82, 100

INDEX

Executive Council, i. 276, 277; ii. 48, 53, 78, 89, 96, 98, 107, 115, 127, 133, 173, 259, 302, 318
Ex-Soldier Settlement Scheme, ii. 52, 54-7, 58, 174

Fashoda Incident, i. 11
Federation, ii. 83-4, 167, 170, 187-90, 197-200, 206, 214-34, 268, 276, 278, 279, 280, 301-2, 315-16
Feetham, Mr. Justice, ii. 251
Felling, Sir Christian, ii. 93, 94, 95, 168, 170, 195, 250, 251, 313
Flax boom, ii. 56-7, 83
Flemmer, A. S., i. 129, 130
"Forced Labour", i. 216, 225, 234, 285; ii. 63, 64, 65-71, 291
Foreign Office, i. 9, 64, 69, 75, 76, 79, 88, 90, 91, 104, 117, 120, 121, 122, 124, 127, 129, 130, 132, 133
Fort Ternan, i. 51, 52, 68, 69, 70, 71, 107, 121, 209
French, activities in E. Africa, i. 10

Galla (tribe), i. 26, 30, 37, 38, 42
Garth Castle, ii. 55
German East Africa, i. 315; ii. 7, 9, 11, 20, 37, 47, 137, 138, 167, 169, 188
Germans, the, ii. 3-7, 9, 10-12, 15, 19, 20, 25, 37, 208, 209, 212, 276
Germany, i. 93; ii. 3, 4, 9, 83, 207, 212
Ghandi, Mr., ii. 140
Girouard, Sir Percy, i. 196, 238, 239, 241, 244, 245, 246, 247, 265, 266, 267, 268, 269, 270, 271, 276, 277; ii. 96
Glenday, V., i. 56
Gold Coast, ii. 37, 191
Gordon, General, i. 51; ii. 222
"Government by Agreement", ii. 88, 249, 255, 311
Governors' Conference, ii. 201, 206, 211, 216, 219, 265, 266, 267, 294
Gowers, Sir William, ii. 216, 219
Great North Road, the, ii. 201, 213
Green, P. C., ii. 140
Grigg, Sir Edward, i. 240; ii. 53, 197, 198, 200, 215, 216, 218, 219, 223, 224, 233, 239, 242, 243, 248, 249, 252, 253, 258, 263, 269, 278, 291, 293, 305, 308, 310, 317
Grogan, E. S., i. 185; ii. 20, 74, 104
Guaso Nyiro river, i. 5, 23, 44, 55, 56, 67, 85, 244; ii. 90

"Half-and-half" principle, i. 246

Hall, Sir Daniel, ii. 263, 264, 309
Hammond, General, ii. 92-4, 96, 97, 98, 168
Harcourt, Rt. Hon. Lewis, i. 196, 264, 269, 279
Hardinge, Sir Arthur, i. 75
Harper, J. F. H., ii. 270, 309, 315, 317
Havenga, Mr., ii. 281
Hayes-Sadler, Sir James, i. 188, 195, 210, 226, 227, 228, 234, 236, 237, 239, 265, 266
Heartwater, i. 297; ii. 30, 89, 90, 91
Hemsted, Rupert, ii. 7, 40, 47
Henn, Sir Sydney, ii. 187, 189
Hertzog, General, ii. 185, 280, 281, 322
Herzl, Dr., i. 117, 118, 119, 129
Hill, Sir Clement, i. 69, 85
Hilton Young Commission, *see* Closer Union Commission
Hobley, C. W., i. 51, 90
Hohnel, von, i. 24-7, 47, 58
Holm, Alex., i. 175
Hoogterp, Mr., ii. 200, 254
House of Lords, ii. 167, 169-70, 302
Hunting in E. Africa, i. 257, 258
Hyde Baker, i. 52, 53

Imperial British East Africa Company, i. 9, 10, 11, 32, 51, 75
Imperial Conference (1918), ii. 111, 112, 156, 166; (1921), ii. 124; (1930), ii. 281
Imperial Institute, i. 169, 280
Income tax, ii. 107
India, i. 34, 64, 68, 71, 76, 150, 171, 175, 176, 205, 206, 285; ii. 7, 32, 71, 75, 76, 110, 111, 112, 114, 115, 116, 118, 119, 121, 122, 123, 128, 129, 138, 141, 142, 144, 145, 146, 148, 150, 152, 161, 165, 166, 187, 224, 234, 259, 278
India, Government of, ii. 125, 134, 140, 141, 142, 147, 150, 159, 166, 225
India Office, ii. 119, 123, 124, 132, 166, 278, 279
Indian Overseas Association, ii. 119
Indian question, the, i. 64, 65, 104, 192, 197, 204-9; ii. 53, 84, 110-66, 167, 179, 180, 183, 189, 194, 214, 224, 232, 259
Indian troops, i. 156; ii. 12, 13, 14, 15, 19, 24, 148
Indirect rule, i. 238, 270-74
Intelligence Service, ii. 4, 5, 6, 16
Inter-Colonial Railway Council, ii. 52
International Missionary Council, ii. 224

Iringa, ii. 25, 201, 202, 208, 209, 210, 212, 262, 268
Irwin, Lord, ii. 132
Italian Somaliland, i. 30, 31, 50
Italy, ii. 171

Jackson, Sir F. J., i. 10, 51, 63, 65, 89, 91, 129, 130
Jackson, J. P., i. 107, 110, 139, 142, 143, 165, 251
Japan, i. 130, 175
Jeanes School, ii. 181-3
Jeevanjee, A. M., ii. 121, 124, 140
Jewish Settlement scheme, i. 117-25
Johnstone, Sir Harry, i. 90
Joint Select Committee on Closer Union, ii. 280, 281, 302, 315-16, 317
Jones, Dr. Jesse, ii. 181
Juba river, i. 4, 30, 31, 37, 38, 241, 245; ii. 187
Jubaland, i. 76; ii. 171-2

Kabaka of Uganda, i. 10; ii. 315
Karungu Bay, battle of, ii. 10
Kenya Farmers' Association, ii. 240
Kenya Land Commission, i. 113, 114, 116, 265, 269; ii. 84, 244, 246, 290, 297
Kenya, Mount, i. 3, 53, 54, 56, 57, 61, 66, 68, 73, 96, 238, 239, 242; ii. 26, 90, 173
Kenya-Uganda Railway—*see* Uganda Railway
Kikuyu (tribe), i. 57, 111-16, 189, 200, 217, 239, 247, 270; ii. 43, 68, 123, 180, 250, 270, 288, 289, 316
King's African Rifles, i. 156, 157, 201, 244, 245, 252; ii. 2, 4, 9, 10, 14, 24, 39-49, 138
Kittermaster, Sir Harold, i. 56
Koenigsberg, the, ii. 5, 20, 25
Krapf, Dr., i. 3, 26

Labour Commission (1911-12), i. 274-6; ii. 53
Labour problem, the, i. 204, 213-36, 274-6, 278; ii. 51, 53, 57-71, 189, 291-3
Laikipia, i. 51, 53, 54, 55, 56, 73, 96, 98, 134, 264, 265, 266, 267, 268, 269; ii. 41, 89, 90, 174-6, 235, 237, 272, 273, 322
Land Bank, ii. 242-3, 252, 264, 308, 314
Land Commission (1917-19), ii. 54
Land Committee (1905), i. 191-3, 197
Land Office, i. 94, 110, 160, 191, 267, 269; ii. 178

Lansdowne, Lord, i. 91, 126, 127, 128, 129, 130, 132
Lansbury, George, ii. 176
Lascelles, Sir Alfred, ii. 103
Lé, Wells of, i. 36, 40
Leakey, Canon, ii. 119
Leakey, L. S. B., i. 219
Legalishu, i. 45, 270; ii. 267, 268
Legislative Council (Kenya), i. 190, 195, 196, 197, 210-2, 229, 236, 261, 262, 276, 277, 279, 285; ii. 24, 36, 52, 53, 62, 78, 85, 86, 88, 89, 93, 94, 97, 98, 102, 104, 112, 114, 115, 116, 120, 122, 127, 134, 153, 154, 157, 158, 160, 165, 176, 195, 199, 200, 215, 219, 227, 230, 231, 233, 236, 241, 242, 259, 260, 263, 269, 270, 274, 290, 291, 293, 301, 311, 312, 319, 320
Lenana, i. 133, 134, 265, 267
Leys, Norman, i. 264; ii. 178
Linfield, F. C., ii. 190
Lion hunts, Masai, i. 259-60
Liversage, V., i. 217
Lloyd George, Mr., ii. 198
Locusts, ii. 248, 255, 256-8, 260, 305, 308, 311
Long, E. C., i. 305, 306-9; ii. 20, 30, 90, 174-6, 235, 271
Long, Viscount, ii. 51
Longido, Battle of, ii. 12, 24
Loroki Plateau, i. 44, 55
Lugard, Lord, i. 9, 10, 11, 51, 70, 71, 72, 270; ii. 192, 226
Lugh, i. 30, 31, 35, 49

M'Call, Sammy, i. 137, 138, 140, 142, 164, 178, 288, 298, 303
McClellan Wilson, W., ii. 281
McKinnon, Sir William, i. 9, 10
McMillan, Sir Northrup, ii. 180
Maize industry, i. 93, 158, 164, 175, 247; ii. 56, 105-6, 195, 250, 258, 273-274, 305, 308, 311
Malaya, i. 125; ii. 95, 103
Mandates Commission, ii. 102
Mant, Sir Reginald, ii. 224, 225, 230, 278
Marsabit, i. 5, 44-7, 55, 56, 242, 244
Marsden, A., i. 110
Martin, James, i. 50-52
Martin, Hugh, ii. 95, 174-6, 178, 268
Masai (tribe), i. 43, 44, 46, 50, 55, 56, 58, 61, 72, 73, 74, 83, 103, 104, 111, 112, 120, 124, 125, 129, 132, 133, 134, 138, 139, 151, 152, 153, 154, 155, 164, 189, 200, 219, 227, 243, 258-60, 264-9,

INDEX

272, 288, 291, 297, 298, 299, 302, 303; ii. 5, 7, 12, 28, 39-49, 68, 91, 175, 176, 196, 244, 246, 248, 270, 289, 290, 323
Masai Move (first), i. 134
Masai Move (second), i. 264-9; ii. 244
Masters' and Servants' Ordinance, i. 275; ii. 61, 69, 70
Maxwell, Judge, i. 115
Meat factories, ii. 246, 249, 264, 268
Meat Rations Ltd., ii. 247, 248
Menelik, King, i. 38, 39, 40, 242
Menkin, A. A., ii. 281
Mesobero, ii. 44, 45
Military Expenditure, ii. 101-2, 294
Milner, Viscount, i. 238; ii. 69, 70, 72, 83, 96, 115, 119, 120, 121, 124, 125
Mining Laws, i. 279
Missionaries, i. 5, 23, 236; ii. 32, 58, 63, 64, 67, 119, 123, 149, 158, 193, 194, 204, 205, 281
Missions, i. 93, 207; ii. 63, 183, 270, 296
Moffat, Mr., ii. 280
Mombasa, Bishop of, ii. 119
Montague, Rt. Hon. S., ii. 111, 126, 141, 157
Montgomery, Colonel, i. 194, 195
Montgomery, R. E., ii. 246-7
Moore, L. F., ii. 186, 202, 214
Muthaiga Club, ii. 190, 236, 237, 260

Nairobi Sheep Disease, i. 297
Nakuru, i. 60, 142, 148, 149, 155, 264, 289, 290, 298, 302, 303, 304; ii. 95, 96, 134, 137, 172, 198, 235, 254, 255, 280
Nakuruitis, i. 138
Nandi (tribe), i. 62, 63, 68, 69, 120, 126, 154, 155, 156, 164; ii. 289
Nandi War, first, i. 68-70
Nandi War, second, i. 70, 154-7, 201
Natal, i. 167, 205, 207; ii. 112, 125, 129
Native Authority Ordinance, i. 270, 276; ii. 65, 70
Native Brains, research on, i. 221
Native Councils, ii. 53, 84, 154, 196-7, 228, 242, 251, 287, 322
Native Education, i. 247; ii. 59, 84, 101, 179-83, 189, 254, 295, 296
Native Industrial Training Depot, ii 180
Native Lands Trust Bill, ii. 269, 290
Native Production, i. 77-8; ii. 51, 100, 192, 196, 250, 291, 297, 305
Native Registration Ordinance, ii. 61
Ndaragua, ii. 90, 174-6
New Statesman, ii. 147

New Zealand, i. 8, 70, 80, 93, 95, 100, 101, 102, 103, 107, 108, 123, 138, 139, 140, 141, 247, 288, 298, 312; ii. 91, 125, 128, 238, 239, 309
Nigeria, i. 78, 238, 270; ii. 37, 144, 191, 204, 250, 257, 297
Nile, the, i. 3, 10, 34, 52, 72, 219; ii. 187, 195, 201, 257
Njemps, i. 50, 52, 60
Njoro, i. 56, 93, 104, 135, 137, 139, 142, 145, 149, 150, 152, 153, 158, 160, 165, 166, 167, 170, 171, 173, 177, 178, 220, 240, 250, 280, 287, 288, 289, 290, 291, 295, 296, 297; ii. 20, 82-3, 95, 96
Norfolk hotel, i. 244, 248, 251, 254, 255, 256, 258; ii. 136
Northern Frontier District, i. 38, 56, 242, 255, 256, 258; ii. 34, 102, 241, 258, 288, 289
Northern Rhodesia — *see* Rhodesia, Northern
Northey, Sir Edward, ii. 25, 51, 52, 55, 60, 61, 62, 63, 69, 72, 73, 74, 76, 77, 88, 93, 95, 96, 104, 105, 108, 112, 114, 119, 121, 122, 126, 127, 131, 242
Nyama, Ltd., i. 299
Nyasaland, i. 156, 227; ii. 14, 25, 37, 38, 51, 67, 201, 213, 214, 215, 221, 226, 322

Official Gazette, ii. 165
Oldham, J. H., ii. 225, 230, 269
Ormsby-Gore, Hon. W. G., ii. 155, 190, 191, 192, 194, 201, 208, 220, 277
Ormsby-Gore Report—*see* East Africa Commission
Orr, Dr. John, ii. 251
O'Shea, T. J., ii. 280
Ostrich farming, i. 166-7
Overstocking, ii. 244-9
Owen, Archdeacon, ii. 64-5

"Paramountcy", ii. 115, 158-9, 198, 276, 277, 279-80, 286, 316
Park, Mungo, i. 27
Parliament, i. 34, 69, 205, 234, 237; ii. 23, 36, 67, 68, 110, 122, 141, 143, 176, 186, 190, 191, 193, 194, 198, 220, 279, 281
Passfield, Lord, ii. 194, 223, 224, 243, 268, 269, 278, 287, 301, 302, 317
Pastoralists' Association, i. 261
Peel, Lord, i. 98; ii. 147
Pegasus, H.M.S., ii. 3
Peters, Carl, i. 10
Phelps Stokes Commission, ii. 181-3

Pipe-lines, i. 309-11; ii. 176
Plant-breeding, i. 170-5; ii. 20, 251
Pleuro-pneumonia, i. 243; ii. 30, 241
Poor Whites, i. 65; ii. 253
Portuguese, the, i. 3, 38; ii. 37, 38
Postma, ii. 6, 16-7
Preston, R. O., i. 61, 66
Prince of Wales, H.R.H., ii. 259
Prince of Wales' School, ii. 253-4
Purko (clan), ii. 41-6, 49, 271

Racing in East Africa, i. 252-4
Railway Advisory Council, ii. 94, 261, 268, 272
Railway—*see* Uganda Railway
Rainey, Paul J., i. 289, 306-9
Ramsden, Sir John, ii. 208
Redwater, i. 289; ii. 31
Reform Party, ii. 98-9
Reitz, Lieutenant, i. 9
Rendile (tribe), i. 43, 44, 45, 46, 48, 54
Resident Natives Ordinance, ii. 61
Responsible government, i. 210, 235, 276, 279; ii. 22, 54, 131, 154, 220, 222, 230-1, 299
Rhodes, Cecil, i. 11; ii. 130, 156, 183-4, 203, 207, 213, 238, 283, 297
Rhodes Scholarships, ii. 253-4
Rhodesia, Northern, i. 235; ii. 38, 67, 186, 201, 202, 203, 210, 211, 213, 214, 215, 226, 263, 277, 322
Rhodesia, Southern, i. 3, 159, 214, 227, 281; ii. 100, 125, 183, 186, 187, 207, 211, 213, 214, 226, 235, 246, 280, 297, 322
Ridley, M., ii. 8
Rift Valley, i. 4, 49, 66, 71, 74, 96, 104, 129, 134, 135, 142, 145, 149, 219, 220, 242, 264, 267, 287, 291, 297; ii. 83, 179, 215, 255, 256, 302, 309, 311
Rinderpest, i. 55; ii. 30, 31
Robertson, Sir Benjamin, ii. 112, 120, 140, 150
Robertson, Colonel J. Kerr, ii. 97, 98
Roosevelt, Theodore, i. 250, 251
Routledge, i. 112
Rowett Research Institute, i. 138; ii. 251
Rudolph, Lake, i. 23, 24, 27, 31, 36, 37, 39, 40, 43, 47, 48, 51, 72, 242
Rust in Wheat, i. 163, 170-4, 176

Samburu, i. 43, 46, 47, 55
Sandbach Baker, i. 143, 145
Sastri, Rt. Hon. Srinivasa, ii. 140, 145-6, 147, 151, 152, 166, 232, 259
Schindler, Fritz, i. 250, 309

Schuster, Sir George, ii. 211, 224, 225, 230
Schwartze, H. E., ii. 315
Scott, Lord Francis, ii. 202, 268, 269, 315
Segregation, i. 127-9, 132-3; ii. 114-5, 120-2, 127, 132, 144, 152, 155, 158, 159
Sendeyo, ii. 48
Shebeyli river, i. 23, 26-9, 30, 37, 39
Shipping crisis, ii. 26, 32
Slavery, i. 210-11; ii. 34, 283
Smith-Dorrien, Sir H., ii. 20
Smuts, General, ii. 13, 15, 19, 20, 24, 25, 37, 93, 125, 126, 128, 129, 130, 161, 166, 183, 185, 188, 207, 281, 322
Somaliland, i. 5, 8, 11, 12, 13, 15, 16, 18, 23, 26, 53, 55, 148, 166; ii. 257
Sotik (tribe), i. 164, 201
South Africa, i. 8, 74, 93, 97, 101, 108, 110, 121, 123, 129, 143, 145, 146, 159, 161, 163, 164, 171, 205, 206, 213, 238, 248; ii. 4, 26, 93, 110, 112, 121, 124, 125, 128-30, 138, 142, 156, 161, 166, 183, 185, 186, 190, 192, 200, 212, 213, 217, 220, 241, 244, 251, 259, 264, 280, 281, 299, 301, 308, 322
South African troops, ii. 23, 37
Soysambu, i. 142, 165, 212, 288, 289, 291-8, 299, 301, 303, 304, 309-14; ii. 17, 20, 27, 28-31, 44, 82, 89, 90, 91, 92, 235, 272, 273, 322, 323
"Squatters", ii. 61, 292
Stanley of Alderley, Lord, ii. 315
Stanley, Sir Herbert, ii. 213, 219
Stewart, Sir Donald, i. 125, 134, 156, 191, 195, 253, 265
Sudan, the, i. 176, 238; ii. 254, 257, 258
Sudanese Mutiny, i. 51
Suk (tribe), i. 48, 52, 53; ii. 246

Tanga, attack on, ii. 12-13
Tanganyika Territory, i. 3, 270; ii. 67, 83, 102, 103, 162, 167, 168, 169, 170, 171, 172, 183, 188, 189, 201, 202, 204, 206-12, 213, 214, 215, 216, 217, 218, 219, 221, 223, 225, 228, 232, 247, 262, 264, 265, 267, 268, 276, 279, 281, 286, 295, 315, 316, 321, 322
Tariff Committee (1929), ii. 265-6
Taveta, ii. 4, 5, 6, 9, 12, 13, 24
Taylor, Charles, ii. 270
Teleki, Count, i. 23, 27, 47, 58
Theiler, Sir Arnold, i. 145
Thomas, Rt. Hon. J. H., ii. 166, 186, 189, 190, 230, 269, 279

INDEX

Thomson, Joseph, i. 3, 51, 134
Thuku, Harry, ii. 123
Times, The, i. 119, 120, 122; ii. 144, 147, 165
Transvaal, the, i. 131, 159, 180, 205, 206, 213; ii. 112, 251
"Trusteeship", ii. 193-4, 219, 220, 229, 248, 276-8, 286, 287, 297, 317
Turkana (tribe), i. 48, 49, 54, 126; ii. 294
Turner, Colonel R. B., ii. 183

Uasin Gishu Plateau, i. 73, 123, 124, 213; ii. 3, 4, 35, 106, 195, 281
Uasin Gishu Railway, ii. 57, 70, 93, 95-8
Uganda, i. 9, 10, 11, 33, 34, 47, 50, 51, 52, 55, 63, 73, 74, 84, 85, 90, 156, 172, 176, 210, 253, 270, 283; ii. 8, 52, 66-7, 70, 72, 78, 83, 92, 94, 95, 97, 103, 107, 132, 144, 156, 158, 166, 183, 187, 189, 195, 201, 206, 214, 215, 216, 223, 225, 228, 232, 250, 257, 261, 264, 265, 266, 272, 299, 295, 296, 297, 305, 306, 315, 316, 321, 322
Uganda, Bishop of, ii. 144, 145
Uganda Railway (including Kenya and Uganda Railway), i. 33, 34, 59, 60, 61, 63, 64, 94, 121, 126, 134, 148, 149, 150, 155, 158, 160, 180, 202, 203, 204, 238, 239, 245, 246, 252, 278, 280, 304, 311; ii. 3, 4, 7, 9, 10, 51, 52, 58, 89, 90, 92-98, 105, 106, 116, 166, 169, 195, 216, 250, 251, 261, 272, 305, 306, 310, 313, 314
Unga, Ltd., i. 177; ii. 33, 106, 107, 240
Unofficial Conference: Tukuyu (1925), ii. 201-6, 211, 221
Unofficial Conference: Livingstone (1926), ii. 213-14, 221
Unofficial Conference: Nairobi (1927), ii. 221
Unofficial Conference: Nairobi (1930), ii. 264, 266-7
Untouchables, ii. 151-2
Usambara Mountains, ii. 13, 15, 19, 25, 37

Vale Royal, i. 6, 7, 8, 16, 24, 25, 26, 60, 68, 85, 94, 99, 137, 170; ll. 213
Van der Weyer, J., ii. 6
Varma, B. S., ii. 140
Vasco da Gama, ii. 34
Veterinary Research Laboratories, i. 143, 297; ii. 28, 30, 31

Victoria, Lake, i. 51, 73, 77, 84, 146, 315; ii. 10, 25, 40, 95, 96, 207, 216, 226, 250, 272
Vigilance Committee, ii. 126, 135, 137, 160-61, 164-5
Virjee, Hussenbhai S., ii. 140
Voi-Kahé Line, ii. 167-70
Vorbeck, von Lettow, ii. 20, 25, 38, 137

Wakamba (tribe), i. 27, 59; ii. 246
Walsh, Captain, i. 15, 16
War Council, ii. 21-2, 23, 26, 31, 35, 54, 105, 106
Watkins, Frank, i. 189
Wattle cultivation, ii. 167
Wedgewood Benn, Mr., ii. 234, 278
Weeks, R., ii. 41, 47, 48
Welby, H., ii. 42, 46
Wessel's Scouts, ii. 4
West Africa, i. 175, 247, 248, 270, 285; ii. 181, 192
"West Coast Policy", ii. 155, 204-6
Wheat industry, i, 213, 247; ii. 20, 32, 33, 35, 106-7, 237, 240, 251, 266
"White highlands", i. 97-8, 208; ii. 116, 130, 132, 153, 155, 159, 192, 288-90, 301
White Settlement, i. 70, 72, 75, 78, 79, 84, 91, 97, 98, 131, 273, 274; ii. 71, 110, 114, 116, 129, 183, 191, 194, 198, 204-5, 207, 211, 253, 276, 277, 280, 283-5, 288, 291, 295, 299-301, 302, 316
Wilson, F. O'B., i. 307, 308; ii. 15
Wilson, Sir Samuel, ii. 232, 233, 234, 259, 268, 278, 279
Winterton, Lord, ii. 132
Wood, J. R., i. 178
Wood, T. A., ii. 53, 140
Wood-Winterton Agreement, ii. 126, 127, 132, 133, 134, 136, 141
Woosnam, R. B., ii. 6, 7

Young, Sir Hilton, ii. 224, 225, 228, 230, 232, 263, 279
Young Kikuyu Association, ii. 123

Zangwill, Israel, i. 118, 120
Zanzibar, i. 4, 9, 10, 31, 35, 51, 75, 108, 210; ii. 162, 163, 171
Zanzibar, Bishop of, ii. 119
Zaphiro, i. 244
Zionist Movement, i. 117, 118, 119, 120, 121, 125